Margaret Powell was born in 1907 in Hove, and left school at the age of 13 to start working. At 14, she got a job in a hotel laundry room, and a year later went into service as a kitchen maid, eventually progressing to the position of cook, before marrying a milkman called Albert. In 1968 the first volume of her memoirs, *Below Stairs*, was published to instant success and turned her into a celebrity. She followed this up with *Climbing the Stairs, The Treasure Upstairs* and *The Margaret Powell Cookery Book*. She also co-authored three novels, tie-ins to the television series *Beryl's Lot,* which was based on her life story. She died in 1984.

MARGARET POWELL

Tales from Below Stairs

Below Stairs • *Climbing the Stairs*

SIDGWICK & JACKSON

Below Stairs first published 1968 by Peter Davies Ltd
First published in paperback 1970 by Pan Books

Climbing the Stairs first published 1969 by Peter Davies Ltd
First published in paperback 1971 by Pan Books

This omnibus edition published 2012 by Sidgwick & Jackson
an imprint of Pan Macmillan, a division of Macmillan Publishers Limited
Pan Macmillan, 20 New Wharf Road, London N1 9RR
Basingstoke and Oxford
Associated companies throughout the world
www.panmacmillan.com

ISBN 978-1-4472-1183-9

A CIP catalogue record for this book is available from
the British Library.

Typeset by CPI Typesetting
Printed and bound by CPI Group (UK) Ltd, Croydon, CR0 4YY

Visit **www.panmacmillan.com** to read more about all our books
and to buy them. You will also find features, author interviews and
news of any author events, and you can sign up for e-newsletters
so that you're always first to hear about our new releases.

Below Stairs

To Leigh (Reggie) Crutchley

with gratitude and affection

1

I WAS BORN in 1907 in Hove, the second child of a family of seven. My earliest recollection is that other children seemed to be better off than we were. But our parents cared so much for us. One particular thing that I always remember was that every Sunday morning my father used to bring us a comic and a bag of sweets. You used to be able to get a comic for a halfpenny plain and a penny coloured. Sometimes now when I look back at it, I wonder how he managed to do it when he was out of work and there was no money at all coming in.

My father was a painter and decorator. Sort of general odd-job man. He could do almost anything: repair roofs, or do a bit of plastering; but painting and paper-hanging were his main work. Yet in the neighbourhood where we lived, there was hardly any work in the winter. People didn't want their houses done up then; they couldn't be painted outside and they didn't want the bother of having it all done up inside. So the winters were the hardest times.

My mother used to go out charring from about eight in the

morning till six in the evening for two shillings a day. Sometimes she used to bring home little treasures: a basin of dripping, half a loaf of bread, a little bit of butter or a bowl of soup. She used to hate accepting anything. She hated charity. But we were so glad of them that, when she came home and we saw that she was carrying something, we used to make a dive to see what she'd got.

It seems funny today, I suppose, that there was this hatred of charity, but when my parents brought us up there was no unemployment money. Anything you got was a charity.

I remember my mother, when we only had one pair of shoes each and they all needed mending, she went down to the council to try to get more for us. She had to answer every question under the sun and she was made to feel that there was something distasteful about her because she hadn't got enough money to live on.

It was very different getting somewhere to live in those days. You just walked through the streets, and there were notices up, 'Rooms to let'.

When we were extra hard up, we only had one room or two rooms in somebody else's house. But when Dad was working, we would go around looking for half a house. We never had a house to ourselves. Not many people could afford a house in those days, not to themselves. As for buying a house, why, such things were never even dreamed of!

I know I used to wonder why, when things were so hard, Mum kept having babies, and I remember how angry she used to get when a couple of elderly spinsters at a house where she worked kept telling her not to have any more

6

children, that she couldn't afford to keep them. I remember saying to my mother, 'Why do you have so many children? Is it hard to have children?' And she said, 'Oh, no. It's as easy as falling off a log.'

You see that was the only pleasure poor people could afford. It cost nothing – at least at the time when you were actually making the children. You could have babies forevermore. Nobody bothered about doctors. You had a midwife who came for almost next to nothing. The fact that it would cost you something later on, well, the working-class people never looked ahead in those days. They didn't dare. It was enough to live for the present.

But, apart from that, people didn't think about regulating families. The whole idea was to have families, a relic of Victorian times perhaps. The more children you had, in some ways, the more you were looked upon as fulfilling your duties as a Christian citizen. Not that the Church played much part in my mother's and father's lives. I don't think they had much time for it or, perhaps it's truer to say, they had time but no inclination. Some of us weren't even christened. I wasn't, and never have been. But we all had to go to Sunday School, not because my parents were religious, but because it kept us out of the way.

Sunday afternoons were devoted to lovemaking because there was not much privacy in working-class families. When you lived in two or three rooms, you had to have some of the children in the same room with you. If you had any sense of decency, and my parents did because I never, during the whole time of my childhood, knew that they ever made love, you waited till they were fast asleep or out of the way. The fact is I never even saw them kissing each other because my father was a rather austere man outwardly, and I was amazed when only lately my mother told me what a passionate man he really was. So, you see, it was only when the children were out of the way that they could really let themselves go.

So, Sunday afternoon, after a mighty big dinner (and everybody tried to have a big dinner on Sunday), was the time spent lying on the bed, making love and having a good old doze. Because, as my Mum said later, if you make love, you might as well do it in comfort. When you're getting middle-aged, there isn't much fun in having it in odd corners. So that's why Sunday School was so popular then. I don't know about now.

My brother and I began proper school together. They let you start at the age of four in those days. My mother sent me there as well because she had another baby coming along and she thought that would be two of us out of the way.

We had to come home for dinner. There were no such things as school meals and school milk. You took a piece of bread and butter with you, wrapped in a piece of paper, and gave it to the teacher to mind, because many of us children were so hungry that we used to nibble it during the course of the morning when we should have been doing whatever we did have to do. It was then doled out to us at eleven o'clock.

My early school days don't stand out much in my mind. It was when I got to the age of about seven that I, as it were, took my place in life. You see, with my mother going off early in the morning to do her charring and me being the eldest girl, I used to have to give the children their breakfast. Mind you, giving them their breakfast wasn't a matter of cooking anything. We never had eggs or bacon, and things like cereals weren't heard of. We had porridge in the winter, and just bread and margarine, and a scraping of jam, if Mum had any, in the summer. Three pieces were all we were allowed.

I always loved going to the baker and buying those round loaves with four corners on top. (I think they were called Coburg loaves.) We used to fight to get the corners because that counted as one piece of bread but it was far more filling than just a slice.

Then I would make the tea, very weak tea known as sweepings – the cheapest that there was – clear away and wash up, and then get ready for school.

The two youngest I took along to the day nursery. It cost sixpence a day each and for that the children got a midday meal as well. I took them just before school time and collected them the moment I came out of school in the afternoon.

At midday, I would run home, get the potatoes and the greens on, lay up the dinner and do everything I could so that when my mother rushed over from work, she just had to serve the dinner.

Generally it was stews because they were the most filling. Sometimes Mother would make a meat pudding. It's funny now when I look back on it, this meat pudding. I would go along to the butcher's and ask for sixpennyworth of 'Block ornaments'. Hygiene was nothing like it is now and butchers used to have big wooden slabs outside the shop with all the meat displayed for the public and the flies. As they cut up the joints, they always had odd lumps of meat left which they scattered around. These were known as 'Block ornaments'.

I used to get sixpennyworth of them and a pennyworth of suet. Then my mother would make the most marvellous meat pudding with it. That tasted far better than those I make now when I pay four or five shillings for the meat.

Directly she'd eaten her dinner, she'd have to rush back to work because she was only allowed half an hour. So I had to do the washing-up before I went back to school again. Right after I came out of school in the afternoon, I would collect the two children from the day nursery, take them back home, and then set to and clear up the place and make the beds.

I never used to feel that I was suffering in any sense from ill-usage. It was just the thing. When you were the eldest girl in a working-class family, it was expected of you.

Of course, Mum took over in the evenings. She came back about six and got us our tea which was the same as break-fast – bread and margarine.

Being a girl, I never went out at night and my parents were very strict about this. But I used to read a lot. We had a free library even then. We also managed to amuse ourselves.

My oldest brother used to give magic shows. He was really very good. Then somebody gave us a magic lantern with slides, of course not moving, and my brother would make up a story about them. We were never bored with an evening. There was always something to do.

Unlike so many people I've met, I didn't really make any lasting friends in my school days. I suppose it's easy to look back and say my mother and father weren't sociable because we weren't allowed to have friends in. Mum had enough children of her own. I never had birthday parties, of course; things like that were undreamt of.

I had two girls at school who were friends but you know what it's like when you're three together, someone is the odd one out and that was always me. I think these two girls came from homes where things were talked about, things like sex, because they used to have a sort of code between them which would make them screech with mirth, and I never understood a word. I remember when I was nearly thirteen years old, one of them, her name was Bertha, wouldn't run around and play with us. And I asked 'Why? Why can't you run about?' 'Oh,' she said, 'I had a bicycle out yesterday and it hurt me, and I can't do anything now.' And they both went off into screams of mirth.

But, being a member of a family, I wasn't worried and, you see, we had the town itself.

2

HOVE WAS a wonderful place, especially for children, and particularly for children with no money. It wasn't built up as it is now.

Take the seafront and the lawns. Each lawn is laid out for people with money now. There are clock golf, putting, tennis, bowls; but there's nowhere for children at all. But then, every one of those lawns was free; there was nothing on them but grass and a shelter, and all around the lawns there were shrubs where you could have the most marvellous games of hide-and-seek. You could take your tea down there, spread it all over the clean grass. There were no park keepers to come and chivvy you.

And immediately behind the town was the country. We only had to walk a matter of minutes from where we lived and there was the country and the farms.

The farmers were so friendly to you; they let you walk around; hang over the pigsty, scratch the pigs, cluck at the chickens and watch them milking the cows. Often the farmer's wife would come out with a glass of lemonade for us.

There were trees to climb, marvellous trees which seemed to have grown just for children.

Back on the beach, there were the seaside shows, the Pierrot shows. It was sixpence or a shilling to sit down in a deckchair and watch it, but, needless to say, we never had money like that. So we used to stand at the back.

Looking back, I think the shows were good. Not in the least smutty because it was meant as a family show.

A soprano would come on and sing a soulful song about lost love, how she once had a lover and the lover had departed through some misunderstanding and she hoped with all her heart they would come together again. Half the audience were in tears, and so were we kids at the back. People believed in things like that then; dying for love, feeling soulful about it, regret, lost opportunities and all that kind of thing. None of this 'couldn't care less' attitude. Then there was the baritone. He would sing songs about friendship, England, and 'Hands Across the Sea'.

All this would be considered very small beer nowadays but we thought it was wonderful and so did the audience.

Then there were the donkeys, and the donkey man who looked after them. Now I've heard it said that people who have much to do with animals get like them both in appearance and mannerisms. So the donkey man resembled his charges. He was old, small, bowed down, grey, and very hairy. He didn't exactly have a beard. Hair seemed to be sprouting out all over him. I thought to myself many a time, if he got down on all fours you could have got on his back and you wouldn't have known you were not on a donkey.

What a poor sorry lot those donkeys were! I suppose they had enough to eat, but donkeys always look such pathetic creatures unless they are well looked after, and these presumably weren't. But the well-to-do children never had to sit on the back of a donkey like the common children. Certainly not! They might get polluted. They sat in a little dogcart, all done up in red leather. It held two. These children with nannies to look after them used to come down in style in large prams.

Not only did the man who owned the dogcart have to walk along the one side, but the nanny had to walk along the other. Because no harm must come to those darlings. Though it didn't matter about us jogging along on the back of the old donkeys getting saddle sores.

Wealthy children were never allowed to play with low-class children like us. They were never allowed to play with anyone but similarly wealthy children. They never went anywhere on their own without their nannies. Some of them had two, a nurse and an under-nurse. The lawns were open to everybody, and they couldn't keep us away from them, but if any child wandered up to us, its nurse would say, 'Come away! Come away this instant! Come over here.' They'd never let them speak to us.

Mind you, we had a kind of contempt for them. They couldn't do the things that we could do. They weren't allowed to dirty their clothes like we were. They weren't allowed to run in and out of the bushes. They weren't allowed to climb all over the seats and walk along the very narrow tops of them. They weren't allowed to do anything exciting. It wasn't their fault.

So we never mixed, never. They played their dainty little games with large coloured balls. They pushed their dolls' prams around and rode on their scooters.

We had nothing except perhaps an old tennis ball, but still we used to have the most marvellous games with absolutely nothing at all.

Perhaps if we had been allowed to mix, we would have become quite friendly but I don't think so because they were brought up with an ingrained idea that they were a different class of people from us altogether.

For instance, I remember one occasion when I was playing on the lawns, I had a coat on which had originally been my grandmother's. It was a plush affair. One of these children came over and started making remarks about my coat. The nanny said to her, 'Oh, you shouldn't say things like that, dear, after all they're poor children. Their mummy hasn't got any money.' And the child said, 'Haw, haw, but doesn't she look funny? I wonder if Mummy has got anything she could give her to wear.' I was simply furious because I hadn't minded the coat. I hadn't felt that because it was my grandmother's coat there was something wrong about wearing it. But although this incident has stuck in my mind I soon got over my feelings of resentment because there was always something to do or something to look forward to, like the yearly visit to the circus.

3

THE BEST circus we ever had was Lord George Sanger's. I suppose his name was George Lord and he turned it around, but we used to think he was a real lord. He dressed up so well we thought he was marvellous, in a leather jacket with fringes hanging all around, a huge Stetson hat and a sort of riding trousers, with shiny boots that came up to his knees in a point with metal studs up the side. We thought that was how a lord should dress. It was something out of this world. We couldn't always afford to go to his circus, but we would do our utmost. Still, you could always walk around and look at all the animals – the elephants, the lions, and tigers. That was all free.

One particular year they came down, I remember, and billed as a marvellous attraction was a man who was shot from a cannon, right across the tent, and landed in a net. Every night we could hear the tremendous 'Boom!' as the cannon went off. This made our longing to go even stronger but it was during one of my father's out-of-work periods. He just couldn't give us the money. It was sixpence each for children to go in. That is for sitting right at the back. So we set about getting the money. We went along the streets knocking on people's doors asking for old jam jars they didn't want. We didn't have any jam jars in our house. When we bought jam it was by the pennyworth in a cup, doled out from seven-pound jars. The grocer was a friend of mine, and used to make a fuss of me. After he'd doled out my penny-worth of jam in a great big wooden spoon, he always used to give me the spoon to lick. It was marvellous.

So we got all the jam jars we could and took them to the rag-and-bone shop. You had to get six, I think, for a penny. Then we went out getting manure. Threepence a barrow we got for it. It was easy because there used to be the corporation cart horses. Every day the cart came around with a sprinkler on the back and watered the roads. When it got to our house, it was the end of the round. The driver used to go into a nearby café and leave his two horses outside. Whether it was because it was the end of the round or whether they were tired, they always used to oblige by dropping a large load of manure. Before the man went into the café, he used to put nosebags on the horses to feed them and tremendous flocks of pigeons would come around to pick up the bits that fell from the bags. We used to run under the horses' legs to shovel up the manure, and the pigeons would fly into the air startling the horses. How we never got kicked to death I don't know.

Then sometimes we would follow a pantechnicon through the street waiting for it to stop and the horses to oblige. So it didn't take very long to fill a barrow with a load of manure.

When I look back on it, we must have been very honest. We didn't just pile it up. We would pat it all down with our shovels so that people really did have their money's worth. It used to surprise us that, with so much of the stuff lying around, people were willing to pay for it.

After several days of this selling of jam jars and collecting manure, we managed to accumulate half a crown which, at sixpence each, was the entrance money for the five of us.

So the great day came. It was like a fairy tale. A girl dressed in glittering tights came on leading four or five elephants. She let the elephants pick her up in their trunks. Then she would lie on the floor and let them step over her.

The lions came on and roared suitably. As part of the act a man put his head right into the lion's mouth. I couldn't watch.

Another thing I couldn't watch was the aerial trapeze.

But the high spot of the evening for us was the man to he shot from the cannon. The night before we went, we'd heard Mum saying to Dad that when this act had been on in America, the man didn't land in the net the right way and he broke his neck. Well, with the callousness of children, we didn't think it was a bad thing at all. Suppose it happened when we went. After all, he had been doing it for several nights and it was time he had a mishap.

It was the very last act of all. We saw him climb in feet first. Then came the 'Boom' we'd anticipated. Out he shot in a cloud of smoke. I must admit I didn't see him sail to the other side of the tent. I suppose he must have done. He landed in the net quite safely, and there was a tremendous burst of applause which we joined in. Mind you, we would have given just as much applause if he had broken his neck.

It was a marvellous evening. I didn't go to sleep that night thinking about it all.

4

ANOTHER DIVERSION which may seem a commonplace now was the cinema but, of course, it bore no comparison with films today. The places by present standards were sleazy.

The one we liked was in the main street. The films were livelier and so were the serials. It used to be on every evening and Saturday afternoon. In the evenings the prices were sixpence, ninepence, a shilling, and one and threepence, but on Saturday afternoon children could get in for three halfpence if you sat downstairs, or threepence if you sat in the gallery. All the well-to-do children, well-to-do by our standards that is, went upstairs and subjected us to an avalanche of orange peelings and nutshells.

Infants in arms went in for nothing. We used to stagger up to the box office with three- and four-year-olds in our arms so that we didn't have to pay for them. The moment we passed the box office, we put them down and let them walk.

We would all go into the cinema at least an hour before the film began. During that hour, a tremendous uproar would go on. There was a woman who always played the piano. Her name was Miss Bottle or so we always called her. She was a middle-aged spinster who had her hair scraped back in a bun with what appeared to be a hatpin skewered through it at the back. She had the most tremendous bosom. Women didn't wear falsies in those days so I suppose it was natural. About a quarter of an hour before she was due to arrive, we used to stamp our feet on the floor and cry out, 'Miss Bottle! Miss Bottle!' She must have been flattered, and when she did appear, Paderewski could not have received a greater ovation than Miss Bottle did. Not that we cared the least about the music or the fact that she played the piano, it was because when she appeared we knew that the film was just going to start.

During the whole time that we were in the cinema, there was nothing but pandemonium. Babies were howling and the kids were screeching. But it didn't matter because they were silent films. We did all the talking that there was.

Just before the film began, the manager used to come on stage with a megaphone and bawl through it, 'Quiet! Quiet!' Then, oozing benevolence, his face wreathed in smiles, he used to say, 'Now, kiddies, you are going to have a marvellous time this afternoon. You're going to see two lovely films, and I know you are going to enjoy yourselves so when you go home, don't forget to tell your mummies and daddies what a good time you've had.' Then his face would change. The smile would be wiped off, and glaring at us ferociously, he would say, 'Look after the babies and don't you let the little buggers wet the seats!' But we never used to care. We used to stamp our feet and scream. Nobody took a bit of notice of him.

Then began the main film and Miss Bottle played all the way through. When I think of the stamina of those pianists! When the action was fierce, she would bang on the keys and put her foot down on the pedal to get it as loud as possible. In the romantic love scenes, she would play soft melodious tunes and the kids used to put their fingers in their mouths and whistle. We didn't care tuppence about love in those days.

The serial was often the most harrowing thing. It also used to be our bugbear because there were some weeks when we couldn't afford to go. Dad would be out of work and he couldn't even give us the three halfpennies we needed to get in. It always happened when the serial had reached a most thrilling episode like the heroine being suspended over a cliff or tied on the railway line or fixed just in front of a circular saw coming nearer and nearer to her. Then up would come the words, 'To be continued next week'. The times I've hung around the cinema that next week waiting for my friends to come out to tell me what had happened. It never occurred to me that she wouldn't really get killed, that she couldn't because the serial had to go on. I used to ask, 'What happened to her? Did she get killed? How did she get away?' So really the serials were a terrible worry to me.

5

THE SHOPS, of course, were nothing like the shops there are now. There were no such things as supermarkets or self-service stores. They were mostly little family concerns.

There was a Woolworth's. I don't think it was called Woolworth's in those days. It was the 'Thruppenny and Sixpenny Bazaar'. Everything in it was either threepence or sixpence. You would have thought that at these prices there couldn't have been much variety but the way they used to get over it was most ingenious. They would separate things. For instance, sixpence for a kettle and threepence for the lid, not sold separately so, you see, it was still sixpence and three-pence. The same with saucepans, cups and saucers and so on. Nevertheless, for sixpence, you could get a great many things.

The pawnshop played a big part in working-class people's lives. Every Monday morning the wives would cart their husbands' suits along to put them in pawn and have enough money to get them through the week. On Friday night or Saturday morning, they'd be along to get them out so that the husbands could wear them on Saturdays and Sundays. On Monday, back they would go again. In very hard times, other things would go in, like sheets and blankets. You didn't get a lot of money on them but even a shilling or two helped you through the week.

Then, of course, the little grocers' shops were a great standby. They were always ready to give tick. Mother would send me along with a note saying could she have this, that, and the other on her list and she would pay at the end of the week. They would let you do it because people always paid when they could. Mostly everybody was poor and relied on getting things on tick. The shops may not have been as attractive as they are today but I'm sure the food had more flavour.

Take the baker's shop on the corner of our road. It was the most wonderful shop to us! You see they really baked the bread there, and the glorious smell greeted us on our way to school in the morning. Even if you weren't hungry the wonderful smell of that bread would make your mouth water. They used to do doughnuts for a halfpenny each. Not the sort of doughnuts that you find now that are a lump of dough. One bite and you haven't found the jam; another and you've passed it. They were gorgeous, greasy, and golden, coated in fine sugar, and loaded with jam. The baker used to make several batches a day. On a weekend when Dad got his money, for a treat we would have some of these for tea. They beat any cakes that I've ever known now. And so did the bread. It wasn't like this kind of bread you eat now that tastes like cotton-wool in your mouth, you can chew it for ever and it's like swallowing lumps of wet dough. It was like cake. Of course by present-day standards, it wasn't hygienic. None of it was wrapped.

When I was a girl practically every street had a pub, in fact some streets had one on each corner.

Saturday night was the main drinking night. The gaiety there had to be seen to be believed. I can well understand why. You see, employers in those days were vastly different from what they are now. Today 'Jack's as good as his master', but in those days he certainly wasn't. It was 'Yes, sir', 'No, sir' and work from morning till night. And work hard because if you didn't there were half a dozen people queuing up to take your place. But when you got in the pub you were your own master. Yes, then a man had money in his pocket regardless of the fact that it was supposed to last him all the week. So he let go. He went in the pub and aired his opinions and there was no boss to dictate to him. He could say what he liked. Mostly the men got over there as soon as the pub opened and the women as soon as they put the kids to bed. Many women took their children with them – leaving them outside the doors.

On a Saturday night, by eight o'clock, it would be absolute bedlam inside. There'd be all the people singing and dancing. There was always music. Somebody would play a concertina; somebody a banjo. Somebody would give a turn singing. The men would be swearing at the top of their voices, and often the women as well.

And the kids outside. Some of them would be in prams; some would be playing; some would open the door and bawl,

'Mum, aren't you coming out? Mum, baby's howling!' And out would come mother. She'd either give the baby something or she'd cuff all her offspring for getting her out and back she would dart in again. Of course, when it came to closing time there was nearly always a free fight on the pavement. They just fought with their fists and shouted obscenities. There was no knocking them down and kicking them in the balls or using knives and bottles like you get now.

There used to be one man whose wife didn't drink. When he came out of the pub, three sheets in the wind, reeling along, he'd look up at his bedroom window. If he saw a light on, he knew she'd gone to bed and he'd bawl out, 'It's no good you bloody well going to sleep, you old cow, because I shall need you in a minute!'

There was nothing else for working-class people but the pubs. They couldn't afford to go to the theatres; the cinema maybe. It wasn't that they spent such a lot. The beer was so strong then. When my Dad was in work he used to come home Saturday at dinnertime and send me around to the bottle-and-jug department to get half a pint of Burton. They used to have only this half a pint between them. But my mother said it was just like drinking wine, it was so strong and smooth that that was as much as they needed. Nowadays you can down pints of the stuff and all it does is fill you full of wind and water.

6

ALTHOUGH WE lived by the sea a lot of our playing was done in the streets. It is nowadays to some extent, but then we used to play proper games. The games were marvellous because not only did you have the pavement, you had the road as well. There wasn't much traffic then.

At Easter, for example, it was street skipping. We'd get a long scaffold rope out, stretching from one side of the street to the other. The mothers would turn the rope and anyone who liked could skip in. Sometimes there would be a dozen all skipping at the same time and singing, 'Hot cross buns, one a penny, two a penny, hot cross buns.'

Another game was Buttons. How my mother used to dread the autumn when Button time came around! We used to draw a chalk square on the pavement by the house and shoot the buttons into it. The first person who managed to get her button into the square and knock somebody else's out won them all. I was an absolute duffer at the game.

Then there was hopscotch time. You drew a big oblong in

chalk on the pavement and squared it off, and numbered these squares from one up to twelve. Then you threw a stone first into 'One', then you hopped into that square, picked up the stone and bopped the way around without touching the lines. Next you threw the stone into 'Two' and hopped and picked up the stone in 'Two' and hopped all the way around again, and so on till you'd put the stone in all the squares. The moment you put the other foot down or you didn't succeed in picking up the stone, you were out.

Marbles was the game everybody went mad about. You kicked a hole in the road about six or seven feet from the gutter. And you could then. The idea was to get the marbles into the hole – and the game developed in the same way as Buttons. Yet another game was hoops. My aunt bought me the largest hoop you could have. It had an iron guide which you hooked on to the hoop and I ran all round the roads with it. You never had to worry about traffic. No child would last very long doing that today.

Then, of course, there was top time. That was a wonderful time because these tops you just wound up with string and you could whip them from one end of the street to the other. You could paste little coloured pieces of paper on the top of them so that when you whipped, it was like a rainbow going round.

Later in the autumn, we used to go up to the Downs and get horse-chestnuts and play conkers. It didn't cost us anything. And as soon as we lost one supply we could always get more.

I don't want to give the impression that life was all games.

There was always school and the holidays weren't as long as they are now, but I always enjoyed going to school because I did pretty well there. I never found any of it hard except things like art, knitting, and needlework. None of those things were any good to me at all. The needlework was my biggest hate. We had to make such ugly garments; chemises and bloomers – as they were called then. Both made of calico. The chemises were wide with sort of cap sleeves and they reached down to the knees. The bloomers did up at the back with buttons and were also voluminous. Whoever bought these awful garments when they were finished I really don't know. I should imagine they were given to the workhouse because I certainly never brought any home. There were always loads of gathers and you had to stroke the gathers. I was absolutely hopeless at it. In the first place, I could never seem to get on with the thimble. So, of course, I used to prick my finger and the garments got spotted with blobs of blood. It started out as a white garment but it was red and black by the time I'd finished. Well, can you wonder at it? There were the most primitive lavatories in the yard but there was nowhere to wash your hands. So I came in after playtime with my hands filthy to do this needlework.

Singing was hopeless too. I always remember the school concert. We had a concert once a year and, as I was always a bit of a big head, I thought that I would be able to do something. The teacher said to me, 'You can't sing.' So she said, 'I know what you can do. You can tell a funny story. I'll write it all out for you and you learn it all off by heart.'

The funny story was about a man who went into a café

and wanted a plate of boiled onions. He got so muddled with it that he asked for a plate of oiled bunions. I thought it was quite funny. So did my family. They got the joke presumably. But when it came to the concert and I got up on the platform I started saying it in a very straight way – sort of parrot fashion, and then I got my onions and bunions all the wrong way round and at the end I waited for the laugh but nobody did except the teachers. They had to laugh. It was terrible. I never felt so mortified in my life. I went as red as a beetroot, and left in a great hurry. They never got me to do anything else. They had no manners at all. They should have laughed. Especially as it was free.

But the great thing about school in those days was that we had to learn. I don't think you can beat learning; how to read and write, and how to do arithmetic. Those are the three things that anyone who has got to work for a living needs. We were forced to learn and I think children need to be forced. I don't believe in this business of 'if they don't want to do it, it won't do them any good'. It *will* do them good. Our teacher used to come around and give us a mighty clump on the neck or box on the ears if she saw us wasting our time. Believe me, by the time we came out of school, we came out with something. We knew enough to get us through life. Not that any of us thought about what we were going to do. We all knew that when we left school we'd have to do something, but I don't think we had any ambitions to do any particular type of work.

7

I WON A SCHOLARSHIP when I was thirteen which was the age one sat for it then. You had to say on your paper what you would like to be. I said I wanted to be a teacher. My parents saw my headmistress but when they found out that I couldn't possibly earn any money till I was eighteen and up to that time they would have to keep me, and not only keep me, but buy my books and clothes, they just couldn't do it. You see, there were no government grants in those days.

I was allowed to leave school because I was in the top class and if I had put in another year it would have been the same work all over again.

Looking back, I wish it had been possible to have gone on with my education but at that time I didn't mind in the least. I didn't think my parents were hard because I knew I had to go out to work, I knew we needed the money so desperately. I had known the mortifications of poverty. I remember when I was about seven – it was early in the Great War. Dad wasn't called up then but nobody was having anything done in the decorating line; the men had gone into the army and money was very tight indeed.

That was when the town opened the soup kitchen. It was in Sheridan Terrace, Hove. A covered stone building with two coal-burning coppers. You queued up for your helping at midday – that was the only time they served it. The soup was terrible. Thin, watery pea soup. I'm sure it was the kind of stuff they doled out to Oliver Twist. I had to go up there with a washstand jug to get it. Mum never knew what shame that washstand jug caused me. It was a white one covered in pink roses. Other children had enamel jugs which seemed to me a far more suitable thing. And to walk through the streets, carrying a large washstand jug full of pea soup pretending you hadn't been up there and got it for nothing, that you've not been accepting charity, well, then you've got to be very clever indeed. I wouldn't let Mother know how it made me feel because there was no one else to do it.

When my father got called up in 1916 the separation allowance was terrible. It really was. Starvation money. That's all you could call it.

Then the coal got in short supply. You couldn't have even half a hundredweight of coal if you had a gas stove. So I used to have to go down to the Town Hall, young as I was, to get a permit. I swore 'black's blue' that we hadn't got a gas stove, that we'd never had a gas stove, that we did all our cooking on the fire, and I never turned a hair. Can you wonder that you grow up with all your wits around you? Then when I'd got this permit, I had to go right up to the depot where the trains came in and wait there in a queue. It was winter, it was freezing cold and my stomach was empty. I pushed the coal back in an old pram and I fainted with the cold. Somebody picked me up and took me into their house. They gave me something to eat and a sixpence but I still had to push the coal back home.

With my father gone, it was a harrowing time. I remember Mother used to confide in me, the eldest girl. I remember when we hadn't anything left to use for warmth and no money to get coal. I said to Mum, 'Get all the wood down. Let's have a fire with wood.' She took every single shelf there was in the rooms and she even took the banisters from the stairs. Things like this make you hard.

I had also adopted a kind of grown-up manner with all the shops. The butcher in particular, he was a great favourite of mine. I used to go along there on a weekend and say, 'I want the biggest joint you've got for a shilling.' He used to say, 'Well, I hope you've brought your own paper.' So I would say, 'Oh, yes, I have. I've brought this bus ticket to wrap it in. That's large enough for your joints.'

Every other morning, Mum got my brother and me up at six o'clock. She gave us sixpence and a pillowcase and we went to the baker's – Forfar's in Church Road. They didn't open till eight o'clock but the earlier you got there, the better bread you got. It took us about twenty minutes to walk it so we had a long wait outside.

If we were first in the queue, we used to look through the letterbox and see just what sort of bread they had. Mostly it was large flat brown loaves. We used to call them cow cakes because they resembled the cow-dung that we saw in the fields. Especially when people had trodden on it.

Sometimes we'd see a currant loaf. It was marvellous if we got a currant loaf.

For our sixpence they used almost to fill a pillowcase with bread.

Best of all were the rolls. If there were any rolls put in, we used to eat them on the way home and never say a word to Mum. We were so ravenous, getting up at six, queuing outside in all that cold, so just eating those odd rolls was absolute heaven.

The best thing that happened around our street during the war was when they billeted the soldiers on us.

My mother had three. An Englishman, a Scotsman, and an Irishman. She had to ask to have the Irishman removed. He made such uproars and all that.

I don't know what the money was, but I noticed there was a change in our standard of living. Mum said my father wasn't too keen about the idea. You see she was an attractive woman and he was in France at the time and couldn't do anything about it.

It made a big difference. All of a sudden everybody sprouted out with new things. Even the tally-man got paid. The tally-man was a door-to-door salesman. He came around and sold sheets and pillowcases, and boots and shoes, and things like that, carrying them in a large case. You paid him so much a week for the goods and a little bit over the odds because he had to wait for his money. You never signed agreements, it was just written down in a book. Selling the goods was easy. Anyone could buy them but when it came to collecting the money it was a different story indeed. When Mother had no money I used to stand at the top of the steps watching for the tally-man. When I saw him coming I used to rush in and bawl out, 'He's here, Mum!' and she used to go and hide. When he came to the door I would answer and say, 'Mum's out.' He never used to believe me and he used to get very abusive, but of course he couldn't do anything. The same with the rent collector. There just wasn't the money.

I would have nightmares about this rent collector and the fact that he might turn us out. Everything got paid eventually but that was the trouble, you see, running up debts so that when your husband got work again, you were still as hard up in a way because you were paying off what had accumulated while he was out of work.

8

I STARTED WORK the first week after I left school. It was a housework job in a bungalow, with a married couple. The wife was an old lady, a semi-invalid, paralysed from the waist down. I worked from seven in the morning until one, Sundays included, for ten shillings a week. I didn't get any dinner because that was the idea of leaving at one o'clock just as they were starting their dinner, but I did get breakfast.

The funny part about this breakfast, although I didn't think so then, was that it was anything that was left from the night before. Sometimes I had milk pudding, sometimes I had macaroni cheese, sometimes I had cottage pie. But I didn't worry. I ate everything there was because the more I ate down there the less my Mum had to give me. Food was getting to be a constant problem with me because although I was only thirteen, I was a huge girl and I had an enormous appetite. And of course the harder I worked, the hungrier I got. My mother used to get so indignant about this breakfast. She said it was such a cheat giving me things like that.

I should have eggs and bacon, and not the old left-overs. But I never used to worry, I couldn't care less what I ate so long as I did.

I didn't stay at that job very long mainly because I began to develop pains in my legs. I presume it was because I was beginning to mature. I remember one morning I had such pains in my legs, I said to the man of the house, 'I can't work any more today. My legs hurt me so much.' He gave me a bottle of liniment to rub them with and said it would do them extra good because it was horse liniment. I was furious. I could hardly walk. So that finished that job.

That first year I had a dozen jobs altogether. These little daily jobs were all the same. I was very young so they paid me a microscopic wage, but at the same time I looked so hefty that they expected a lot out of me.

One job which I had lasted only a week. It was to push a cantankerous old lady around in a bathchair. She had once been somebody by the aristocratic way in which she spoke, but she was reduced to one old retainer to look after her and a large-sized house.

Every morning it was my job to go there and help this old lady into her bathchair. And that was a business, believe me, what with the bonnets, the capes, and the button boots. All the time I was doing this for her she was nagging at me. When I got her ensconced in this bathchair I had to push her round to the shops, and then go and say, 'Mrs Graham is outside. Will you please come out for orders?' Can you imagine nowadays going into a shop and asking the shopkeeper to come out for orders? But in those days, although she was as poor as a church mouse, with her aristocratic manner, the shop keepers would come out, very obsequiously bow and scrape and later send everything that she ordered.

Nothing I did was right for her. Either I hadn't got her into the right position outside the shop or the sun was in her eyes or I'd jolted her back.

One particular day, it was a lovely summer morning and she wanted me to push her along the seafront. We went down to the West Pier, about a mile and a half. Then she wanted me to arrange her chair so that the wind was at the back of her and yet so she could still see the people. She was at her worst that day, and she moaned the whole journey, so that after I tried to get her into position about six times and still it wasn't right, I just gave up. I didn't say anything. I just walked away and left her. I never did know what happened to her or how she got back or anything.

When I told Mother she was taken aback at first, but when she told Dad he saw the funny side of it and all through the week he kept saying, 'I wonder if that old girl is still stuck at the West Pier?'

After that, as a change from housework, I got a job in a sweet shop. Every child's delight. I was allowed to eat as many sweets as I wanted. I was soon sick of them. The reason I got the sack from there was that all my brothers and sisters and their friends used to come in with their halfpennies and farthings. I used to dole them out sweets *ad lib* and the owner saw all her profit going.

The job I was really waiting for was to work at the local laundry, but you had to be fourteen before they would start you there. I went at thirteen and a half, thinking that, as I was such a big person, they would take me on, but they asked to see my birth certificate so that was that.

As soon as I was fourteen I went there and got taken on as a sorter. I was put in a room on my own and had to sort the linen from the Hotel Metropole, the biggest hotel in Brighton. That was my job for the first six months. Afterwards I got to running around for everybody, a bit in the ironing room and a bit in the washroom.

I worked from eight o'clock until six for twelve and six-pence a week. Not a lot of money and no meals. But it was lively, far livelier than doing housework, especially the iron-ing room. The language and the atmosphere there reminded me of Dante's *Inferno*.

It was one of my jobs to go into this room with a watering-can to sprinkle the floor, because there were no mechanical means of removing the dust and with the clothes being continually moved around the floor used to get covered with a fine white powder. If by chance you sprinkled the water on the feet of the ironing women instead of on the floor, they used to swear like Billingsgate fishwives. I'd never heard anything like it in my life, even on a Saturday night along our street, and they used to tell the foulest jokes and screech with mirth at my incomprehension.

What a sight I must have looked. It was the time when girls were wearing boots that came up to the knees but I had a pair that came just above my ankles like my father's boots. I was already taking size eights although I was only fourteen. In the morning I never knew whether they were Dad's or mine until

I had examined them well. So what with that and the jumper my mother had knitted me (she had run out of the wool when she got to the back so it was a different colour from the front) and my hair straight back, and the goitre from which I was suffering, I must have looked like a drawing by Boz.

When I got to be fifteen and was due for a half a crown rise, I got the sack. They had no need to pay you fifteen shillings a week. Girls of fourteen could do what I was doing. So that any excuse they found to get rid of you, they did.

9

WHEN I CAME home from the laundry and told my mother I'd got the sack she was very annoyed. I expect she was a bit fed up, with all the various jobs I'd had since I left school, and she said, 'I did think you were settled at the laundry. You were mad keen to go there at fourteen, and now you've got the sack at fifteen. Oh well, there's nothing else for it, you'll have to go into domestic service, that's all.'

I hated the idea but I never even thought of moaning about it. I dare say I could have appealed to my father because he always made a big fuss of me; although Mum was the guiding light in our house – Dad left everything to her. We've always done as my mother told us to do. Children did at that time.

So I said, 'All right, then.' I didn't know that much about it – and my mother told me what a good job it was; all the benefits that accrue from going into service; good food and lodgings and that. The money you do get is all your own.

Of course, like a lot of things seen in retrospect, my mother looked at her years in domestic service through a vista of married life, with a husband always out of work in the winter, with seven children and never enough money for food, never mind about clothes. Her years in domestic service seemed a time when at least she did have a certain amount of money that she could call her own.

She forgot the tales she used to tell us – how she went into it when she was fourteen years old in 1895, and how she had to work like a galley slave; an object of derision to the other servants.

So when I reminded Mum of all this, 'Ah,' she said, 'life is different in service now; the work's not so hard, you get more free time, and the outings and money are better.'

So I said, 'Well, what could I be in service, then?' and she said, 'Well, as you hate needlework' (and I always did hate needlework) 'there's only one place you can go and that is into the kitchen. If you're a parlourmaid you've got to mend all the table linen, and if you're a housemaid you've got to mend all the house linen, and if you're in the nursery you've got to mend, and even make, the children's clothes. But if you're a kitchen maid, then you don't have any needlework to do at all.' So I said, 'All right, then, I'll be a kitchen maid.'

I went down to a domestic agency, of which there were a great many at that time; and many posts for kitchen maids, because it was the lowest position in the house for a servant. Yet it's funny, you know, if you wanted to be a cook and you had no money to pay for training, the only way you could learn to be one was by starting as a kitchen maid.

I was offered various posts and eventually I settled on one

in Adelaide Crescent in Hove, because it was fairly near to where we lived. It was the home of the Reverend Clydesdale and his wife. My mother came with me for the interview.

They were tremendous houses in Adelaide Crescent; they started off with a basement and went right up to an attic, there were a hundred and thirty-two stairs in all, and the basements were dark and like dungeons. The front of the basement, with iron bars all down the bay windows, was the servants' hall. When you were sitting in there all you saw going by was people's legs, and when you were on the other side of the basement hall, which was the kitchen, a big conservatory overhung that, so you saw nothing at all. It had one tiny window high up in the wall which you couldn't see through unless you got a ladder. The light had to be on all day long.

The Crescent is one of the most imposing in Hove. The houses were Regency style, and even now, although they are all flats, they haven't altered the façade, and it still looks very much as it did with gardens right down the centre. Of course, at that time only the residents had keys and were allowed to use the gardens, but that certainly didn't apply to the servants, I can assure you.

When my mother and I arrived at this house for the interview we went to the front door. In all the time I worked there, that was the only time I ever went in by the front door. But the front door it was on this particular day. We were ushered into a hall that I thought was the last word in opulence. There was a lovely carpet on the floor, and tremendously wide stairs carpeted right across, not like the tiny little bit of lino in the middle we had on our stairs. There was a great mahogany table in the hall and a mahogany hallstand, and huge mirrors with gilt frames. The whole thing breathed an aura of wealth to me. I thought they must be millionaires. I'd never seen anything like it.

A butler opened the door to us and my mother said that this was Margaret Langley who had come for the interview as a kitchen maid. A very tiny little butler he was. I'd always thought that butlers were tall, imposing men. In the hall we saw a rather elderly gentleman and the lady who was to interview us. We were shown into what was obviously a nursery – a day nursery.

My mother did all the talking because I was overcome with wonder at this room, for although it was only a nursery, you could have put all the three rooms that we lived in into it. Also I was overcome with shyness; I suffered agonies of self-consciousness in those days. And the lady, Mrs Clydesdale, looked me up and down as though I was something at one of those markets, you know, one of those slave markets. She seemed to be weighing up all my points.

My mother told her that I had been doing daily jobs. She didn't mention the laundry because she didn't think that was any recommendation. People thought that laundries were hotbeds of vice in those days because of the obscene language of the girls who worked there.

Mrs Clydesdale decided that because I was strong and healthy I would do. I was to have twenty-four pounds a year, paid monthly. I was to have one afternoon and evening off from four o'clock to ten o'clock, and alternate Sundays off the same hours, and I was never to be in later than ten o'clock under any circumstances. I was to have three print dresses, blue or green; four white aprons with bibs, and four caps; stockings, and black strapped shoes. I was always to say 'Sir' and 'Madam' if I was spoken to by Mr and Mrs Clydesdale, and I was to treat the upper servants with great respect and do everything the cook asked me to do. To all these things my mother said, 'Yes, Madam, no, Madam', and all these things she promised on my behalf that I would do. My spirits sank lower and lower. I felt I was in jail at the finish.

When we got outside I told Mum how I felt but she'd decided that the job would do for me. So that was that.

The trouble was the uniform. My mother worked it out that it couldn't be done — all these things that had to be bought for me — under two pounds. I know that it sounds a ridiculously small sum now, but two pounds was untold wealth to us then. We hadn't got two pounds but anyway she managed to borrow it and she fitted me out.

On the day I was due to go there she got her old, battered tin trunk that she'd been all through domestic service with, and I packed the few things that I had in it. Apart from the uniform my own clothes were very few indeed. I was dressed up in a blouse and skirt and a coat that had belonged to my grandmother.

I said to Mum, 'How are we going to get the tin trunk down to Adelaide Crescent? Are we going to have a taxi?' She said, 'You must be stark, raving mad. Where do you think we are going to get the money from? Dad's going to borrow the barrow.' Dad worked for a decorator at that time, so he was going to load the trunk on to the barrow and wheel it down there. We must have looked a peculiar lot – my Dad walking in the road with the tin trunk on the barrow, and Mum and I trailing along on the pavement. When we got there Dad carried the tin trunk down to the basement.

As she said goodbye my Mum put her arms around me, which was very unusual because in our family we didn't indulge in any outward show of affection. I felt as if I could have howled and howled. And yet they weren't going miles away, they lived in the same town, but to me it was a terrible thing to see my mother and father retreating and leaving me in this alien environment. I thought, 'Oh, no, I can't stay here', but I wouldn't say so. I knew I'd got to work as my parents couldn't afford to keep me.

The first person I saw was another young girl just about my own age. She told me she was Mary, the under-housemaid, and she said, 'I'll help you upstairs with your tin trunk.' Help me upstairs! I'd never seen anything like it! I never thought there could be so many stairs in a house.

From the basement until you got up to two floors below the attics there were back stairs for the servants to use, so that you never interfered with 'Them', and 'They' never saw you running up and down the stairs or anything. And of course the back stairs were very different from the front stairs. They only had linoleum on them, the same as our stairs had at home.

It was a good job I didn't have many clothes because I don't know how we would have got this tin trunk up to the room.

When we did get there I said to Mary, 'What do I do now?' She said, 'The first thing you do is to change straight away into your uniform and come downstairs. And by the way,' she said, 'you'll have to do something about that hair of yours, you can't come down like you are.' I had very long hair because it was before the days of people having their hair cut off. I'd tried to put it up in a bun to go into service and Mother had helped me to do it, but it was all falling down and I didn't have half enough hairpins. Anyway Mary said, 'I'll help you.' She scraped it all back off my face; I had pulled it forward in an effort to make myself attractive. But Mary said, 'The cook won't let you have your hair like that. When you've got your cap on none of your hair must show in the front at all.' So she scraped it all back and she screwed it in a bun at the back, and not only did she use all the hairpins I had but she gave me a dozen of hers as well. I felt like a pin-cushion at the back. When I put my hand up I could feel nothing but hairpins, and when I looked in the glass at my face with not a scrap of hair showing, I thought I looked hideous. Little did I know I was going to look hideous the whole time I worked there, so really it made very little difference starting off like that.

I got the uniform on, and oh how I hated it! As a kitchen maid I had to wear this uniform morning and afternoon. I didn't change into black like the upstairs servants did. It was a blue uniform, not navy blue, a sort of between navy and saxe blue. Then I put on one of those wide aprons with a bib and straps over the back that buttoned on to the ones that went round your waist, and then the wretched cap. I hated that cap until I got to be a cook, and I never wore a cap then. I had a battle royal with one woman I worked for over it, but I'd never wear a cap as a cook.

When I was dressed Mary said, 'Now we'll go down to the kitchen.' When we got down there it was teatime for the servants. That's one meal the kitchen maid doesn't have to get, the under-housemaid gets it.

10

I THINK ONE of the worst ordeals was meeting all the servants, although compared with some of the other houses I worked in later, there weren't so many. There was a butler; a parlour-maid instead of a footman; two housemaids – upper and under; a governess; and a gardener/chauffeur; the cook and me.

The first thing I was shown before I sat down and had my tea was a list of the kitchen maid's duties. When I looked at this list I thought they had made a mistake. I thought it was for six people to do.

Kitchen maid's duties – rise at five-thirty (six o'clock on Sundays), come downstairs, clean the flues, light the fire, blacklead the grate (incidentally, when you blackleaded the grate you didn't have nice tins of liquid polish, you had a hard old lump of blacklead, which before you went to bed at night you had to put into a saucer with water and leave soaking all night before it would assume any kind of a paste to do the grate with. I didn't know this, and nobody bothered to tell me. I tried to do it next morning with this lump; I thought you had to rub it on the stove. No one told me anything. Why people should assume I knew, I don't know), clean the steel fender and the fire-irons (that steel fender, without exaggerating, was all of four foot long, with a tremendous shovel, tongs, and poker all in steel, which all had to be done with emery paper), clean the brass on the front door, scrub the steps, clean the boots and shoes, and lay the servants' breakfast. And this all had to be done before eight o'clock. The things that were written down to do after breakfast throughout the day, well, I'd never seen such a list in my life.

So what with the uniform, the cap, my hair, and the list of duties, well, when Mary said, 'Come and have your tea and meet all the servants,' I felt that life couldn't hold anything worse for me. I was in the lowest pit. I thought, 'How could my mother let me come here and tell me that things were better now, you didn't have to work so hard, you've got more free time, and people think more of you?'

So I went into the servants' hall, and when I say I met the other servants, don't think I was introduced to them. No one bothers to introduce a kitchen maid. You're just looked at as if you're something the cat brought in. One of them said 'She looks hefty enough'. It was just as well I was hefty, believe me.

I sat down and had my tea, but how I ate it with all these servants looking at me, I don't know. Fortunately my mother – and father – had always been very insistent on table manners. We were never allowed to sit anyhow at the table, we always had to use the right things.

50

I hadn't yet met the cook; she was out, she'd gone to see a film. The cook had a lot more free time than anyone else; the cook could go out any afternoon she liked, so long as she was back in time to cook the dinner at night. Naturally, she was the one I was most keen on meeting because it was with her a large part of my life would have to be spent.

Mary told me that Mrs McIlroy — a Scots cook she was — was quite a pleasant person, but I took that with a grain of salt because Mary wasn't under her, so it didn't make a lot of difference what Mary thought about her.

After tea I went and had a look at the kitchen. That was enough to strike a final note of depression.

Occupying one whole side of the kitchen was the range, and I stood and looked at the thing in amazement. We had a kitchen range at home, but my mother never cooked on it, she had a gas stove. But there was no gas stove in this kitchen, only this tremendous range, which was to become to me, although I didn't know it at the time, a nightmare. It had ovens each side of it, one big and one small, and it had been so pol-ished up with blacklead by the previous kitchen maid that you could almost see your face in it. It never looked like that after I did it somehow, I don't know why. As the cook said, some people can polish and some can't. In front of it was the steel fender, and that also was polished to a silvery brightness.

Opposite it was a dresser with great big cupboards on the lower half of it and five shelves on the other half, all plain white wood. Not the small kind of dresser we had in our own little kitchen at home, but one that could take a whole dinner set, and when I say a whole one I don't mean the kind you buy now which are really only halves; a hundred and twenty-six pieces of china were ranged on the shelves, and on the flat part of it, which was the top of the cupboards, were an enormous soup tureen, vegetable dishes, and sauce boats. It was my job, written down in my duties, to take this whole lot down once a week and wash every single piece of it, and scrub the dresser.

On the third wall there were two doors; one led into servants' hall. It used to be quite an enjoyable occupation when we were sitting in there having our meals to look at the legs of the passers-by in the street and to give a face to the legs. If you saw a fat pair of legs go by you would say, 'Fifty if she's a day', and somebody would say, 'No, not her, she's got duck's disease or water on the knees.'

Incidentally, I never know why they called it a servants' hall. It didn't resemble a hall, it was just a room. But everywhere I went the room the servants sat in was called a servants' hall.

The other door led into the butler's pantry. Although it was called a pantry it was not a place where food was kept. There were two sinks, one to put the soap in to wash all the silver, and the other with plain water to rinse it and to wash all the glasses. The butler and the parlourmaid between them did all the silver and all the glassware; not the knives, that came into the kitchen maid's province.

Another door in the fourth wall led into a long passage from the back door to the kitchen – a huge place, all stone-flagged. In this passage, hanging on the wall, was a long row of bells with indicators above them to show where they rang from, and it was my job every time a bell went to run full tilt out into the passage to see which bell it was. We had whistles in the house. You pulled a plug out in the wall and whistled up to the various rooms to see if you could catch anybody to tell them they were wanted. If you didn't run like mad out into the passage, the bell would stop ringing before you got there, and you had no idea whether it was from the blue room, the pink room, first bedroom, second bedroom, fifth bedroom, drawing-room, or dining-room. So you would come back to the cook and say, 'I don't know which bell it was.' 'You must be quicker,' she'd say, 'otherwise all hell will be let loose upstairs.' But what could you do? If you were in the middle of something you couldn't drop it straight away. I was always in trouble over these bells at first, but at last I mastered the art, and nobody shot out quicker than I did when they rang.

The kitchen floor itself was all stone, not nice shiny stone flags that you see new, but just sort of large bricks. They had to be scrubbed every day. Down the whole length of the room was the kitchen table; a heavy great thing on four of the hugest square legs I have ever seen, and it had been scrubbed to a whiteness that would have been the envy of any washing powder today, although we only had soap and soda then. That was the cook's table which, Mary informed me, I had to set out.

She said to me, 'You know how to set a cook's table, don't you?' I said, 'Yes, I know how to put things out for cooking,' but little did I know how to set it out, really and truly.

That same evening, about six o'clock, Mrs McIlroy, the

cook, came in, and a very pleasant person she seemed. She came up to me and actually shook hands, which was more than anybody else had done.

She was a woman about fifty, a Scotswoman, rather short with grey hair, very down-to-earth type of person, rather plain, but she had such a pleasant personality that you never really noticed how plain she was.

Later on, after I had got to know her better, I said, 'Mrs McIlroy', the Mrs was just a courtesy title; most cooks, if they had not married and if they were a Miss and they were getting on in years, were called Mrs not only by the people they worked for, but by the other servants as well. 'Mrs McIlroy,' I said, 'I wonder you've never got married,' and I piled the old flattery on because I found it always paid off, especially when you happened to be under the person, 'you've got such an attractive personality', nearly choking myself when I was saying it. She said, 'Well, it's like this, my girl. When I was about twenty-five I looked in the mirror and I said to myself, "Girl, a good plain cook you've decided to be, and a good plain cook you're going to be all your life. It's certainly sure you're plain and it's certainly sure no one is going to want to marry you." That's how I found it was too.'

That first evening after she'd introduced herself she said, 'Well, girl, we've got to get on with it. You'll lay up my table, won't you?' 'Oh yes,' I said, and she went up to her room.

All I put out was a knife, a fork, and a spoon, the flour, the salt, and a sifter. I thought that was all she'd need for cooking the dinner. Luckily for me, Mary came out while I was doing it, and after explaining with a fit of giggles that my idea of laying out a cook's table was hopeless, she said, 'I'll show you how to do it. I'll show you before Mrs McIlroy comes back, not that she will grumble, but she might start laughing when she sees what you've put out.' Mary began. There were knives of all kinds, all shapes and sizes, big long carving knives, small knives for paring fruit, pallet knives, bent knives for scraping out basins with, and then metal spoons, not the ordinary type – they were like a kind of aluminium-coloured spoon – huge ones, about six of them. The largest ones had the measures on them, from ounces right up to dessert-spoonfuls. She put out two sieves, a hair sieve and a wire sieve, and a flour sifter, and an egg whisk. Naturally, there were no electric whisks in those days. In fact, there weren't even the ones with the wheels, you had a kind of wire contraption that you had to beat by hand. Then there were two kinds of graters, one fine one for nutmegs, and one to do the breadcrumbs on; there was a big chopping board and a small chopping board, three or four kinds of basins, paprika pepper and cayenne pepper, ordinary salt, pepper, and vinegar. Half the table was covered with these things. All these implements had to be laid out twice a day; for lunch, although the lunch was only three courses, and for dinner again at night, when there were five or six.

When I saw all that I said to Mary, 'She can't use all those things.' 'Oh,' she said, 'you've not seen anything. By the time dinner starts in this house you will be running around wiping things because cook used them once and she wants them again. She uses some of these things two or three times in the course of preparing the meal.' It turned out to be true.

11

THE AMOUNT of food that came into that house seemed absolutely fabulous to me, the amount of food that was eaten and wasted too. They often had a whole saddle of mutton. You don't see saddles very much now but they were gorgeous things. And sirloins. Sometimes with the sirloin they would only eat the undercut and the whole top was left over, so we used to have that for our dinner. Even so, we couldn't eat everything and a lot got thrown away. When I used to think of my family at home where we seldom had enough to eat, it used to break my heart.

The milkman called three times a day – at half past four to five in the morning he would leave some milk, then he would come round again at ten o'clock with more milk and any other orders that you wanted. Naturally, he carried cream and eggs with him, but if you wanted butter or cakes which he sold, or anything like that, he came yet again at about two o'clock in the afternoon.

I've never seen such milk and cream and eggs. Pints of

cream nearly every day was nothing in that household, even when they weren't entertaining, when there was only Mr and Mrs Clydesdale and the young daughter and the governess. When I was first there the milk was served from a great big churn with a handle. Not the kind of churns they roll around on railway stations, or did do, but a churn he carried in his hand. But very soon after that it did change to bottles, which was very much cleaner, of course, because the cans used to smell.

Most of the shopping was ordered from a grand shop in Hove, like Fortnum and Mason's, only you had to be a member to use it. I suppose in a way it was a rich man's Co-op. I don't know if you got a dividend.

They had departments for everything; greengrocery, butchery, cakes, and ordinary groceries.

Mrs Clydesdale would come down about ten o'clock and give cook her menus for the day, and if Mrs McIlroy wanted anything she hadn't already in, she would just ring up and ask them to send it around. That's all you had to do with tradesmen in those days. Just ring them up. In fact, the butcher and the greengrocer would come round for orders when they thought cook knew what she wanted for the day, and in less than half an hour they would be back with it.

Fish we never had from them. A man used to come up from the beach, bringing the fish in a bucket filled with sea water, still alive. I used to dread having to see to these fish because when I cut their heads off they jumped and squirmed.

One day he brought up a giant plaice, and when I laid it on the board to chop its head off it jumped right up in the air and its sharp fin made a wide scratch right down my nose. Mary looked at me and said, 'Whatever have you done to your nose?' I said, 'A fish flapped up and scratched me.' It was a long time before I heard the last of that. I never tried the same thing again. I used to get the heavy steel poker and hit them on the head with it. I never found out where the vulnerable part of the fish was, but my way worked all right.

The same fisherman used to bring lobsters up alive. I used to put them in a bowl in a larder. It was a huge larder, not just a place with shelves all round, it was like a room on its own, with a heavy slated floor and slated shelves which were stone cold even in the summer.

I used to put these lobsters in a bowl on the floor, but when I went in at night to get them for dinner they were never inside it; they had got out and were crawling around. I used to pick them up, often getting a nip for my pains. I never knew where the safest part was to get hold of them.

I hated dropping them into boiling water. Mrs McIlroy said they were killed the instant they touched the boiling water, but were they? I never used to believe they were because I am sure they used to give a terrible squeak as I dropped them in.

Mrs McIlroy had no 'arrangement' with the shops, but nevertheless when she paid the quarterly bills some little gift would often be given to her, and at the end of the year quite an appreciable discount, as they called it, was paid to her.

It was the cook who really chose the shops, so when she

went in they laid the red carpet down for her. Because, although ours wasn't such a large staff, the food was of a very high quality. So that, apart from her salary, any cook could count on a regular bonus from the shops at which she dealt.

But to get back to my daily round. I found that what I had thought was work for six was, in fact, work for one, and that one was me from now on.

Up I got at five-thirty, dragged myself downstairs, and presented myself to the kitchen range. I lit it, cleaned it, and lit the fire in the servants' hall.

Then I'd tear upstairs to do the front door, which was all white paint and brass – a thankless task, particularly in the winter, for when I'd got it all bright and shiny the wind from the sea tarnished it again. So by the time Madam saw it, it was something to find fault with.

Then there were fourteen wide stone steps to be scrubbed. Back downstairs again, and there was Mary waiting with all the boots and shoes.

I remember the first morning. She said, 'Carrie' (that was the head housemaid) 'says she hopes you know how to clean boots and shoes.' 'Well, of course I do,' I said. After all, I'd done them at home. But I didn't know how to do them the way they wanted them done.

The Reverend, he used to wear boots all day; black boots in the week and brown boots on Sundays. In the evenings he changed into black patent shoes. Madam wore black or brown, often both during the course of the day. Then there were the governess's, and Leonora's. These I did and I thought they looked very nice indeed. Well, the toes shone anyway.

When Mary came down for them she said, 'Oh, they won't do. They won't do at all.' I said, 'What's the matter with them? They look all right to me.' 'All right,' she said, 'I'll take them up if you like but Carrie will only sling them back at me.'

About two minutes afterwards down she came again and said, 'It's like I said, they won't do. You haven't done the insteps.' 'The insteps?' I said. 'I never knew you had to clean underneath the shoes.' So I did that, gave them another polish, and Mary took them up again.

Seconds later back she came and said, 'You haven't done the bootlaces.' I said, 'Haven't done the bootlaces!' 'Don't you know?' she said. 'You have to iron all the bootlaces, take them all out and iron them.' I thought she was joking. 'Iron the bootlaces?' I said. She said, 'Yes.' You see in those days they weren't the narrow little bootlaces they are now, they were quite half an inch wide. In fact Mrs Clydesdale's and Leonora's were nearly an inch wide.

So I had to take the laces out of the shoes and iron them. Of course, there were no electric irons, just flat irons. They had to be heated in front of the fire and that took nearly a quarter of an hour. Never in all my life have I seen such a footling procedure.

After that I had to clean the knives because there were no stainless ones in those days. I did this with a large round knife-machine; it had three holes into which I shook the knife-powder, a sort of emery powder. Then I put a knife into each of these holes and turned the handle.

BELOW STAIRS

I felt like an organ-grinder. Indeed the whole business became a musical affair – I sang as I turned.

> *'A young man stood within the court,*
> *'Twas some poor girl he had made sport,*
> *He heaved a bitter, bitter sigh*
> *When she upon him cast her eye.'*

(By then three knives were done, and I'd put another three in.)

> *'She sued him for a thousand pounds*
> *For breach of promise on these grounds.*
> *But on the day they should have wed*
> *He did a dive from church and fled.'*

(Next three).
> *'Not au revoir but goodbye, Lou,*
> *I've got a better girl than you.*
> *She loves me for myself you bet,*
> *And we have bought a basinet.'*

(Then the last three would go in for the last verse.)

> *'The jury looked at him and grinned.*
> *The Judge could see she'd got him pinned.*
> *She won the day, but don't forget*
> *She hasn't got the money yet.'*

By now it was time to take Mrs McIlroy a cup of tea. Then I laid up breakfast in the servants' hall, and at eight o'clock the staff had their meal.

After we'd had our breakfast it was time for Mrs McIlroy and me to cook for upstairs.

Like most of the meals this was very different from what we had. Mrs Clydesdale thought only about our nourishment, so we used to have things like herrings and cod and stews and milk puddings, but none of these nourishing foods ever found their way upstairs. So I was forced to the conclusion that even their internal organs differed from ours, inasmuch as what nourished us did them no good at all.

There were always economies which had to be made. During my years in domestic service I noticed that all economies began with the servants and always ended with them too.

The breakfasts they had upstairs were always huge, whether they had visitors or whether they didn't; there were bacon and eggs, sausages, kidneys, either finnan haddock or kedgeree – not one or two of these things but every one.

I couldn't help thinking of my poor father and mother at home. All they had was toast. And all this food going up to them, who never worked. I just couldn't help thinking of the unfairness of life.

If I said so to Mrs McIlroy she couldn't see it, she just accepted her lot. She thought there ought to be the people who had the money and the people who didn't. 'Because,' she said, 'if there weren't the people who had the money, what would there be for people like us to do?' 'But,' I said, 'couldn't it be equalled out more – more equitably – for them not to have so much, and for us to have a little bit more? Why do you and I have to work in this dungeon with the barest of comforts while they have everything upstairs? After all,' I said, 'don't forget, Mrs McIlroy, our board and our lodging is part of our wages. The two pounds a month that I have in money is supposed to be supplemented by the board and lodging. If the lodging is of the kind that Mary and I have in that attic, and the food is meagre, and the outings are so small,' I said, 'how are we getting an equitable wage?'

Even at that early stage I used to think about these things. Maybe through my father, because the inequalities of life used to cause him a lot of heartache. Mother didn't take the same notice. So long as she could just have a drink now and again and give us enough to eat, which she could in the summer, she didn't seem to mind so much, but Dad felt these things more.

After breakfast had been washed up we started preparing lunch.

Lunch, according to Mrs McIlroy, was a very simple meal. Soup, fish, cutlets, or a grill, and a sweet. One of the things she taught me was how a dish should be sent up. For instance, when it was cutlets, she would mash the potatoes and roll them in egg and breadcrumbs, in little balls, slightly larger than walnuts, and then she would arrange them in a pyramid on a silver dish and the cutlets would stand on end all round with a little white frill on each bone and parsley at intervals around the dish. It really looked most attractive.

For us the main meal was the middle-day meal because at night we just had anything that was left over. Although it was our main meal I noticed we never got three courses, we only had meat and sweet; fairly substantial, but not cutlets or fillet steak or anything like that. When it was fish, it was her-rings or cod. Still, there was always enough of it, and as I'd never been used to luxurious living, I always ate anything there was.

12

THE MAIN meal was always at night, even when there were only Mr and Mrs Clydesdale, their little girl Leonora, and the governess. These last two had their meals in a separate place altogether except on Sundays, when Leonora was allowed to have her meals with her parents. It was always five, some-times six courses.

It would start with soup of some kind. Mrs McIlroy was very good at making clear soup. We used to get lovely bones from the butcher which she'd stew in a saucepan on the side of the range all day long with herbs in a little muslin bag, and with a carrot, onion, swede, or turnip. Towards the end of the evening she would take all these out and put in eggshells, not the eggs themselves, just the shells, and vigorously whisk it. Every bit of scum used then to come to the top, and it was my job – and a jolly long job it was too – to skim everything off the top. When I'd got as much off as I could with a spoon, I had to get greaseproof paper and lay it gently on top of the liquid so that it kept on absorbing the fat.

Sometimes I had to lay over a dozen pieces. By then the soup was clear – a pale, faintly golden colour, but as clear as water.

Sometimes it was tomato soup; of course it wasn't out of tins. No soup was out of tins. For tomato soup again there was the stock – we always had a stockpot going. When I got to be cook I did too. Every single bone that was left over from saddles of mutton, or legs of mutton, or sirloin, every bone or every bit of vegetable we didn't use went into the stockpot. For tomato soup Mrs McIlroy used to melt butter (we never used margarine; everything was butter) over the side of the range, so that it just gently melted. She then thickened it with flour, added the stock, the tomatoes cut in half, and the whole lot was mixed until it thickened. Then I had to put it through a wire sieve. A long job it was too, getting all the pips and skins out of the way.

Mushroom soup was another speciality of Mrs McIlroy's. Made rather similarly, except that the mushrooms had to be put through a hair sieve. She said that if you put them through a wire sieve you got tiny little pieces because they were so soft they went through too easily.

A hair sieve was like a wire sieve in shape, but instead of being covered in wire, it was covered in very fine hair – it felt like horse hair but yet it seemed a lot finer than that.

About five minutes before Mrs McIlroy was going to send it up, she would put a whole gill of cream into the tureen – a great big china one with a ladle with a long handle. It always used to remind me of that saying about the devil and the spoon. I used to say, 'They're supping with the devil all right, up there with that spoon.'

If there was any left Mrs McIlroy used to give it to me because there wasn't enough to share among everyone. I was always hungry, and I used to eat everything there was to eat. She used to say, 'You'll go off your food in the finish, you do when you're with it.' I never did. I think it was the years of semi-starvation when I was a child. Even now I can eat anything there is to eat.

Often there was an entrée for the next course. Sometimes Mrs McIlroy used to do pieces of chicken in aspic jelly. She used to make her own aspic jelly, with stock and gelatine; nowadays it's all bought ready made. If they'd had chicken the night before and there was some left over, I used to cut it up in small pieces and Mrs McIlroy would make this aspic with the gelatine, the stock, and the seasonings, place these pieces of chicken into it, and then put it in an icebox. We didn't have any refrigerators, of course.

We used to have a big metal galvanized box, and every morning the iceman would come around with a large lump of ice, which I put in a tray on the top of the box. The food that needed chilling was put in there. Having a larder that was practically all made of slate and in the basement into the bargain, very little food went bad. In any case, nobody tried to keep food, it was brought fresh in every day.

Then would come the fish course. Sometimes salmon if salmon was in season, sometimes lemon soles, sometimes turbot, each with the appropriate sauce; hollandaise, tartare, or mayonnaise. It was my job to make the mayonnaise sauce.

And what a job it was too. I never thought I'd get it right. First I would drop one egg yolk in a basin, then add olive oil, one spot at a time, only one spot, and I kept stirring and stirring and stirring, until I got a lovely thick yellow mixture, rather like custard. But if I tried to hurry it – to put the olive oil in a bit quick – the whole thing curdled and I had to throw it away and start all over again. I threw away a lot of mayonnaise sauce in my time!

Then came the main course, sometimes a round of beef, sometimes, if they had visitors, it would be a whole saddle of mutton, sometimes just a leg of lamb.

Mrs McIlroy used to make a beautiful sort of glaze. I really never knew how she did it. You can buy it out of bottles now, but she used to make her own out of a kind of burnt sugar. It used to melt and go a lovely toffee colour, and she would spread this over the leg or saddle before she sent it up; it really looked glorious.

Then the sweet. This could be anything, but was nearly always something cold; perhaps a chocolate whisk, which used to be made with grated chocolate, eggs, and castor sugar; or perhaps fruit, fresh fruit with sugar boiled down into a syrup and tipped on top of it; perhaps a compote of oranges, or a compote of bananas; not always a savoury because the Reverend Clydesdale wasn't very fond of savouries. He sometimes liked sardines or anchovies on toast. Nothing too fancy.

Then came cheese and coffee. That was their dinner.

What we had at night were the left-overs of the day before or a macaroni cheese or welsh rarebit. It wasn't Mrs McIlroy's fault, she wasn't allowed to give us more. Some of the maids used to moan like mad and say they never got enough to eat. I didn't moan, but I used to feel it wasn't fair.

Although their dinner at night wasn't until eight, I had to get things ready for Mrs McIlroy before six o'clock because as well as laying out the table, everything she cooked was prepared by hand. For instance, if she was making a cheese soufflé, which was a thing they were very fond of, Mrs McIlroy used to do it with Parmesan cheese because it's a lighter cheese in texture and in weight than the ordinary kind. Now today, of course, you can buy Parmesan cheese ready grated in bottles; in those days you had a lump of it, and believe me, it was as hard as a rock, and I used to have to grate this on the fine side of the grater. That took quite a long time, and some of my knuckles at first.

If it was horseradish sauce, that had to be done by hand too. Grating horseradish is far worse than doing onions. The tears used to stream from my eyes. I used to dread having to do it. If it was creamed spinach, this had to be put through the sieve and that was another long chore.

The worst job of the lot was when they had minced beef cake. The raw beef, generally a fillet, had to go through the mincer. This wasn't easy. But then I had to get it through a wire sieve, still raw, so you can imagine how long this took. I thought it was impossible when I first tried, but I found I could do it if I kept on long enough.

The sieved beef was then mixed with herbs and a yolk of egg, tied up in a piece of muslin, and dropped into a little stock and simmered for not more than twenty minutes. So that when it was cut open the steak was still more or less raw, but because it was so fine after going through the sieve, it tasted as if it had been cooked until it was tender. It was a marvellous thing but it took a lot of work.

If they were serving game they had potato crisps with it. Nowadays everybody buys potato crisps in bags or tins, but in those days they had to be done by hand. First of all you peeled the potatoes, then you got a clean tea cloth and laid it out full length on the table and sliced the potatoes by hand so thinly that when you held them up you could see right through them. They were like little rashers of wind. You laid each one separately on the cloth. Then you covered them up with another cloth until they dried. Then you melted fat – lard, not dripping because that was too coloured. (We used to get our lard not in half-pounds, but in whole bladders as they used to call them. They were about the size of a rugby football and about the same shape.) You melted a portion of that in a frying-pan, a very deep one, and when it was boiling and blue smoke came off, you dropped these crisps in, one by one, because if you dropped two in at a time they stuck together; they wouldn't separate out. By the time you got the last one in, the first ones were already cooked, so it was one mad rush to drop them in and get the first lot out again. If you left them a minute longer than you should, instead of being pale, golden crisps, they were dark brown chips, as hard as rocks.

When my mother asked me if I'd learnt much cooking I said, 'No, Mum, there isn't any time', but I suppose I really was absorbing knowledge, because when I took my first place as a cook, I was amazed at the things I found I could do.

13

ALTHOUGH MR CLYDESDALE had a gardener/chauffeur and a car of his own, on two mornings a week he used to have a hackney cab call at the door, with a decrepit old horse in the shafts. It looked as if it should have been in the knacker's yard. It was driven by an elderly man called Ambrose Datchet.

This Ambrose Datchet, so he told me when he used to talk to me (which wasn't very often because he mainly talked to the cook), had been a gardener in a large household, far bigger than my mother or I ever worked in. It had two stewards, two chefs, seven footmen, six housemaids, and over twenty-eight gardeners, of whom he was one. He started off as a hallboy, but he didn't like working inside, and when he saw the footmen, who always had to walk around in uniform and wear white gloves and even wigs, he said he couldn't stick that life, so he went to the outside and became a gardener.

I used to hear him talking to Mrs McIlroy about the things

that used to go on in this great big place where he worked. I listened all agog – you know how it is when you hear anything you think you're not supposed to hear, you think it's something out of this world. Well, according to this Ambrose Datchet, the most outrageous affairs used to go on in this household, and strangely enough, not so much among the women servants as between the footmen and stewards and the people upstairs; not only the people who owned the house but the visitors too. Once I heard Mrs Mellroy say, 'Not her ladyship!' Ambrose Datchet said, 'I saw it with my own eyes.' So Mrs McIlroy said, 'What, with her?' 'Her, and with him too,' he said. 'He was a very handsome young man.' I gathered it was one of the footmen having an affair with both the lady and the master of the house.

Mind you, what Mr Ambrose Datchet saw with his own eyes must have meant he had eyes at the back of his head, because if I heard him say, 'I saw it with my own eyes' once, I must have heard him say it a hundred times.

I remember a story he told me once about a raw country girl who went into service – it was her very first place – and the lady said to her, 'Elsie, I like my breakfast at eight o'clock in the morning.' So Elsie said, 'Oh, that's all right, Madam. If I'm not down, don't wait for me.'

When Ambrose Datchet came back from these outings with Mr Clydesdale he used to be allowed to come down in the kitchen. If it was the summer he'd have a glass of lemonade, if it was the winter he would have a cup of cocoa. He would sit there and jaw to Mrs McIlroy and sometimes to Mr Wade, the butler.

When it was time to go, he used to walk right through the kitchen into a sort of yard place at the back. I thought at first he was going to talk to our gardener/chauffeur, but when he came back Mrs McIlroy used to say, 'Hello, Ambrose. Been to shake hands with your best friend?' I hadn't the faintest idea what they were laughing at, but the fact that they looked at me made me go as red as a beetroot. After it was explained to me, I used to laugh too. Mrs McIlroy, although she looked a bit prim, she could say things with the best of them.

Most mornings Mrs Clydesdale went out for her constitutional. I used to dread it when she came back because she used to scrutinize the front door. The brass on that front door was something too terrible for words. The door handle was all convoluted and the Brasso would get into the cracks of it, and there was a tremendous knocker, the shape of a big gargoyle. That was all nooks and crannies, and there was a big brass letterbox too. The doorstep was also all brass. Some mornings when it was bitterly cold and my hands were covered in chilblains, I used to skip a bit. I didn't leave anything showing as far as I knew, but she could usually find something.

If the bell used to ring two minutes after she came in, I knew what it was for. The parlourmaid would come down and say to me, 'Madam has sent down a message that she wants to speak to Langley' (that was me) 'in the morning room.'

My legs used to feel like rubber at the very thought of going up there, because I knew what she was going to say; I knew it was about the front door. She would start off with a very ambiguous remark, 'Langley, whatever happened to the front door this morning?' Well, she could have equally meant that it looked a picture as that it wasn't done very well, but I knew perfectly well what she meant. Then she would go on to say, 'Langley, you have a good home here, you have good food and you have comfortable lodgings and you're being taught a trade, and in return I expect the work to be done well.' By this time I was in tears, what with feeling so inferior. I was only fifteen years old; by the time I'd been in service a bit longer, I got much harder, and it never used to make me turn a hair when they said these kind of things to me.

When I got back downstairs, even Mrs McIlroy used to be sympathetic. She'd say, 'Oh well, never mind, girl, just remember their bodies have to function the same way as ours do.' I couldn't see what difference that made, and in any case their bodies could function in comfort. All we had was a lavatory in the basement which was the haunt of all the fauna, hairy spiders, blackbeetles, and every other kind of insect.

Many a night Mary, who used to share the attic bedroom with me, used to wake up and want to go to the lavatory. She was frightened of going down all those stairs alone, so she used to wake me up to go with her. We used to creep down, trying to avoid the stairs that creaked – just like criminals. As a matter of fact, I reckon Mrs Clydesdale would have thought we were criminals, because she would have said that servants should be as regular in their habits as they were in anything else, and not go to the lavatory in the night.

One morning when Mr and Mrs Clydesdale were out, Mr Wade came down and asked Mrs McIlroy if she could spare me for a bit.

Mrs McIlroy and Mr Wade were quite friendly, although Mrs McIlroy always thought Mr Wade had a secret in life. Later on, when I had been there some months, he came home 'drunk to the wide', and he was found wearing one of the Reverend's suits. He got the sack there and then. When we went into his bedroom at the back of the butler's pantry, we found a cupboardful of empty whisky bottles. Maybe that was his secret.

Anyway, this particular morning, when Mr Wade came down and asked if she could spare me, Mrs McIlroy said, 'Why?' 'To see the ten o'clock totterers,' he said. 'The ten o'clock totterers, Mr Wade?' 'Yes,' he said. Mrs McIlroy said, 'All right, I can spare her for half an hour,' so we went upstairs, opened the front door and looked.

Up and down Adelaide Crescent were the cars with the smartly uniformed chauffeurs. They wore knee breeches and shiny boots, peak caps, and white gloves. Some of the uniforms were grey, some green, some blue. The chauffeurs stood rigidly to attention beside their cars, ready for when their employers came out.

Almost on the stroke of ten the Crescent sort of sprang into action. It started at the house next but one to ours. The door opened and out came an old gentleman. He was helped down the steps by the butler, then came the old lady on the arm of the housemaid, the under-housemaid carrying a footstool and a horrible old-looking lap dog. The pair were ushered into the car, the footstool was arranged under the old gentleman's feet, and the dog was tenderly placed on the old lady's lap. The chauffeur leaned in and carefully wrapped a rug around both of them. No wind must blow upon them (though goodness knows, some years after that the bitter winds of adversity blew all around them), and off they went. This scene was repeated all around the Crescent. These were the ten o'clock totterers.

Then Mr Wade said he would show me over the house, because, being a kitchen maid, during all the months I had been there, I had seen nothing except the back stairs. All I had done was to go from the basement to the attic.

What a contrast it was to our domain. Beautiful thick carpets everywhere, all colours, Turkey carpets and Chinese carpets in the morning room, the drawing-room, the dining-room, and the bedrooms. Lovely massive armchairs, great big thick velvet curtains, lovely beds with mattresses so thick that no princess would have felt a pea if she had slept on them, like she did in the fairy tale. Everything reflected the life of ease and comfort.

I thought of our bedroom that was so tropical in the summer, and so freezing cold in the winter, that when we left the water in our wash jugs at night, a layer of ice formed on it, and we had to break that to wash in the morning. We couldn't even have a bath in comfort, all we had was a hip bath. For that we had to carry up every drop of water from the bathroom, two flights below, and carry it down to the lavatory when we wanted to empty it. And with a hip bath, I never knew what to do, whether to get right in, sit in it with my bottom down and my knees up under my chin, or to sit in it with my legs hanging outside. Either way I got stone-cold.

Then I thought about the so-called servants' hall, which

was our sitting-room, really. They had lamps, beautiful reading lamps with lovely shades. The only light we had in our servants' hall was one bulb with a white china shade. The floor was covered in old brown lino, with horrible misshapen wicker chairs which had once graced their conservatory and weren't even considered good enough for that now. Depressing walls that were shiny brown paint halfway up, and a most bilious green distemper for the top half, the barred windows and one table with an old cloth; that was our sitting-room.

Mary and I had the worst bedroom, it's true, because we were the two lowest – but even Mrs McIlroy's was only furnished with the cast-offs from upstairs. The bed was one Leonora had at one time or another and wasn't considered good enough for her now. The bits of rugs were once in their bedrooms. Wherever you looked the difference was accentuated. If only they had made some attempt to furnish ours with a few new things. Why did we always have to have the cast-offs?

One job I particularly hated was when it was the gardener/chauffeur's day off, and I had to take out the horrible little dog of Mrs Clydesdale. It was a pug dog and it was so fat and overfed that it was almost square. It was called Elaine, but I couldn't imagine any Lancelot taking a fancy to that Elaine. I used to walk it up and down Adelaide Crescent, and of course it kept hanging round the trees. All the errand boys – there were hundreds of errand boys in those days – used to whistle after me and say, 'I see you've got your monkey with you, where's your organ?' I loathed that job.

14

IN MY FIRST months there I made one mistake after another. I particularly remember one day when I was doing the front door – I was a bit late this particular morning – the newsboy came with the papers. As I went to put them on the hall table, Mrs Clydesdale came down the stairs. I went to hand her the papers. She looked at me as if I were something subhuman. She didn't speak a word, she just stood there looking at me as though she could hardly believe that someone like me could be walking and breathing. I thought, what's the matter? I've got my cap on, I've got my apron on, I've got my black stockings and shoes; I couldn't think what was wrong. Then at last she spoke. She said, 'Langley, never, never on any occasion ever hand anything to me in your bare hands, always use a silver salver. Surely you know better than that. Your mother was in service, didn't she teach you anything?' I thought it was terrible. Tears started to trickle down my cheeks; that someone could think that you were so low that you couldn't even hand them anything out of your hands without it first being placed on a silver salver.

I was so miserable about this that I wanted to go home; it seemed the last straw. I thought, I can't stand domestic service. I don't think I ever felt so wretched before or after that. But I knew I couldn't go home, because we had only three rooms – we lived in the bottom half of a house, two rooms on the ground floor and one in the middle – and since I had come into service, my mother's father had died, and my grandmother had to come and live with us. So now there just wasn't room. I didn't even say anything to my mother about it. What was the good of making them unhappy as well? In any case I think she'd just have said, 'Take no notice.' She'd have been right. That's what you had to do if you wanted to keep any pride at all – just take no notice.

Although we weren't forced to attend church, it was taken for granted that we went at least once on Sunday, preferably in the evening. It interfered less with their comfort if we went in the evening. One day the Reverend asked me if I had been confirmed. I said, 'No, I haven't.' He wanted to know why; so I said, 'Well, my mother didn't bother about it, she never mentioned it to me, and now I'm fifteen I don't think it's worth bothering about.' After all I couldn't see what it had to do with being a kitchen maid whether I was confirmed or not, I mean it made no difference to my work; but of course the Reverend was greatly concerned with my religion and with my moral affairs.

In fact, all my life in domestic service I've found that employers were always greatly concerned with your moral welfare. They couldn't have cared less about your physical welfare; so long as you were able to do the work, it didn't matter in the least to them whether you had back-ache, stomach-ache, or what ache, but anything to do with your morals they considered was their concern. That way they called it 'looking after the servants', taking an interest in those below. They didn't worry about the long hours you put in, the lack of freedom and the poor wages, so long as you worked hard and knew that God was in Heaven and that He'd arranged for it that you lived down below and laboured, and that they lived upstairs in comfort and luxury, that was all right with them. I used to think how incongruous it was when the Reverend used to say morning prayers and just before they were over he'd say, 'Now let us all count our blessings'. I thought, well, it would take a lot longer to count yours than it would ours.

For ever below stairs we were making fun of the Reverend. At the time most of it went way over my head. It must have been because of my parents – bad dirty jokes and things like that had never come into my life. I remember when I was cleaning the vegetables, turnips, and salad, one of the maids looked at what I was doing and said, 'Oh! Turn up and let us.' Everybody went into screams of laughter – but I didn't know what it was all about.

They used to go on about the Reverend and the eight children he had by his first wife. They'd compare him with Catholic clergy who don't get married; and say that they wondered how he could ever get up in the pulpit and talk about the sins of the flesh, with a lot more innuendoes that

I didn't really understand at all. I wasn't naïve; I mean I could see very well that for a clergyman who is supposed to preach about spiritual life, and life hereafter, then to have a tremendous family of eight daughters – well, it wasn't really on, although I suppose in those days eight wasn't such a lot. It was just that he was a clergyman, and then him getting married again in an effort to get a son and heir, and having another daughter, well, you couldn't help laughing. You really felt it served the old thing right. I know now I should have given up the ghost after eight daughters and all that went with it. When I got further on in service, of course, and understood what they were talking about, I used to add my quota to it.

One lacks moral courage, because I did stand for lots of the things I didn't like later on when I was in service. If you didn't do them they thought you were stuck up, and after all you had to work with the servants. Not only work with them, you had to live with them, and almost sleep with them. You shared rooms, so it was up to you to keep on good terms with them. They were your whole life.

15

I STAYED FOR a year in Adelaide Crescent. Then I decided that I'd try my luck in London. I'd always heard that it was a marvellous place, and that fortunes were to be made there. Not that I believed the streets were paved with gold, or all that baloney of course, but that there was more opportunity in London than there was in a small provincial town.

When I announced this idea at home, the consternation that reigned with my parents, you'd have thought I'd said I was going to Timbuktu. My mother immediately remembered that she'd read an article in a newspaper about how all young girls disappeared as soon as they got to London and were never heard of again. It was well known, she said, that those women, and by 'those women' of course she meant prostitutes, originally were innocent young girls who'd gone to London in the same way that I was suggesting, and been lured away by promises of easy money and a life of luxury. I remember saying, 'Oh, don't worry, Mum. I'll tell them when I'm standing on the corner that I'm only waiting for a bus.' That didn't console my mother. My father never made much fuss about anything. I can't think why Mum did because I wasn't such a wildly attractive girl that any young man was going to take one look at me and decide that he needed me to decorate his harem. I suppose she thought it was a sort of disintegration of the family. People were much keener on families in those days than they are now.

Anyway, in spite of all her protestations and prognostications, I decided I was fed up with living in Hove, so I got the *Morning Post*, and answered an advertisement for a kitchen maid at a place in Thurloe Square, Knightsbridge.

The wages were an advance on what I had been getting, four pounds a year more. I know it doesn't sound very much now, but of course money did go further in those days.

My mother wanted to come to London with me. 'You'll get lost, you won't find the place.' 'But Mum,' I said, 'I've got a tongue and a voice and two legs, I can talk, I can walk, there's buses and undergrounds.' I'd never been to London before, I didn't know a soul there.

I said, 'I'm sixteen now, and I'm going to do it all on my own.' It made me feel very much superior to my brothers and sisters, especially to my older brother because elder brothers always lord it over you.

The size and dignity of the houses in Thurloe Square frightened me at first. And the interview with the lady of the house, Mrs Cutler, was even more intimidating than the house itself. When I told her my name was Margaret Langley I could see she considered it a highly unsuitable name for a kitchen maid. It was more like the sort of name you'd have if you were going on the stage, not one to work down in the basement with. I could see she thought it should have been Elsie Smith or Mary Jones. They were the sort of names that kitchen maids had. Margaret Langley would be flighty.

That was always the bugbear of people that employed you. They were always so afraid that you were going to be flighty. The parlourmaids often used to tell us that when they were waiting on people at the ladies' 'at homes' which they had once a month, they heard them talking about their servants. That was one of their main topics of conversation. Then they'd say, 'Yes, I had to get rid of her. She was flighty.' You were flighty if you used the slightest little bit of make-up. People didn't use a lot of make-up in those days, but if you used any, or if you had your hair waved, or if you wore coloured silk stockings; brown silk stockings were all right, but if you wore coloured ones, and I mean on your off-duty periods not when you were on, you were flighty, and flighty girls came to bad ends.

I've never been able to understand why, and I still can't. A bad end meant that we, the so-called lower classes, would get ourselves into the family way. I would have thought we were the last people to go in for illegitimate babies, because we had no means of supporting them, and there were not the homes to go to then. Nowadays you're almost encouraged to have them, with the facilities for girls going into homes and having them looked after when they leave there. Things are made so easy and there is no publicity. In those days you were an outcast if you had a baby outside marriage. So why they should have thought we were so ready to kick over the traces I don't know. Perhaps it was because in their heart of hearts they realized our life was so dreary that any young man that would take you out, regardless of what he wanted in exchange for it, was a treat.

I know that I would never have dared kick over the traces – not because I didn't want to, but because I was too dead scared. I hadn't even the faintest idea just how far I could go without any after-effects, if you know what I mean. So I just had to keep to the straight and narrow because I didn't know where the broad path would lead me.

Despite my name my present path was leading me to Mrs Cutler. I felt as if I was being smothered by her and smothered by the room. Everything was in velvet. Velvet was in vogue at that time. The drawing-room curtains were brown velvet, the three-piece suite was brown velvet, the picture frames had a velvet surround, and Mrs Cutler's bosom was draped in purple velvet. She reminded me of Queen Victoria inasmuch as she also would not have been amused. Life was real, life was earnest for people like her. I wasn't the type that Mrs Cutler wanted. She really wanted a London gal. It was always gal to those people.

Nevertheless she decided that she would employ me. She thought I would do. Probably it was my hefty size and good health that got me the job. I certainly needed both.

When I went there I found they had their married daughter living with them and her three children. They, of course, needed a nanny. Not only a nanny but an undernurse, and nursery meals too. Later on in life I never ever took a place where there were nannies and children, and where they had to have separate meals in the nursery.

The nanny would come down with all the airs and graces of a miniature employer, saying what the children wanted and what she wanted. There were always feuds between the nursery and the kitchen. There always were and there always had been. The parlourmaid, the housemaid, and the cook always thought nanny and nursemaid considered themselves better than *they* were, and they did, of course.

They were a sort of liaison between us and the people upstairs. In lots of ways I think it must have been a problem for them. They were more with the people upstairs; they took the children into the drawing-room in the evening before they went to bed, and they sat in the drawing-room with 'Them', and yet of course they weren't of 'Them'. And when they came downstairs they weren't of 'us' either, because we always thought that they were on friendly terms with 'Them' upstairs and that meant that anything we said about 'Them' would be repeated upstairs. Probably it wouldn't have been but that was what it seemed it might be.

The cook, of course, used always to be furious at the nanny coming into the kitchen. The kitchen was the cook's domain. Only the mistress of the house was allowed in it and her only once in the morning to give her orders. The nanny coming and asking 'What is the menu for today, cook?' or 'Mrs' if she was called 'Mrs'. Well, that infuriated the cook to start with, but if the nanny asked for different food for the children, then the feathers really used to fly.

The cook's name in Thurloe Place was Mrs Bowchard, and

she was an absolute old harridan. The other servants in the house were: the kitchen maid, which was me; instead of having a butler or footman – they weren't very keen on men servants in the house, except that Mr Cutler had a valet – there was a parlourmaid and an upper-parlourmaid; upperhouse-maid and under-housemaid; the nanny and nursery maid; a chauffeur and a gardener and a gardener's boy. It wasn't a large staff for a house that size, but judging by present-day standards, you really did two people's work, so you can say more or less that there were six people to run the house, because you don't count the nanny.

The cook was sour. Looking back on it now I would say she was soured by the constant stream of kitchen maids that kept coming and going. They never did stay long. You could generally get a job as a kitchen maid; nowadays, of course, they lay the red carpet down for you, but even then there wasn't a queue for the job. The trouble with kitchen maids, to anyone who wasn't a kitchen maid, was that they were always larking about with the tradesmen.

Perhaps it seems as though my life was one long tragedy. It wasn't. I worked jolly hard and I got miserable often, but no one can be fifteen and sixteen years old and be miserable all the time. Like all the kitchen maids I used to lark around with the tradesmen, especially the errand boys. They were one of the notable sights of London, the way they used to go through the streets with a bicycle laden sky-high, whistling all the latest tunes. And they were cheeky little devils.

And the kitchen maids were cheeky, too, and Mrs Bowchard was soured by the constant procession and the cheekiness and larking around. So she made my working life a misery. She was always carping and always complaining. It wasn't that I was more inefficient than the previous kitchen maids, it was just that I was young. It was a condition that I can assure you she did her utmost to rectify. After a day with Mrs Bowchard you didn't feel so very young.

Another thing about Mrs Bowehard was she suffered from a curious complaint which was called 'melegs'. Doctors wouldn't know about it, but it was always 'melegs'. 'Melegs' prevented her doing so many things; melegs wouldn't let her climb all those stairs to the attics where we all slept, so she had to sleep in the basement; melegs wouldn't let her do anything that anyone else could do for her; melegs wouldn't let her sit down and tie up her shoes so I always had to do that. There was nothing I hated more than having to stoop down in the morning, put Mrs Bowchard's shoes on, and tie them up, and stoop down and untie them and take them off at night. I suppose it's a no more menial task than waiting on all the servants at table, but I felt like one of those little boot-blacks out of Dickens. I really did hate having to do that. It wasn't part of my job, but mind you if you've got to work under the cook, you've got to do what she says, otherwise your life's going to be worse than it is.

Mrs Bowchard had a cat. It was an enormous black and white animal, really a handsome cat I suppose you'd call it. She used to call it 'His Lordship', what I called it I won't repeat. I've never been a lover of animals but 'His Lordship' brought out fierce hatred in me. He was such a supercilious-looking animal. Personally, I think that all cats are supercilious. They gaze at you as though you were less than dust. Mind you, it was a very clever cat, I've got to admit that. He used to sleep in the cook's bedroom. He slept under her bed and a quarter to seven every morning without fail when the alarm went off, that cat used to come out from under the bed, go to the door, put his paw up and rattle the door handle; that was the signal for Mrs Bowchard to get out and open the door and let the cat out. When she did that he used to stroll along the passage, come into the kitchen and stand there and gaze at me. He didn't move, he just stood there until he got my eye, and that was the signal that I had to take Mrs Bowchard along a jug of hot water and a cup of tea. It infuriated me. I used to say, 'I wonder the old girl don't give you a note to put in your mouth and bring along for me. Get out of it.' But, do you know, he wouldn't go. If I shooed him to the door he would stand there until he saw me go along with her jug of hot water and cup of tea. It was really clever, even though I didn't feel like that about it then.

Twice a week we used to have a cod's head delivered for this animal, and I had to cook it for him and remove all the bones. Mrs Bowchard would sit gazing at this cat with the most doting expression. '... and don't forget,' she'd be saying, 'to take all the bones out, "His Lordship" mustn't get a bone in his throat, must he?' I used to get livid. But I would do it and then I'd put some down on the floor for him, and you know that wretched beast would sometimes just sniff at it and walk away with his tail and nose in the air. Of course if he did it when the cook wasn't there I'd move him even farther away with the toe of my boot. But that animal got so clever that he wouldn't even look or smell that fish if I was on my own. Oh, he was clever.

Mrs Cutler did a lot of entertaining; two or three times a week there would be a dinner party for at least twelve people, sometimes more, and with all the courses, there was never any time to wash up in between. As soon as one course had gone up you were rushing around getting the plates ready and dishing up the other, so that by the end of the dinner I'd be surrounded by everything under the sun; saucepans and plates and dishes, not the silver because the parlourmaids had to do all the silver and the glasses, but I had everything else to wash up. The things would all be piled up in the sink and on the draining-board, and on the floor in the dark dank old scullery.

The sinks were shallow stone ones, a dark grey in colour, made of cement. They were porous, not glazed china or stain-less steel like you get now, and the dirty water sort of satu-rated into them and they stank to high heaven. That washing-up was what you'd call a chore these days. It was a bore too. After I'd done it, and that took some considerable time, there was still the servants' meal to get laid up and later washed up.

There were six or seven of us altogether, and the valet.

Mr Cutler I had very little to do with. I only saw him as a sort of shadowy thing going in and out. He never came down into the kitchen; even if he'd thought about it, it would be as much as his life was worth. He was something in the City. I'm not well up on these peculiar sort of jobs that necessitate your going off in the morning about ten o'clock and coming home about four in the afternoon, but he didn't do anything very strenuous. He used to go off with a rolled-up umbrella. I asked Mrs Bowchard what he did, when she was in a rather more mellow mood than usual. 'Don't ask me,' she said, 'bugger all.' Still I think he was something in the City.

As I say he had little to do with us. His valet of course saw a lot of him. Now you would think that a valet would be a sort of kingpin in a household. I don't know whether it was always the same, but this one seemed so feminine. Whether it's the nature of their job (although valeting is not really an effeminate job), or whether it's because they're in domestic service and they're living so much with females I don't know, but we used to look on him as one of us. Still valets wouldn't have bothered me. I wasn't going to marry into service. And he seemed inordinately old. I suppose he was about forty-five, but when you're only sixteen, forty-five seems like your grandfather. I was only interested in anyone who was likely to be a permanency. One's whole life was devoted to working to that in those days; getting a permanent boyfriend. And anyone in service was out. So I never took a great deal of notice of the valet.

As I say, it was reciprocated. The cook made more fuss of him than anyone else. She quite liked him. But nobody treated him as though he was a man. They all spoke and made jokes with him as if he was a woman. His hands were so soft, and he was so soft spoken, he didn't seem masculine. More like a jelly somehow, to me. I assume of course he could sire children. I presume he was all there, organically speaking. But you couldn't imagine him trying. He wasn't married and he'd got to forty-five. Maybe he never wanted to get married, I don't know. Looking back, I suppose he was perhaps homosexual, but we certainly never knew of it by that name. One vaguely knew that there were men who 'went with men' as the term was phrased in those days, but even so I never knew anything about it, I don't think anybody else did much. If it went on anywhere in our vicinity it would be very much under cover and nobody talked about such things. If anyone had said the word I wouldn't have known what they were talking about.

The boot-hole was the domain of the kitchen maid. I spent a lot of time in there, among the knives and boots. Mind you, nobody ever dreamt of ironing laces in that place.

When I spoke to Mrs Bowchard about putting the iron on, 'Iron the bootlaces,' she said, 'what are you talking about?' I said, 'Well, in my last job I had to take the bootlaces out and iron them.' 'I've never heard such rubbish, don't do it here,' she said. 'If they don't like it you can tell them to get their own bloody bootlaces out and do them.' She did stick up for me in that way.

Anyway, this boot-hole was really a refuge for me from the demands of that old harridan of a cook. She'd never go into it because it was a very low-pitched place and was festooned with spiders' webs. I used to knock them down just for the pleasure of going in the next day and seeing them spun again.

I know you'll laugh at me, but spiders today don't spin the way they used to. They'd spin their webs from wall to wall in the most intricate designs. If Robert the Bruce had been in there, believe me he'd have had an absolute bun day, he wouldn't have known which one to watch to get him up to start all over again.

It used to take me an hour every morning to clean all the boots and shoes, and I used to make them shine like a mirror. I'd got really expert at it by then, I was even congratulated at that place on doing them, but I used to feel a bit like Cinderella sitting in that boot-hole in an old sacking apron and thinking of all the things I would like to do: not that I ever expected any Prince Charming to come along with a glass slipper, I can assure you. After all when you wear size eights you don't expect Prince Charming to come walking round with one that size for you, do you?

16

MRS BOWCHARD had a sister in London who was also a cook, and this sister had married a butler and they worked together in the same house. I used to think how awful it was, marrying a butler and then working in the same house still carrying on your jobs of cook and butler.

It's not like being a cook in a house and having your bit of 'how's your father' with the butler. It's not the same with your husband, is it? Legitimate fun never seems quite the same somehow, does it? It doesn't to me anyway, maybe I've got the wrong idea on it, but I've known cooks who've had a lot of fun with butlers. I thought, well, fancy marrying one and for the rest of their life being in domestic service together; talk about a pair in harmony.

Mrs Bowchard's sister and her brother-in-law worked for a Lord something or other, I forget what his name is now, and they used to have their free evening at the same time. Naturally, they had to, otherwise they'd never have any free time together.

On their evening out they used to call round and see Mrs Bowchard. Talk about a busman's holiday, they must have been steeped in domestic service. They must have had it running in their veins instead of blood. Just imagine one evening out a week, and one Sunday a fortnight, coming round to some other domestic service place and having a meal with your sister who is also a cook. If I couldn't have thought of anything better to do on my evening out than that, I'd have shot myself.

After Mrs Bowchard had done the dinner, she, the two visitors, and the valet would retire to her room. I had to serve their dinner in there before I served the rest of the servants in the servants' hall. You can imagine what my life was; the rest of the servants used to moan like mad because their supper was late, but what could I do? In the order of rank the visitors were more important than the parlourmaids and the housemaids.

Mrs Bowchard's brother-in-law, Mr Moffat, was a very large man with a huge ponderous stomach and a double chin. He used to laugh a lot, usually at his own jokes. His laugh used to start down in the pit of his stomach and his being so fat, it used to ripple up in waves until it reached his double chin and that would flap in sympathy with the rest of him. I was fascinated by it.

He was always talking about his job and how important it was. He would say, 'I said to his Lordship', 'I told his Lordship', 'His Lordship consulted me'; honestly, if you listened to Mr Moffat for long you'd think that his Lordship couldn't do a thing, couldn't make a decision without Mr Moffat's advice.

When he was mellowed by the port and cigars – Mr Cutler's port and cigars – he used to get very arch and sort of frivolous. I thought it was a very incongruous trait in a man of his size, and his age too, and with his so-called dignity. He used to say to Mrs Bowchard when he was in one of these moods and I was waiting on them, 'How are we shaping?' (He was referring to me.) 'Are we learning all we can in the way of cooking? Remember the way to a man's heart is through his stomach.' I used to think to myself, I'd get lost looking for your heart. After he'd said this his whole mound of flesh would shake like a jelly as he had another good old laugh. Mrs Bowchard, whose high colour showed that she'd also consumed an amount of Mr Cutler's port, would say, 'Yes, as kitchen maids go, Margaret isn't too useless.' If Mr Moffat was more mellow than usual he'd even speak to me direct. That was a great condescension, a butler who worked for a lord, and who was consulted by a lord, speaking to a kitchen maid direct. I used to feel I was expected to curtsey. He'd say to me, 'Well, my girl, do you like it here?' What could I say with Mrs Bowchard sitting there? I'd have liked to have said, 'It's the lousiest place I've ever been in,' but I didn't dare.

It's funny, you know, when I think of it now, that I didn't dare. Can you see young girls of sixteen now being frightened to say anything? They'd turn round and say, 'Stuff it', and double quick too.

When I didn't answer he used to say, 'Have you a boyfriend? Ah! When I was your age I used to be a one with the girls; as a young footman I used to have many a kiss and cuddle in the footman's pantry.'

When I used to go to bed at night Gladys used to say to me, 'What was old fatty talking about down there?' because she could hear him with his rumble of a laugh. I used to say, 'He was telling me all about when he was young and what a Don Juan he was.' Then she'd say, 'Well, if he was like he is now with his fat belly, it'd just be "take a tip from me," wouldn't it?' then we'd go off into fits of giggles.

Mrs Moffat, as befitted anyone who had Mr Moffat for a husband, was a meek and mild person. I often wondered if she was meek and mild when she had dealings with her kitchen maid. But everything that Mr Moffat said was gospel truth to her. I don't know what Christian name Mr Moffat had but she never used to call him by it. It was always, 'As Mr Moffat said to his Lordship', or, 'When Mr Moffat was serving Lady so and so', or, 'Mr Moffat told John' (that was one of the foot-men). It was 'Mr Moffat this', 'Mr Moffat that'. Her whole life was wrapped around Mr Moffat. What personality she had, if she'd ever had any, and presumably she must have had to have attracted him in the first place, unless it was her cooking that appealed to him, was submerged in him so that in a way although Mr and Mrs Moffat came to dinner with Mrs Bowchard, it was only one person – Mr Moffat.

When I was serving I went to Mr Moffat first, and poured him out his port first. He was the kingpin. He was imbued with the importance of the establishment he worked for. You know, I suppose that's what people mean when they say that the servants live for them.

In Mr Moffat's case it really was so, he aligned himself with his Lordship. When his Lordship went out to dinner

Mr Moffat went out to dinner, because in his mind's eye he saw what his Lordship was doing. When his Lordship was presented to noble personalities, Mr Moffat was also presented to them. I could tell that because he told us things in detail that he couldn't possibly have known because he wasn't at the functions. That, of course, was the kind of servant that people really liked, because if you submerged your whole personality in your employers, they were going to get the very best out of you. I think that's why I was never such a good employee because to me they were a means to an end. A means, at the time, of living, and the end was to get out of service as fast as I could.

Living in such close contact with the other servants, a lot of quarrels went on. You can't coop up a lot of females, perhaps it even applies to men, without words passing, and what words too. But it didn't matter how much we servants quarrelled among ourselves, a united front was always presented to them upstairs.

We always called them 'Them'. 'Them' was the enemy, 'Them' overworked us, and 'Them' underpaid us, and to 'Them' servants were a race apart, a necessary evil.

As such we were their main topic of conversation. The parlourmaids used to come down and tell us. It would go something like this. 'You know if I lived in a little country place I wouldn't bother about servants at all, they are only a nuisance to me; they quarrel among themselves, they want more money, and they don't want to work hard, and they don't do the things the way you want them, but there, you see, I have a certain position to keep up and so I must employ them.'

Mrs Cutler certainly looked upon us as necessary evils, so in that house we were always united against 'Them' upstairs. In the opinion of 'Them', we servants must never get ill, we must never dress too well, and we must never have an opinion that differed from theirs. After all it was perfectly obvious, wasn't it, that if you'd only stayed at school until you were thirteen or fourteen, your knowledge was very small in comparison to what they knew upstairs. So if you had to have opinions why not take them from those upstairs who knew more than you did?

It was the opinion of 'Them' upstairs that servants couldn't appreciate good living or comfort, therefore they must have plain fare, they must have dungeons to work in and to eat in, and must retire to cold spartan bedrooms to sleep. After all, what's the point of spending money making life easier and more comfortable for a lot of ungrateful people who couldn't care less what you do for them? They never tried, mind, to find out if we would have cared more by making our conditions good and our bedrooms nice places in which to rest. No, it wasn't worth spending your money because servants never stayed with you, no matter what you did for them. After all was said and done, only 'Them' upstairs needed luxury living, only 'Them' could grace the dining-room table and make witty conversation. I mean there's got to be a stratum of society in which people can move around graciously and indulge in witty conversation, and no one can do this if they work hard. So make life harder for those who work for you, and the less inclined they'll feel for any kind of conversation.

But if 'Them' upstairs could have heard the conversation the parlourmaids carried down from upstairs, they would have realized that our impassive expressions and respectful demeanours hid scorn, and derision.

17

MR CUTLER was fond of shooting. He was in Africa for some years and if the trophies in the house were any indication, he spent a great deal of his time shooting things there.

The hall was absolutely festooned with antlers of this and antlers of that, I don't know what the animals were, all I know is that some were curved and some were straight and it was my job to get up and dust them.

Back in England, of course, with there not being the same kind of animals, he shot at birds. I got sick of the sight of grouse and pheasants and partridges. These were sent down from wherever he was shooting as quickly as possible, they were hung until they were high, and high they certainly got believe me.

They used to hang in the basement passage from an iron rod, and many a morning when I came down I would find just a head hanging there and the body on the floor. The maggots had eaten clean through. Then it was considered high enough to cook for their dinner.

It was my job then to pluck them without breaking the skin and then to clean the insides. A foul job; they reeked to high heaven.

When the cook served the pheasant she'd keep the head with all the feathers on it, and the tail feathers, and when the bird went up to the meal its head would be placed at one end and the tail feathers at the other.

Another distasteful job was cleaning the hares he shot. They seemed simply full of blood. I think they must be vampires and live on blood. In the cold weather they used to hang for two weeks at least, and you needed the strength of ten to remove the skin from them.

I used to try and get it off in one go because anything like that, rabbits' skins or hares' skins, were my perks. The rag- and-bone man used to give me ninepence for a hare skin that was pulled straight off without being torn in any way.

The cook, she would never let me wash the hares. I had to get them clean with tissue paper. She said that if you washed hares or washed game of any kind it took the flavour away. She didn't like you washing anything, she always reckoned that you washed the flavour down the sink.

Mrs Bowchard loved cooking jugged hare because of the port wine. This was always sent down into the kitchen when we had jugged hare. The parlourmaid used to bring it from the dining-room, two wineglasses full, but never more than one glass ever went into the cooking. Mrs Bowchard always used to try and drink it secretly so that I could never say afterwards, 'Well, Mrs Bowchard had some of it.' I used to watch out of the corner of my eye. One glass used to go into the jugged hare, the other glass went down Mrs Bowchard's gullet. If she knew I'd seen her she'd say, 'Oh well, it's the cook's perks. Everyone does it.' Perhaps everyone did; I remember doing it myself later.

Still Mrs Bowchard was a very good cook. Cooking was really something in those days because you had unlimited materials. There was none of this business as in the war when they told you how to make a fatless or eggless cake which was the most appalling thing you ever ate in your life; you used vinegar and lard. People just deluded themselves if they thought it was worth eating.

Even nowadays when you see an economic recipe and they say you can't tell the difference from the original, well probably you can't if you've never eaten the original, but if you have there's a vast difference. It's like using margarine instead of butter, the top of the milk instead of cream, having cheaper cuts of meat instead of the best, and having frozen salmon instead of fresh salmon. None of it tastes the same.

The food was marvellous then because it was always fresh even butchers and fishmongers never had things like deep freeze. They used to have a cold room but it didn't freeze things, so that all the food you had was fresh; it had a flavour.

Nowadays they are at their wits' end to put things on the market to put back the flavour into food, the flavour that's come out with freezing. But it can't be done. No one can delude me into thinking that it can be, but of course if you've not had it the old way you don't know the difference.

Today when people talk about their jobs they always

mention the 'fringe benefits'. As I've said cooks used to get fringe benefits from the stores they dealt with. You'd have thought that cast-off clothes might have found their way downstairs, but they didn't. They didn't care to give them to the servants because they wouldn't want you to wear them while you were living in their house, and of course they wouldn't want you to leave so that you could wear them somewhere else. They preferred to give them to societies.

All these people interested themselves in charities, they were all on this board and that board. If you read the papers you would see Lady this, and Mrs that, had a stall here and a stall there.

Mrs Bowchard used to make cakes for the stall Mrs Cutler ran for helping fallen women. Mrs Cutler used to be very keen on helping the fallen women, from a distance. Like a lot of people, she could be generous if she was not involved. It was to charities like this that they used to send their old clothes.

I remember the head parlourmaid being very annoyed once because there was a nice coat with a fur collar which Mrs Cutler had had several years. The head parlourmaid knew that she'd very soon be getting rid of it and she felt sure it would come to her because she'd dropped a few hints which seemed to have had an effect, but no, it was packed up and sent to a charitable institution.

There wasn't very much given away to us. At Christmas, we got presents of cloth to make things with, aprons, and horrible sensible presents.

Although I'd made such a fuss about going there, during

the two years that I stayed in Thurloe Square I saw very little of London. I was always too tired to go and look. Yet before I went I got a book on various aspects of old London. Where people had stayed, like Carlyle, Wells, and Dickens, and I thought how marvellous it would be to walk around and to be able to say that I'd been there, because I was always mad on history and reading.

But I was always too darned tired, I just wanted to go to the films where you could sit in darkness, where it didn't matter that you hadn't dressed up.

On my day off I used to go to the nearest cinema and get all my romance second-hand. It took a lot less energy. I often thought I wouldn't have had the strength if a marvellous lover had swum into my life. I couldn't have done anything about it.

Once a fortnight I used to get a Sunday evening off with Gladys the under-housemaid, and we used to stroll around Hyde Park.

Gladys was a year older than me and she'd lived in London all her life. Her home was in Stepney, she had eight brothers, and ten sisters. She could hardly remember when her mother wasn't having a baby. She told me lurid tales of life in Stepney, the overcrowding that there was, and bugs in the beds, the filth, and the drinking, and the fights on Saturday nights. I thought it was marvellous to listen to, although I wouldn't have wanted to be there.

According to Gladys, her father drank like a fish and he came home most nights roaring drunk and incapable. I used to think he couldn't have been so incapable otherwise her mother couldn't have had nineteen children, could she?

Gladys wasn't a pretty girl by any means, neither was I, but she had a very lively personality and she certainly knew how to look after herself. Coming from a place like Stepney I suppose she had to, with all those brothers and sisters and a father who drank. She'd learnt how to take the buffets of life and still come up smiling. No one could put much over on Gladys. She used to give me a lot of good advice. One of the things she told me, she said, 'Never, never at any time when you meet a boyfriend, let on that you're in domestic service, because if you do you'll only be called a skivvy and you'll never keep him.' So I said, 'What shall I say I do then?' 'Oh tell them any old yarn, tell them you work in a shop or in a factory.' I said, 'Well, factory girls aren't any better than us.' 'They are in a boyfriend's eyes,' she said. 'Anyone that works in domestic service is a skivvy and they never bother about them. The very fact that our hours are limited is enough to put anyone off for a start.' I followed all this instruction but I really couldn't see it mattered much because the only young men that we ever met were the Red Coats from the Knightsbridge Barracks, the soldiers.

They never had any spare cash at all, or if they had, none of them ever spent a penny on us. All we ever did was wander round the park for hours on end or listen to the soapbox orators at Marble Arch. We had to be in at ten o'clock sharp, so the goodbyes weren't prolonged. A lot of inane remarks from the men and a lot of giggles from us, a few kisses and further promises to be sure to meet them at the same time next week, but neither Gladys nor I had any intention of having permanent dates with such ill-paid escorts.

It wasn't our idea of romance to walk around Hyde Park for hours on end with a couple of Red Coats and never get anything out of them.

Gladys and I were avid readers of those women's magazines of the time; things like *Peg's Paper*, *The Red Circle Magazine*, and the *Red Heart*. Between their pages many a poor and lonely heroine ended up marrying some Rudolph Valentino sort of man, or a Rothschild with loads of money. Of course the girl, in spite of her upbringing, always had a lovely almond-shaped face and beautiful liquid violet eyes, and although Gladys and I hadn't got these attributes, it didn't prevent us from dreaming that we had and that one day our prince would come. My idea of heaven at that time was a place where there was absolutely no work to do.

Gladys had a very vivid imagination, maybe Stepney is a place where vivid imagination is the only thing that keeps you going. She used to be able to rattle off details of an imaginary job to any boyfriends that she got to know. It was useless for me to pretend that I did any other sort of work except physical work because my hands were always so red and raw, and that was a dead give-away. How could they be anything else because there weren't rubber gloves in those days, or if there were kitchen maids didn't wear them, and barrier-cream certainly hadn't been invented. Even if it had, by the time I'd done the front stone steps and the brass in the morning and all the washing-up that followed done in strong soda water, it wouldn't have made any difference.

I think one of the things I hated most was doing the steps with hearthstone. Nowadays if you do hearthstone your steps, and not many people do, you can buy it in a packet of powder, but we used to have a big lump like a beach stone, and had to rub it hard on the steps. There you were in a sacking apron with your bottom sticking out and the errand boys throwing cheeky remarks at you. In the beginning I tried to do the steps from the bottom one up, but I couldn't because I tipped forward. They had to be done from the top down.

Another pet hate was cleaning the copper saucepans. Every time they were used they got filthy. All the bright polish would be tarnished after every meal. They had to be cleaned with a horrible mixture of silver sand, salt, vinegar, and a little flour. You mixed all this into a paste and then rubbed it on with your bare hands. You couldn't put it on with rags because you couldn't get the pressure that way, you dug your hand into the tin where you had previously mixed it all up and you rubbed it on the copper outside. It was a foul job. Every morning I had to do it. Mind you they looked lovely when I'd done them, they used to hang all along the wall in the kitchen, right from the very tiniest little saucepan, which didn't hold more than a teacup full, to the most enormous one in which you could put three Christmas puddings side by side. And there was a big fish-kettle as well. I used to get so miserable sometimes that I used to wish that they'd all get ptomaine poisoning from them. I was always being told that if I didn't clean them properly they'd get ptomaine poisoning. If they had they might have changed their saucepans.

They did eventually change them I heard afterwards

because the new kitchen maid flatly refused to clean them. I often wonder what would have happened if I'd refused to. I suppose they'd just have given me a month's notice.

After I'd been there a year I did give in my notice, and a very nerve-racking procedure that was. First, of course, I had to tell Mrs Bowchard, the cook, and that brought on, as I knew it would, a long diatribe on the ingratitude of young people in general and kitchen maids in particular. 'You train them,' she moaned, 'and for what? As soon as they've picked your brains they go off somewhere else.' She continued in this strain for some moments, glaring at me all the time.

It was a lot of tripe. She never taught me how to do any of her special dishes, the things I really wanted to know. All the ordinary stuff you can pick up out of a book, but every good cook has specialities with that little something that's not in any cookery book. Many a time I'd ask her what made a particular thing taste like this or how it turned out like that, but she would never tell me, 'that's the cook's secret', she would say. It was most unfair because when you go as kitchen maid you've taken the worst job in the house, you work harder than anyone else and you wait on servants because you eventually hope to have the best job in the house, the cook's. So it really is up to the cook, if you are doing a good job for her, to return it by helping you.

Anyway, my notice. I got over the ordeal of telling her. The next thing of course was to see Madam. I really don't think there was much to choose between them, they were both terrifying ogres as far as I was concerned. But the performance when you want to see Madam and you are only a kitchen maid! First you've got to ask the parlourmaid to ask Madam if she could spare you a few minutes of her time, and you have to say it in the tone of voice that shows you know Madam's time is so very precious.

During the year that I'd worked there I don't think that I'd seen Madam more than a dozen times, because when Mrs Bowchard knew that she was coming down to the kitchen, if I looked particularly scruffy which of course I often did, she'd just shoo me out until Madam had gone. No one considered that the reason why the kitchen looked so clean, the table white as snow, and the copper saucepans as burnished gold, was the reason you were so scruffy. So, as I say, I really only saw Madam about a dozen times and even then I don't think she saw me. She didn't appear to because she looked right through me.

Anyway, through the parlourmaid Madam graciously gave me an audience at ten o'clock the next morning and I gave her a month's notice. She naturally wanted to know the reason, 'Aren't you happy here?', with the slightly indignant air that meant how could anyone work in her house and not be happy? And, 'You wouldn't find a better place anywhere', and she was sure I must have learnt a lot. I said that the work was too hard and the hours were too long. Well, much to my astonishment she said she'd get help for me, that if would stay on she would get an odd-job man to help out. I would still have preferred to leave, but I was so overcome anyone really wanting me that I couldn't get over it. I found myself agreeing to stay, and I even said that I liked the job.

I must have been stark raving mad. But you see no one

had ever wanted me to stay before except one boyfriend, and I knew what he wanted me to stay for.

Even Mrs Bowchard, that old harridan of a cook, looked slightly less grim when I told her that Madam had asked me to stay on. She said, 'Is she giving you more money?' I'll bet if I'd said yes she'd have been up there herself the following day. So I said, 'No, she isn't giving me any more money but I'm going to have an odd-job man to help out.' Of course, she had to say, 'Girls aren't what they used to be in my days, you all want pampering now. But never mind,' she went on, 'it's better than having to train another girl. I'd sooner you stayed than have to start all over again. When you've had one kitchen maid you've had them all.' On she went. I'd heard it all before. I didn't take any notice.

Anyway, every morning except Sunday we used to have a man called Old Tom. I don't know if he had a surname, we only knew him as Old Tom. He used to come in at six o'clock and he worked for an hour and a half, and I can't tell you what bliss it was not to have to go out and do those front steps. It didn't matter Old Tom doing them. Nobody throws ribald remarks at a man scrubbing with his rear sticking up to high heaven. He used to do the boots and shoes, and get all the coal in as well, it was absolute heaven. I stayed there another year after that, I didn't find it nearly so hard. It was too good to be true.

18

EVERYTHING NOW went on very much the same in the house – the same routine broken by dinner parties and 'at homes'.

The 'at homes' didn't really affect me, not workwise, but they interested me. Everybody used to have them once a month – Mrs Cutler's used to be on the first Thursday, and there'd be a constant procession from half past three to about five. Mostly women, but a few gentlemen – they'd just come in, say, 'How do you do?', have a cup of tea, and rush off again, presumably to someone else's 'at home'. 'Keeping in the swim' I suppose they called it.

In the swim! The parlourmaids I know would have liked to have pushed their heads under and drowned them. The parlourmaids had to do all the work; cutting platefuls of thin bread and butter and anointing them with some stuff called Gentlemen's Relish. I don't know if you can still get it, or why it was called that. I didn't like the nasty salty stuff. I suppose it gave gentlemen a thirst for the drinks they had at around half past five.

Madam was always on the look-out for new ideas for these 'at homes', and used to badger the cook and parlourmaids. Sort of putting one over on the Joneses. I suppose they still do it today at debs' dances – trying to get the latest beat band, and things like that.

But it didn't affect me like the dinner parties. Although it meant a lot of extra work and a bad-tempered Mrs Bowchard, there was always a sense of 'occasion' about these dinner parties. You could feel it in the kitchen, but you could see it upstairs.

I always used to try and pop up to the dining-room before dinner. The table would be laid out with a lace cloth that was a family heirloom, it was a wonderful thing, all handmade, and you can imagine the size it was to stretch out on to a dining-room table that had two more leaves put in it. It was the most marvellous one of its kind I've ever seen. In the centre was a crystal epergne, the silver was all Georgian. With that, and the two crystal chandeliers with the candles lit, it used to look like a scene from the Arabian nights.

I do think that when you had a cloth on, even if it wasn't a lace cloth but a snowy white damask, it looked a lot better than all these bits and dabs of mats do today, stuck all over the table.

Mrs Bowchard was never the soul of amiability, but on a dinner party day she was something too terrible for words. A sort of aura of grimness and unapproachability enveloped her. You would have thought she was cooking for Buckingham Palace and a regiment of Guards all at once. It used to make the work that much harder. But the most exciting part about these dinner parties was the chauffeurs who used to bring the guests. They would stay and sit in our servants' hall while their employers were upstairs.

You never saw such a fluttering in the dovecote as there used to be on these occasions. There we were, six or seven of us women who hardly ever spoke to a man and whose femininity was so suppressed that we got to be like female eunuchs. We would suddenly realize that we'd got a sex, that we were real females. So noses would be powdered, hair all fripped up, and waists pulled in. People had waists in those days, there were none of these shifts. Bosoms were stuck out, and rears stuck out, so if you pulled the waist in, you looked like an hourglass, but it was fashionable then. Even Flora, the head parlourmaid, and Annie, the head housemaid, both well over forty and resigned to a life of spinsterhood, would become one of the girls for the night. Our servants' hall would be a sort of magnet for the females, even the sewing-maid and the nursemaid would find some excuse or other to come down. And all because of these chauffeurs in their uniforms.

Probably they were the most nondescript collection of men in private life. It's like the soldiers in the war, isn't it? They all looked so handsome when they were wandering around in uniform, but if you met them in civvies you wouldn't cross the road to speak to them, well half of them anyway, especially the American ones.

To Gladys and me these chauffeurs looked simply wonderful, and to be actually able to speak to these hundred-percent men in leggings was something too glorious for words.

It's a sad fact that uniform does nothing for a woman at

all, it just accentuates all the wrong bulges, but even the most insignificant male seems to look masculine when he's got a uniform on. Maybe because it's cut to show off whatever points he has got (I'm not being vulgar), I mean to accentuate them.

They were, of course, delighted to be the centre of interest. What man wouldn't be if he had five or six females fluttering around him, plying him with biscuits, and cups of tea, and hanging on to his words with bated breath. Men are very susceptible to flattery. Even a man with a face like the back of a bus, if you tell him he doesn't look too bad, believes you. You can stuff men up with any old yarn. They believe anything. You've only got to gaze into their eyes, and sound as though you mean what you say. I've tried it so I know it's true.

They used to tell scandalous stories about the gentry. Anybody upstairs was called the gentry in those days. We would hear all about their employers. The good, the bad, the spicy. They used to talk about their affairs. A lot of the male gentry had what was known in those days as a love nest, a flat they'd set up for some woman, and the chauffeurs used to drive them to it. That was really the extent of their knowledge. They never went into the flat, they never actually knew what went on. But to listen to them you would have thought that they'd partaken of the love feast. Using the royal 'we' like Mrs Bowchard's brother-in-law, they would take us through the whole ceremony in all its amorous detail. They couldn't have known it but, I suppose, it wasn't hard to surmise.

In any case some of them were chauffeur/valets and I've no doubt were looked upon as a sort of respository of secrets by their employers. They knew that they were never likely to talk on social terms to anyone that mattered, and it probably got it off their conscience if they had one. Anyway, men like to talk about that sort of thing.

I used to work for a man myself who had a little place on the seafront. And when the rest of the family were in London he often used to pop down and go round to this little love nest.

People used to expect it of men. Mind you, if it was a woman doing it . . . Now there's the unfairness of life, you couldn't set up a love nest for a man, and yet maybe you would like to. It's like those 'red light' districts, isn't it? Why should men have the advantages in their sexual life? When all's said and done women can have husbands who don't supply enough, and I think there should be places where they can go where all the men have been vetted and are ready to oblige for a small fee. We are the underprivileged sex, really and truly, in every way of life.

But to come back to the chauffeurs – it may seem a nasty kind of conversation for them to have had, but it was the same with all the upper servants. Their own lives were so devoid of excitement that they had to find all their life vicariously. Sexual life, social life, every sort of life.

Employers constantly, by the things they talked about in front of servants, left themselves open to blackmail. But we would never have known how to set about it. That sort of thing has come with more education, with the greater freedom of the press. We had the feeling that what they upstairs did, although it was a subject of scandal and gossip and laughter, was their privilege. Not because they were better than us, but because they had money and it was no good having money if you couldn't deviate from the norm.

It was shortly after I had agreed to stay on with Mrs Cutler that something happened which still stands out in my mind like a scene from a Victorian melodrama. It was discovered that Agnes, the under-parlourmaid, was going to have a baby.

Nowadays it's all so vastly different; so much do they want you now in domestic service that I'm sure that if your employers found you were going to have a baby they'd say,'Yes, well bad luck. But you'll be sure and come back when you've had it, won't you?' You see them advertising, saying one child not objected to. They're as good as saying all right, you've got an illegitimate baby, we're quite prepared to accept the child as well.

In those days it was slam the door, dismissal with no money, your own home probably closed to you, nothing left but the streets or the workhouse.

Gladys and I shared a bedroom with Agnes and although I'd seen her being sick as soon as she got out of bed, I didn't realize that it was one of the symptoms of having a baby. I just thought she had sudden bilious attacks. It did seem strange that as soon as she got on her feet it happened, and that she was all right during the day, but that's what I put it down to.

Eventually Gladys, who was far more versed in all these

things than I was, asked her outright if she was pregnant. It sounded a terrible word that 'pregnant'. Agnes admitted that she was and implored us to keep it a secret. It hadn't gone very long and it didn't show yet.

But clothes in those days weren't designed to conceal your tummy. You had a waistline with a belt and it was very difficult indeed. I wished with all my heart that I could help Agnes but I hadn't the faintest idea what to do. It was Gladys who knew a bit, and she did try.

She bought bottles of pennyroyal pills which were supposed to be very good at getting rid of it, Beecham's pills, and quinine. But all they did for Agnes was to make her spend half the day in the lavatory. Then on Gladys' instructions we used to lug hot water up the stairs to fill the hip bath for her. Then we'd tip tins of mustard in it, until it was absolutely yellow. That was supposed to be another good thing, hot mustard baths. Maybe it would have been if Agnes could have got her waist in it, but she couldn't. Then she tried carrying all the heavy weights she could, and when it was her day off she used to go in the park, climb on to the park benches and then keep jumping off. It sounds amusing, but it was a terrible thing for her. She tried shifting furniture. She would pick up a massive armchair, they were huge in those days, and move it from one part of the room to the other. But none of it did any good.

Eventually, of course, she couldn't hide it from Mrs Cutler, and poor Agnes was told to leave at the end of week.

It's impossible nowadays to imagine what it must have been like for her. Although Gladys and I were terribly sorry

about it, it was like when you go into hospital and somebody's dying of something, you've got that faint feeling of
rejoicing that it isn't you, and Gladys and I both felt that;
above our sympathy we were thankful it wasn't us that were
in this predicament.

Although Madam told her to leave at the end of the week
she did give her a month's wages. But the very fact that she
did this convinced me in my suspicions as to who the father
was. Agnes would never tell. I didn't expect her to tell
Madam, but she wouldn't tell Gladys and me who it was, and
I knew she knew, because she wasn't the sort of girl that
would have gone with any Tom, Dick, and Harry; it just had
to be one man and one man alone. I suspected it was a nephew
of Mrs Cutler's. He was very young, probably in his early
twenties, and a very handsome man. He had such an attractive voice that even to hear him say good morning used to
make you feel frivolous. It sent shivers all up and down you.
I suspected him because on several occasions I discovered
him on the back staircase, which was our staircase, a place
where he certainly had no right to be at all. He used to say
good morning or good afternoon to me in this marvellous,
attractive voice of his. Some of the Americans have voices
like that I have since discovered.

I think Mrs Cutler was worried, because I think she knew,
or she was nearly certain it was this nephew. She questioned
Gladys and me closely and though we said we didn't know,
she didn't believe us.

Even though she thought it was her own flesh and blood
that was responsible I had to listen to such a long lecture on

the evils of such wanton behaviour. No nice young man would ever suggest such a thing to a girl he hoped to marry. Have you ever heard such drivel because that's one of the things they always suggested. Whether they're likely to marry you or not, they like to try their goods out first. I've never been out with a man that didn't suggest it, believe me. And Mrs Cutler went on that no decent girl would ever let a man take advantage of her.

Well now, that's another ridiculous remark, because the ratio of girls to young men was so high that if you had a young man and you cared about him and he suggested this, it seemed to be the only way to keep him. You had a hard job not to do it if you were not going to be stuck without a young man at all, and if you were dying to get out of domestic service, which most of us were. What did Mrs Cutler know about human nature in the basement? The only thing that kept me and those like me from straying off the straight and narrow was ignorance and fear. Ignorance of how not to have a baby, and fear of catching a disease. We were always told that you only had to go with a young man and you'd catch venereal disease. That's why so many deviate now because those two fears have gone, haven't they? The disease can be cured, and the baby can be taken care of, even if you have it. Now they encourage you to get rid of it before it gets to anything.

But Agnes wasn't like Gladys or me; Gladys came from an enormous family, had a very hard life, and was a realist; I was just frightened of what might happen. And ignorant. I did know roughly what you had to do to have a baby, but I didn't know what you could do and *not* have one. But Agnes was a soft girl, very sentimental, starry-eyed, and when she went to the films she would come back with all dreams and things.

I remember she used to have a crush on Cesar Romero. Gladys and I got turned out of the cinema when we went to see Cesar Romero because I said to Gladys, 'Hasn't he got lovely teeth?' and she said, 'Yes, and I bet he's got another set at home.' And we laughed so much they made us leave. But to poor Agnes, Cesar Romero was a god.

So you can imagine if it was Mrs Cutler's nephew with that marvellous voice of his, he would know how to treat a girl, and make her feel she was really something, not just an under-parlourmaid with no money and no position. And Agnes was a pretty girl too, and her prettiness was natural, she never used any artificial aids. I can quite see how she was overcome. And he bought her presents, I know because she had some silk underwear. She said it came from her home, but I don't think it could have.

All right, it may not have been him, but I have a very strong suspicion that it was, and Mrs Cutler did too. Anyway what was he doing on our back stairs? They didn't lead anywhere except to the maids' bedrooms.

But going back to ignorance, fear, and straying off the straight and narrow, the whole idea of lovemaking was tied up with the idea it was sinful and revolting. Even the married relationship was often ruined because of this way of thinking.

I remember about a year after I was married I chanced to meet a girl I'd known in service and we went into a tea shop to talk about old times. She told me she'd been married for five years, and when I made an inquiry into whether she had any family she burst out, 'Oh, I hate all that side of married life. I can't bear George even to kiss me because I know he's leading up to "that".' She would never put it into words, it was 'that'. Well, I remarked that her mother couldn't have felt like that, she'd had twelve children, the mother had. She said, 'Oh, it was my Dad, he'd never leave her alone. Even when she was hanging the washing on the line he would creep up behind her, and in the daylight too!' I was thrown half-mast at this! Laugh? Her 'in the daylight too', it sounded so funny. And when I said to her, 'Well, it was a blessed interlude on a wash day,' she was so incensed that she stalked out and I had to finish my tea on my own. But I couldn't help bursting out, could I? It was a pleasant interlude.

Although much of what I have said may make you think I was envious of the lives of other people this wasn't really the case. It was the inequality and the unfairness that struck me so much of the time. But there was one person of whom I was both jealous and envious: Miss Susan, the eldest of Mrs Cutler's grandchildren. She was only two years younger than I was, but what a different life hers was from mine! She was almost as tall as I was, and she had the same sort of hair colouring, but there the resemblance finished completely, because Miss Susan was and had everything that I wasn't and hadn't. She had masses of clothes, a horse to ride, a tennis court to play on. She could speak French, play the piano, sing well; I was envious of her life, envious of all her accomplishments. Not all the time. But when she came down into the kitchen to ask for something and I was at the sink, you know, immersed in bowls of greasy water, washing saucepans, my hair straight as pump water, clad in a sacking apron, and there she was, only two years younger than me, tripping in, dressed up to the nines, and with her cultivated voice asking for something which I would immediately have to rush to get for her, I wouldn't have been human if I hadn't felt envious. Everything was done for her, the under-nurse used to brush her hair, her bath was got ready, even the toothpaste used to be laid on the brush ready for her.

Sometimes she came with a message for the cook, and Mrs Bowchard would be all smiles for Miss Susan. It would be, 'Oh yes, Miss Susan', 'No, Miss Susan', 'Certainly, Miss Susan'. And when she had gone Mrs Bowchard would say to me, 'Doesn't she look a picture, she's a sight for sore eyes, a ray of sunshine.' It seemed to hurt. Once I had the temerity to say, 'If only she'd had to work down here for a week she wouldn't be such a ray of sunshine.' Mrs Bowchard, she was furious with me. She said, 'You're just eaten up with jealousy because you could never hope to look like that, even if you had money you couldn't look or behave like Miss Susan.' I don't think I really begrudged Miss Susan her place in life, it was just the contrast was so marked when she came into our kitchen. And you see she never spoke to me or even noticed me. You would have thought she would have done. I was another young girl of about her own age. So I thought she was stuck up, but it could have been she was being tactful, that she noticed the contrast between what I was and what she was, so I might have been doing her an injustice now that I look back on it.

19

CHRISTMAS IN domestic service was nothing like the Christmases we had at home. I remember the excitement there was at home even with little money, the excitement of waking up early, the rush into our parents' room for the presents and stockings. We didn't have turkeys or Christmas trees, but we had plenty of laughter and there was always enough food to eat.

Christmas in Mrs Cutler's house was a very formal and elaborate affairs. There used to be a large tree in the dining-room which was decorated by the nanny.

On Christmas Day after breakfast all the servants had to line up in the hall. Being the lowest in status I was at the end of the line. Then we had to file into the dining-room where all the family, Mr and Mrs Cutler, and the daughter, and the grandchildren, were assembled complete with Christmas smiles, and social-welfare expressions. The children looked at us as though we were beings from another world. And I suppose to them we were really sub-beings from a sub-world.

It used to remind me of those adverts with blacks all walking along. I used to keep kidding Gladys, trying to make her laugh. But you couldn't really laugh, it was such a solemn occasion. Talk about Christmas! When we got to the Christmas tree we deferentially accepted the parcels that were handed to us by the children, and muttered, 'Thank you, Master Charles, thank you, Miss Susan.' Oh I hated it all.

Then we had to go to the Master and Madam and were given an envelope containing money; I used to have a pound and Mrs Bowchard had five pounds. The presents were always something useful; print dress lengths, aprons, black stockings, not silk, of course, they never gave you anything frivolous; black woollen stockings. How I longed for some of the things they had, silk underwear, perfume, jewellery, why couldn't they have given us something like that? Why did we always have to have sensible things? I think that the reason they used to give us uniforms was because they knew we couldn't buy them out of our measly wages. Besides if we were to have perfume or silk we would go astray. So I hated this parade of Christmas goodwill, and the pretence that we also had a good time at Christmas.

We had to work like trojans, coping with their dinner parties and the other entertaining that went on upstairs. All right, we had a Christmas tree in our servants' hall that they'd bought, but they never put anything on it; we had to decorate it up with tinsel and bells and things, and they didn't put their presents on it. We had to line up before them in Indian file accepting their alms. That was Christmas there.

It was a replica of all the Christmases I had in domestic

service. Formal and elaborate, a lot of entertaining by them, but nothing much for us. I dare say in the very large establishments they would arrange a servants' ball like they do at Buckingham Palace. But from what I know of that sort of thing it never took place at Christmas, it was always well afterwards.

About two months after Christmas we had to start on the spring-cleaning. That was a major operation, and lasted for four weeks. Spring-cleaning in those days was done with nothing, I mean no Hoovers, no mechanical aids, no modern detergents, nothing. People don't spring-clean nowadays, they just keep their houses clean all the year round.

During these four weeks I got up at five o'clock every morning and I worked until about eight o'clock at night. Then I had to get supper for the servants after that. We all worked these hours, but, of course, I remember mine in particular because it was mine that made me tired, not theirs! I used to crawl up to bed, too weary even to wash. I know it sounds dirty, but you work from five till eight doing spring cleaning in an old-fashioned house where they have coal fires in every room, and you'd be very weary.

The first job was to scrub all the stone floors in the basement using a mixture of soap and sand. Those stone floors in the basement weren't like those very shiny tiles that you see in front porches or kitchens nowadays. They were pitted and those pittings used to get filled with dirt, and only a mixture of soap and sand and a scrubbing-brush would get it out. All the iron and copper saucepans had to be cleaned on the outside even more than usual, and the huge steel fender and fire had to be polished until it looked like new, every bit of china had to be washed (there was enough to stock a shop), and the long kitchen tables, and the chairs and the dresser all had to be scrubbed until they were white. My hands used to get raw and bleeding and my nails broken and jagged.

Upstairs it was easier for the house- and parlourmaids, there wasn't so much scrubbing. The carpets were the worst things there. In those days people had hundreds of little china ornaments all of which had to be washed.

Spring-cleaning the silver was a major operation. In this particular house, and in the majority like it, the silver was stored in a safe and the working silver was put in it every night. The safe was a sort of room that led off the dining-room, its door concealed by a screen. You could walk right into it. There were tea sets, not just one, a number, coffee sets, candelabras, table centres, and silver salvers; it used to look like an Aladdin's Cave. They used jeweller's rouge, not one of these white pastes in tins that are used nowadays, then polish with a leather and a brush. It was a long operation to make sure that none of the stuff was ever left in the little cracks and crevices.

Although we had to work these long hours we didn't get any extra money. But as a treat for this particular job Mrs Cutler used to book us seats at the theatre. Half of the staff went one week, and half the next. I remember the last show I went to, it was a comedy. But I didn't really enjoy it because we were in the expensive seats, sitting among the well-to-do, and I felt conspicuous wearing a somewhat shabby black coat and a pair of black cotton gloves which I didn't dare take off because my hands were all red and raw. I remember the following morning the cook said to me, 'Did you have a good time?' I said, 'Oh it was all right.' So she said, 'Well, don't forget to say thank you tomorrow morning to Madam for the evening out that she gave you.' So I replied with great boldness, 'Well, Madam hasn't said thank you to me for all the extra work I've done for her.' I thought the cook would have suffocated with rage. 'You're here to work,' she said, 'and if you don't like the job we can very soon get another kitchen maid.'

Anyway, by this time I'd been a kitchen maid nearly three years, and after three years of being the lowest, and the lowliest-paid servant, I reckoned I could get by as a trained cook. At least I knew how to cook vegetables, make sauces and I thought I'd learnt a few other things as I'd gone along.

So I looked in the papers and at last I saw an advertisement . . . Good plain cook wanted; it was for a house in Kensington. So I wrote. I had to put two years on to my age because I thought if I told them how old I was they wouldn't employ me. I was sure they would consider eighteen too young to be a cook. I got a reply and was asked to go for an interview.

On the appointed day I presented myself at the house, not without some trepidation, because it's a tremendous jump from kitchen maid to cook. When I got there the usual inquisition followed. Madam started off with, 'How old are you?' 'Twenty,' I lied. 'Is your home in London? Are you afraid of work?'

Now of all the ridiculous questions to ask anyone, 'Are

you afraid of work?' There's a good many people who're not afraid of work who don't like it. If she'd have said, 'Do you like work?' it would have been just as silly. My idea of heaven at that time was a place where you didn't have anything to do except sit around fiddling with your harp.

This lady had a title, she was Lady Gibbons. But I could tell straight away she wasn't of the gentry. She told me there were three in the family; herself, Sir Walter Gibbons, and a son. 'How much money were you thinking of?' she asked. I heard a voice that didn't sound like mine saying, 'Forty pounds.' 'Forty pounds!' she echoed, as if I'd asked for the Crown Jewels. Then there was a pause as if she thought I'd reconsider it. I didn't. 'Yes,' I said, 'and I want one whole day off a month.' Her face fell still further. 'If I give you a whole day off every month,' she said, 'the housemaid and the parlourmaid will want one too.' I said nothing. Just sat silent.

I've always found it's the best defence, be quiet, don't answer, then they felt that although you disagreed with them you realized it wasn't your place to argue with your betters. This attitude usually paid off. In any case although servants were still two-a-penny, the first rumblings of revolt at wages and conditions were beginning to be heard, and it wasn't so easy to give next to nothing and hardly any time off.

I got the job. Forty pounds a year and my day off a month as well.

Once again I had the unpleasant task of giving a month's notice to Mrs Cutler. This time there could be no inducements and she wouldn't offer me more money because once you give one servant any more money, everyone would ask for more. Once again I went through the ritual of making an appointment to see her as though she was some royalty. I laid on the old smarm and she laid on a little lecture. It could have been a lot worse.

The unpleasantness came from Mrs Bowchard. It wasn't that she had any personal animosity against me, she just didn't like kitchen maids, she didn't really like anyone that was that much younger than herself. For a whole month I was subjected to a barrage of innuendoes about my capabilities as a cook. She'd say, 'Suppose they ask you to make so and so, how would you do it?' I didn't know how to do it, because I hadn't had a chance of learning, and I'd say, 'I'll get it out of a book.' 'Meg,' she'd say, 'you can't cook from a book, you learn from practical experience.' I'd say, 'But you've got to start.' 'I didn't start when I was eighteen, I was twenty-five before I thought I was anywhere near good enough,' she'd sneer. 'Times are changing, aren't they?' I'd reply. 'For the worse for Lady Gibbons. You only know how to do vegetables.' And then she'd start on about their digestions, how she hoped they'd got good ones; digging at me all the time.

Then of course I had to leave everything spotless so that when the new kitchen maid came it would all look marvellous. I knew just how Mrs Bowchard would be. When she got the new kitchen maid I would be praised, 'Ah, when I had Margaret, she was a good girl, she used to do this, that, and the other.' The last fortnight was the worst of the lot, but knowing I was going I didn't worry. I stayed as pleasant as I knew how to be.

The only one I was sorry to leave was Gladys. We'd got on

like a 'house on fire'; she'd come from a home as poor as mine, and she never built castles in the air. We'd just got on fine. One thing I did vow to myself was that if ever I was good enough a cook to have a kitchen maid I'd never be as foul to her as Mrs Bowchard had been to me.

20

I ARRIVED AT Lady Gibbons' full of confidence if not much knowledge.

I got my first shock when I went to the servants' hall. There I found the housemaid, Jessica, but no parlourmaid. Jessica told me that there was a constant procession of housemaids and parlourmaids; nobody would stay long because of Lady Gibbons' temper. 'She's an absolute cow,' Jessica said. 'Mean as a muck-worm, eyes like a gimlet, and a nose like a bloodhound.' I thought, well this is fine, this is a lovely job I've come into. I said, 'What do you mean, a nose like a bloodhound?' She said, 'If you use the gas stove because you've let the fire get low, you'll find her at the top of the kitchen stairs bawling down, "Are you using the gas stove, cook?" She can smell it. That's what I mean.'

The following day I came to realize how parsimonious Lady Gibbons was. I'd come from a house where the cook just telephoned for everything she wanted. Where vast quantities of milk and cream, eggs, and butter were used every day;

where caviare and pâté de foie gras were quite commonplace, and where any left-overs would be thrown in the pig bucket.

That first morning Lady Gibbons came into the kitchen, she walked into the larder and inspected every bit of food there. I'd never seen anything like that happen before, nor since. She peered into the old bread crock, she even counted the crusts. She looked into the flour bin and the vegetable rack and the ice box, and she ended up by counting the eggs. I was absolutely dumbfounded. I kept on imagining Mrs Bowchard's face if Mrs Cutler had come down and done the same thing. She wouldn't have stayed five minutes, she would have given her notice there and then.

My next shock was when she told me that she did all the ordering and that anything I wanted I'd have to ask for. She had a store cupboard in the basement and everything was all doled out to me in minute quantities, and the cupboard was then locked. I was never given the key.

For instance, the jam was ladled out of one of those big seven-pound jars as though it was so much gold dust. And the same with tea and other things – just enough for each day. Mind you, perhaps in some ways this was an advantage, inasmuch as I was very inexperienced and I wouldn't have known what to order, and running the store cupboard would just have been an added worry.

I think I should explain that when you go to a house as a 'good plain cook' you don't get a kitchen maid. Nor was there the large staff that I'd known before. There was just me, a chauffeur, a housemaid, and parlourmaid, and as I've said, often only one of the last two.

When it came to what to call me, Lady Gibbons was in a quandary. The two other cooks I'd known had been called 'Mrs' even though they weren't married; a sort of courtesy title, but Lady Gibbons said I was too young to be called 'Mrs'. She called the other servants by their surnames, but I didn't like that, so we settled for 'cook'.

She wanted me to wear a cap, but I wouldn't. It always struck me as a badge of servitude. I know nurses wear caps but somehow it's different with them. In any case it was a hideous cap, so I left it off. Lady Gibbons didn't like it, but she couldn't really do anything about it.

During the morning the parlourmaid used to have to go upstairs to help the housemaid make the beds. And while she was upstairs Lady Gibbons asked me if I would answer the front door. I used to wear print dresses with short sleeves that finished at my elbow; one morning she came down with a cap and a pair of white cotton armlets that fitted from the wrist up to the elbow, and she said, 'Oh, I've brought you these down, cook, because I think you would feel more comfortable if you went to the front door wearing them.' She didn't think I would feel more comfortable at all, what she really meant was that *she* would feel a lot more comfortable. So I said, 'Oh yes, thank you, M'Lady,' because you used to have to say 'M'Lady'; naturally, being a titled Lady, you didn't say Madam. 'Yes thank you, M'Lady.' And I just put them away in my drawer. I never did put them on. She never said anything more. She knew the rules; they were not written down but they were all there unwritten. She knew that she could no more compel me to wear a cap and those armlets than fly.

When I started cooking I found out that it was quite true what Mrs Bowchard had said, that there was more to it than following the books, more to it even than experience; you had to have a kind of instinct about it, and I didn't seem to have much in the way of instinct at that time.

One dish I came a cropper on was beef-olives. I'd watched Mrs Bowchard make these, she used to use the best fillet steak, cut it into thin slices, and then put a little veal forcemeat on each slice, roll it up, tie it with very thin twine, and cook it in a casserole. When you've cooked them you cut the twine off and serve them up. It's a dish which is full of flavour. Lady Gibbons was very fond of salt beef, and would have it as a hot dish on a Sunday perhaps, served with carrots and boiled onions. It was very economical. When it was cold she used to want me to make beef-olives with it. Well, when you cut and fold a slice of cold salt beef, it cracks everywhere. I used to tie them up in little bundles, putting string this way and that. Then of course when they were cooked I couldn't get the string off, it had embedded itself in. So I sent them up as they were. When the three plates came down all the bits of string were round the edge in a sort of silent reproach.

This sort of thing didn't dampen my spirits. I was as lively as a cricket at that time. It's a funny thing, but the less cooking you know how to do, the more competent you feel. It's only when you know how to cook that it worries you when it goes wrong, because when you don't know, you don't know it's gone wrong. The more experienced I got the more I worried. I soon realized when a dish wasn't perfection. Not that I could have hoped to have a dish that was perfection at

Lady Gibbons' because even the best cook in the world can't make a dish out of poor ingredients.

The reason I was so cheerful was because of my metamorphosis of kitchen maid to cook. The difference in status can only be understood by somebody who's been in domestic service. As a kitchen maid you're a nobody, a nothing, you're not listened to, you're even a skivvy to the other servants. All right, as a cook with only two other servants you're not looked upon as God Almighty, but I didn't want that. I didn't want to be better than everybody else, I just wanted not to have somebody continually carping all the time at me.

Although Lady Gibbons was an old cow, I usually only saw her in the mornings when she came down to give orders. She used to moan about some of the things I did. After I'd been there a week, for instance, she came down and looked at the kitchen table and she said to me, 'Cook,' she said, 'this table's getting awfully yellow.' I said, 'Is it? Must be the colour of the wood, M'Lady.' So she said, 'Well, it must have changed its colour since you came here then.' But it didn't dampen my spirits.

After I'd been there a few weeks, Jessica the housemaid left. The new parlourmaid, Olive, was only fifteen years old. A parlourmaid only fifteen years old, even under-parlourmaids are often older than that! Lady Gibbons generally got very young girls as housemaids or parlourmaids and what she called 'trained' them. She did this because she got them very much cheaper, and also because she was getting so well known among the fraternity of domestic servants that she couldn't get anybody that was experienced.

Olive was a country girl. She came from a remote little village three miles from a railway station or a bus. She was exceptionally good-looking with beautiful eyes, lovely black hair, and with a most placid disposition. She needed it at Lady Gibbons'. She became a life-long friend of mine.

Sir Walter was a quiet man, he seemed to be sunk in reveries of past glories, and was oblivious to what went on around him. He'd been somebody abroad. I don't quite know what. With the East India Company perhaps; he certainly had a brown complexion. Lady Gibbons would sometimes expound about Sir Walter, 'When Sir Walter dined with the Maharajah . . .', so I got the impression that he had been somebody at one time.

And I also got the impression that his marriage to Lady Gibbons had been his greatest mistake and had dragged him down socially. She spoke like a fishwife and seemed to have had no kind of education at all. Talk about Gibbon's 'Decline and Fall', she was it.

He only ever came to life at meal times. I remember Olive reporting to me that he had commented that good cooks were a dying race so he had a sense of humour. Looking back he needed it with some of the dishes I served. I remember another occasion. In that house the food lift was situated in the kitchen, and when pulled up went through the dining-room floor, thus noises in the kitchen could be heard. I'd been singing merrily all the evening as I sent up each course, and Sir Walter evidently couldn't stand any more of it because he came to the lift and called down, 'Cook, will you sing "God Save the King" and finish the concert?'

137

But Lady Gibbons used to impress all of us with the importance of her title. She used to say, 'When you speak of me don't call me Lady Gibbons, say "Her Ladyship", and similarly when you're speaking to Sir Walter, don't say "Yes, Sir", say "Yes, Sir Walter, No, Sir Walter".' One day Olive came down with a water jug on a salver, and she walked round the table saying, 'Water, Sir Walter? Water, Sir Walter?' much to our amusement.

Although there were only three in the family the work wasn't all that easy. I still had to get up early to light the kitchen range; Sir Walter couldn't have his bath until that range had been on some time. Then I had to get an early breakfast for the son, about half past seven in the morning. He went to business. Then there was our breakfast at eight o'clock, and Sir Walter and Lady Gibbons' breakfast at nine. Then before she came down at ten to give the orders I had to scrub out the kitchen and the scullery, and tidy the servants' hall and the larder, because she used to look at everything.

The parlourmaid, poor Olive, had plenty to do, especially in the winter when the coal fires had to be lit. She had to carry scuttles of coal from the basement to the ground floor for the dining-room, and to the first floor for the drawing-room. And they had a fire in the breakfast room as well. These three fires had to be lit every morning by eight, and only half a bundle of wood was allowed for each. Some mornings poor Olive could do it on her head, but other mornings when the wind was in the wrong direction she just couldn't get them to go. She used to keep dashing up and down carrying cups of paraffin. And the tears ran down her face, mingling with the soot.

The housemaid was lucky, because they were so mean they never had fires in the bedrooms.

An odd thing happened there which I've never seen before or since. They used warming-pans. Now warming-pans really went out long before that time, but Lady Gibbons had two. One used to hang in the hall as an ornament, but into the other one we used to rake the hot coals from the range each night and run them over the beds. I used to think we were better off, because on winter nights I used to put bricks in the oven and we used to wrap them up in a bit of flannel and put them in our beds. Believe me, I am sure we used to have better benefit from those bricks than they did from their warming-pans.

There was only one attic room and Olive and I shared it. I could have had the room on the floor below, but I let the housemaid have that because I wanted to be as far away from 'Them' as I possibly could be. Lady Gibbons thought it was very unusual that the cook should share, because she always had a room of her own, and the housemaid and parlourmaid shared. But I preferred the attic.

At Lady Gibbons' I had every Sunday afternoon and one afternoon a week off, as well as the whole day once a month that I'd stipulated. Olive only got alternate Sundays. But when it was possible we used to go out on Sunday afternoon together to a tea-dance. They sound quite hectic affairs and would be today probably, but then they were very innocuous dos. You mostly went with a partner. If you went with a girl you might have to dance with her all afternoon.

But you went there of course in the hopes of picking up a

boyfriend. That was really the only opportunity you had of meeting one. If you went to watch a film, for instance, and a young man sat next to you and started nudging you and all that, you naturally thought the worst. Anyway, you could hardly see what he was like in the dark, and you couldn't very well converse. When anyone nudged me he usually turned out to have a face like Frankenstein's monster and morals of the farmyard, so I didn't dare chance it often. But at a tea-dance you could study the opposite sex and if there was anyone you fancied you could go all out to get them. And believe me when we went all out we went all out.

You see I was determined to get married. I didn't want to be an old maid. In those days people put on a very contemp-tuous expression when they talked about 'being on the shelf', or being a spinster. It meant you were lacking practically everything. Nowadays women who don't get married have often had all the sex they want and all the security. They just don't want to take a man for life, which I don't blame them for in the least. But I needed one to support me. I couldn't see myself being a cook for the rest of my time. I wanted one to take me on for life.

Olive, as well as being a good-looking girl, was an excel-lent dancer, far better than me, and as she was so attractive she always got plenty of partners. And the reason for her success was confidence.

She'd been brought up in a village and she'd always gone to the village dances. Parents used to take even their young children. So they learned early, and they had all the confi-dence in the world. I didn't really know how to dance at all.

I could never follow anyone. Being of a rather aggressive disposition, I was wanting to lug them around, instead of letting them take me around.

My only asset was that I could talk, and that's a doubtful asset on a dance floor. People don't go to dances for conversation, they go to dance and to see who they can collect to take home later. It really did me a disservice to be able to talk because I deviated from the norm in my conversation. It should go like this: the boy says to you, 'Do you come here often?' and you answer, 'Oh yes, fairly often,' then he says, 'Lovely floor, isn't it?' then you say, 'Oh yes, very springy.' Then he'd say, 'It's a good band, isn't it?' and you answer, 'Yes, it's got good rhythm, hasn't it?' Instead I'd talk to my partners about historical London, or ask them if they read Dickens. They must have thought I was some kind of freak. They'd never even heard of Dickens, let alone read any of him.

I was beginning to lap up culture; even in those days I always found time for reading, I mean books that were worth reading.

Sometimes I would try talking about Conrad, books a boy would like, Henty even, or O. Henry. But they'd never read anything like that at all, and I'd get dropped like a hot cake.

But Olive, she was a soulful, sentimental sort of girl, and would gaze up into their faces with a loving expression and have all the right answers at the right times. And she was a good dancer as well.

I've always found that when two girls go around together one of them's always more attractive than the other, and it was the same with Olive and me. She was much more attractive than I was. It's the same when you collect two boy-friends, there's one that's handsome and the other who's got a face like the back of a bus. I suppose it's nature's way of compensating.

Olive, although she'd come straight from the country and was only fifteen, used to collect boyfriends like bees round the proverbial honey pot. She knew how to talk to them too and keep them sort of dangling. There's an art in that sort of thing.

Naturally I got the dud one. Sometimes he wouldn't be too bad and I would think, well this is it. Another time it would be a receding chin, a vacuous kind of a creature, and I'd just stick him for one evening and then throw him up.

Although you may want to get married you've got to watch it. If you don't like a weak-chinned, vacuous kind of an individual for even a few hours, you're not going to want him sitting opposite you at the table every morning and every night of your life, are you? Olive used to say, 'You're too particular, what's it matter? Have him until you find another.' But how can you find another if you're going out with the same one all the time? 'Oh yes,' she said, 'you can.' She could. As I say there's an art in that kind of thing, I didn't get to know it, I never had the social graces. When I moaned about one, Olive used to say, 'Any port in a storm,' but it was never as stormy as that at the age of eighteen. Later on when I did get married I got a reasonably good-looking one.

Although Olive must have had endless opportunities, she didn't make the same mistake as Agnes. She seemed to have her head screwed on the right way. Again I put it down to village life.

Olive had been brought up in a Sussex village called Ripe. It sounds like a Cockney immoral assault. It wasn't the same as villages nowadays, with the young people trying to get away at the earliest opportunity. They had a social life, and the centre was the village hall.

People used to take their children to the various functions, thus from a very early age they mixed with the opposite sex. So it was that Olive never got as embarrassed with the opposite sex as I did. It's all very well to talk about country boys being yokels, but a boy's a boy and a man's a man in any place.

Another thing about a village is that if you put a foot wrong everyone knows about it – so you're a bit careful where you tread. But if you do stumble there isn't the condemnation you get in a town. People there live much closer to nature, and they know that when a boy and a girl get together things can and may happen. Mind you, if they did, the parents of the girl, if not of the boy, certainly expected him to marry her. Olive told me that many a girl that got married in white was already on the way to the family way. In fact, some people considered you a bit of a snob if you weren't, after all babies were God's gifts, the way they arrived was only incidental. And, village folk are in contact with the animals that are breeding all the time. In any case there's very little else to do and the opportunities are so profuse, I mean you're wandering round country lanes, there's no lights, it's pitch dark. Opportunity's the great thing, isn't it?

In a town it's vastly different – it's such an impersonal

place, you don't get the same chance to go out as a family; you don't get to know the opposite sex. If you get pregnant the man can slip through the net and you're left with a baby and the reputation 'she goes with everyone'.

I once went to stay with Olive at Ripe. Now I've talked about the social advantages of village life – but living in a town certainly had compensations. To start with the village was three miles from the nearest bus stop, so that meant over an hour's walk with my luggage. There was no water laid on, no electricity or gas, just oil lamps at night, and you washed yourself in an enamel basin on a built-up brick arrangement with a hole to get rid of the water – you tipped it down the hole and it just cascaded on the floor all over your feet if you didn't stand back; I got caught by it the first time. You got water from a well in the garden. There was nothing to wind it up with, you just knelt on the ground and stuck the bucket in. It was full of little squiggly things that looked like tad-poles. Olive said they got boiled before you have them in tea. I thought I wasn't very keen on boiled tadpoles. And everything tasted of smoke. Her mother only had an open fire to cook on.

I shared a bed with Olive, a lovely comfortable bed it was one of these feather mattresses you just shake up. I thought it was the last word in comfort. But there was the most terrible scratching noise going on overhead. I said to Olive, 'What's that?' She said, 'Oh, it's only a rat up in the roof.' *Only* a rat up in the roof! I nearly died. 'Search the roof and get it out,' I demanded. 'It never comes out,' she said, 'it's got a nest up there.' I nearly passed out.

The sanitary arrangements were of the most primitive. They were right down the garden path, and believe me they needed to be. It was the most attractive place in the daylight overgrown with rambler roses, but when you went in! It was one of those awful arrangements which the man every so often had to dig out and bury. And it had one of those seats with two holes. The sort for Darby and Joan who couldn't bear to be separated. Talk about two hearts that beat as one! Heaven knows it was lethal enough when only one had been in. I shouldn't think two could have come out alive.

But it was Olive's home and she was very happy there.

They used to say in towns about villages that everyone knew your business; of course, everybody *does*, but you know their business too, so it's one close-knit community which I think is a good thing. I live in a town, and I couldn't even tell you the names of the people that live two or three doors up the road. Nobody speaks to anybody and it's considered the greatest compliment if you're known as a person who keeps herself to herself. But this kind of attitude doesn't help herself to get herself a himself, does it?

21

As TIME went on Lady Gibbons was getting more and more morose. I think by the things she let drop that money was rather tight, and that Sir Walter had made some rather unfortunate investments. Perhaps that was why she was so mean, that there really wasn't very much money.

When Christmas came round I had to cook a turkey and I made a very sad job of it. I couldn't get on with that kitchen range, either I made it too hot, or it wasn't hot enough. This time it was too hot and the turkey got burnt. I scraped it all off as much as I could with the nutmeg grater, I put brown breadcrumbs over the worst of the burns. I hoped for the best and I sent it upstairs. I expected to hear an explosion of rage from Sir Walter, through the service lift. But all was quiet. When Olive came down I said, 'Didn't he say anything?' 'Not a thing,' Olive replied. 'What about her?' I said. Olive said, 'Well, her face changed colour a bit, she turned it around, and she looked at it from all angles, but nothing was said, not from any of them.' So when two or three days had gone by and Lady Gibbons had still said nothing, I began to think that perhaps it had been all right.

But on the fourth morning, out of the blue, old Lady Gibbons said to me, 'Cook, whatever happened to the turkey?' I said, 'Turkey, M'Lady?' She said, 'Yes, turkey.' So I said, 'Well, it did get a bit burned.' So she said, 'A bit burned! It was just like a cinder, and when Sir Walter went to cut it, the flesh just fell off.' I said, 'Well, that's a sign of it being tender.' 'It wasn't a sign of it being tender with your turkey,' she said. 'It's a pity we're not all vegetarians, because that's the only thing you can cook.' So I said, 'Well, your Ladyship, that brings me to a matter I wanted to speak to you about.' I noticed she went pale at this – she thought I was going to give in my notice and that most obviously wouldn't have suited her. Burnt offering was better than no burnt offering. 'It's this,' I said. 'I thought that I might take a few cookery lessons in the afternoons.'

I really had thought about this and the turkey sort of sealed matters. You see it had been my biggest failure and after all turkeys do cost a lot of money. The wretched bird was on my conscience. 'That's a very good idea,' she said, her face relaxing and the colour coming back into it. Then her jaw stiffened. 'But you'll have to pay for them yourself, of course.' That leopard couldn't change her spots either.

I looked around and settled upon a place with the title of 'Léon's Grand School of Continental Cookery'. It was a very imposing building from the outside, though afterwards I discovered that the part he had was very small indeed, just one large room in a very decayed condition. But the lessons were cheap, 2s 6d for a class lesson and 5s for a private one. I took the six class lessons first.

Monsieur Léon was middle-aged with a head of bushy hair which he covered with one of those tall chefs' hats. He certainly looked professional, and there's no getting away from the fact that he was a good cook. He taught us to make some marvellous things out of very little. This pleased Lady Gibbons.

For instance one of the lessons was making puff pastry. It rose as high as I've ever seen pastry rise, and yet he used margarine. Mind you, he never let us taste it which was probably as well.

All the time he was teaching he'd keep up a running commentary like these French people are supposed to do. 'Voilà', he'd say, and 'Comme ci, comme ça', and 'oui, oui'. Well, I didn't even know what they meant, but it sounded frenchy to me, so I took it at its face value.

When I had my first private lesson I went round to the back of his table and got in close contact with his two gas-stoves and the things that were around them. I've never seen anything like it in all my life! There were saucepans galore, with bits of food in them that must have been there from time immemorial, and there was enough penicillin in those saucepans to cure a hospital I should think, if they'd known about penicillin then. The frying-pans were stuck on to the gas stoves by congealed fat and the smell, well the smell just finished me off. 'Monsieur Léon,' I said, 'it's all bloody filthy,' then I fainted, absolutely passed out on the floor.

When I came to Monsieur Léon was bending over me

giving me a drop of brandy, and himself about half a glass.
He was talking in a voice from which all trace of French
accent had gone. I said to him, 'Monsieur Léon, you're no
more French than I am.' 'Course I'm not,' he said, and then
under the influence of the brandy he became very confiden-
tial. 'I was in the cookhouse in France during the war doing
army cooking,' he said. 'That gave me the rudiments of it,
then I deserted. I had a girl there, we got married as a matter
of fact,' he said. 'Well, she up and left me afterwards, but I'd
picked up quite a bit about cooking. Then I came back to
England,' he said, 'and I set up this place.' 'What is your real
name?' I said. 'Percy Taylor,' he said. 'How could I have
started – Percy Taylor's School of Continental Cookery? I
wouldn't have got a single pupil, so I called myself Léon and
I used some of the French words I'd picked up. I used to
know a lot more but I've forgotten them now.' 'Yes,' I
thought, 'and you've probably forgotten your French cooking.' Anyway, that was the last time I went to him. Lady
Gibbons had to make do with cooking à la Margaret.

One thing she and many like her couldn't abide was
breakages. In domestic service breakages are an occupational
hazard particularly when you've got a lot of washing-up to
do. But no one would recognize this, Lady Gibbons least of
all. It was always the same when I dropped anything. 'What
is it this time, cook?' I'd tell her. 'Oh no, not that,' as though
'that' was her dearest possession. Now it's a peculiar thing; in
all my years of domestic service I noticed that it didn't matter
what got broken, it was always something that Madam
'particularly treasured', or it 'cost a lot of money', or it was

'a family heirloom', or it was 'irreplaceable', or it had 'sentimental value'; it was never just an ordinary thing that you could go to the shop and buy. It used to remind me of a furniture remover who was packing china and broke a plate. And the owner said, 'Oh dear, that plate was over a hundred years old,' so the fellow said to her, 'Oh was it? Well, it was high time it went then, wasn't it?'

One morning Lady Gibbons came down and announced that the family would be going into the country for two months, somewhere in Yorkshire, and the house was going to be shut up. She said she'd found another place for Olive with a friend. I was astonished at Olive letting her find a place for her. Nothing would have induced me to work for a friend of Lady Gibbons because very often you find that people's friends are very much like them. She said she was going to take me with them. There was a cook there already and I was to be the house parlourmaid.

All this without so much as 'by your leave', and do you mind having your status changed, and do you mind going to Yorkshire? What did she think I was, some chattel that she could move around? I was determined that nothing on earth would induce me to go to Yorkshire, not even if she was to offer me double money. Not as parlourmaid. I would have suffered agonies of embarrassment having to serve at table; I suffered agonies just going in the room where they were, never mind waiting at table on them.

When I told her I didn't want to leave London she said that this place where they were going was right in the heart of the country, in beautiful surroundings. If only she'd have known that settled it for me. I'd had enough of the country when I stayed at Olive's place.

I could imagine Yorkshire. I visualized some spot right in the middle of the moors, and me stuck there with old Sir Walter and Lady Gibbons. I disliked the country in any case, for when you've seen one cow, or one tree, you've seen them all in my opinion. A cow's got four legs, a tree's got branches, but they don't do anything, do they? I like talk, people, and things that move around with a purpose.

When old Lady Gibbons realized that I was determined not to go, she wanted to get me a temporary job; you see she wanted someone to come back to. The fact that otherwise she'd have to give me a whole eight weeks' holiday with pay was nearly killing her. Anyway I said, 'Well, I'm very sorry, M'Lady, I don't care for temporary work. I'll take it, but if the position suits I would feel I would have to stay. So I shouldn't rely on me being here when you get back.' That was enough for her, I knew she wouldn't let me go.

She didn't say anything then, she had to make it look as if *she*'d made the decision, but the next day she came down, and said that Sir Walter and she had thought that under the circumstances it would be better not to shut the house down, and that I could stay to keep an eye on it; I could live at home if I wanted to. She would pay me my wages and fifteen shillings a week board. That was just fine. I got two months' holiday with pay. Something unheard of. I was in the seventh heaven.

The strange part was that when she came back I only stayed another four months. Perhaps I'd got used to not working there. When I gave in my notice I said that the doctor felt it wasn't good for my health living in a dark basement with the light on all day.

When you gave in your notice, you always tried to give the impression that you were loath to leave, you just had to make it seem that you were sorry to go. It was because of the reference; you couldn't get another job without a good reference. Nowadays, of course, people forge them. If I'd have known anything about it, I would have forged mine. It's all my eye and Betty Martin that they should rely on what the last person you worked for said. She might try to spite you because you left her. If people were the soul of honour, whether they liked you or not, they'd give you a good reference if you deserved it, but people just aren't like that. I don't know whether Lady Gibbons swallowed my story but she did give me quite a good reference, she didn't praise me up to the skies, but she said I was honest, hard working, and a good cook. What more could I expect?

22

AFTER I'D finished at Lady Gibbons' I decided to try temporary work for a change. I thought that by doing temporary work I wouldn't stay long wherever I went, that I'd do lots of different jobs in a short time and that in that way I'd get a lot of experience. It's very seldom that two people have the same ideas about cooking. Some people like made-up dishes, other people like plain food, some are particular about sweets, others about savouries. So I thought I'd quickly gain knowledge and experience by doing a variety of jobs.

It didn't work out like that. I discovered that generally the people who advertised for a temporary cook only did so because no self-respecting cook would ever stay with them permanently. The first job I took was at Stanley Gardens in Notting Hill Gate.

In recent years it's become notorious because of a murder that was done there. At the time I was there it was a collection of large, ugly Victorian houses that were already going seedy.

The people I worked for were Jewish, a Mr and Mrs Bernard. They weren't orthodox Jews, although they didn't eat pork or bacon, but they didn't observe all the things that orthodox Jews do, like keeping all the teacloths and the cutlery and utensils used for milk separate. Later on in my life as a cook, I worked for two other Jewish families who were very generous but Mr and Mrs Bernard certainly didn't fit into that category. They were just plain mean, and made Lady Gibbons seem like Lady Bountiful, though they were more easygoing than she was.

For example, my bedroom and the bedrooms of the housemaid and parlourmaid were furnished with an absolute minimum. Beds were rock hard, and for blankets we had plush curtains with all the bobbles still hanging on them. I had green, and the other two had red. The quilt had been cut in half so that there was a fringe one side and the other that went by the wall was just a plain hem. There was one chair, and a corner fitment to hang clothes, not a wardrobe, just a few hooks with a curtain across. Then a washstand with a broken leg propped up by books.

Mrs Bernard suffered with phlebitis, and she was for ever complaining about it and showing her leg to all and sundry. It used to drive me up the wall. When I went to bed at night I used to try to creep up the stairs like a mouse, because if she heard me passing her bedroom she'd call out, 'Who's there? Oh it's you, cook, come in.' And I used to have to go and gaze at this horrible leg that she spread out on the bed. It was a most unlovely sight. All swollen up, like a bladder of lard. I suppose I should have felt sorry for her, it must have been painful and certainly she couldn't get around very well. But I couldn't because of this constant parading of her woes, and the very sight of her opulent bedroom and the comparison with ours used to infuriate me. There she'd sit all day in bed eating chocolates and displaying her leg. I think she got to be proud of it. Anyway she felt it was part of our job to look sympathetic.

Edna, the parlourmaid, had to take up a brown roll and a pat of butter last thing just in case she got hungry in the night. If it wasn't eaten, she used to send it down for us in the kitchen. But I'd never use it for the simple reason that this brown roll and butter used to stand on the night commode. Talk about hygiene!

Mr Bernard was a benevolent-looking old gentleman, but this benevolence was only superficial. They talk about beauty only being skin deep, but benevolence is only skin deep, believe me. If Mrs Bernard couldn't come down to the kitchen to give her orders, Mr Bernard used to come down. He always tried to get me into a confined space, like the larder or the scullery, and then he'd put his hand on my arm, or shoulder, and his fingers were as bony as a bank-clerk's. 'Shall we work out the menu?' he used to say. I don't know where he thought the menu was. Then he'd hang over my shoulder while I wrote. I wouldn't have minded this weak display of amorousness if there had been anything attached to it, like a pair of stockings or a box of chocolates, but there never was. He didn't want to do anything more than fondle your neck, I know, but there's no pleasure in that from an old man, is there?

He used to do the shopping. Every morning he'd go to the Portobello Market. If we wanted a salad he'd bring back a lettuce and a beetroot, or a lettuce and tomatoes. Never anything else. To make a salad with. I ask you. He said it provided scope for ingenuity. But even ingenuity requires some raw materials, doesn't it? I wasn't a miracle worker. I wonder he didn't bring the water down to see if I could turn it into wine for them.

The trouble was they couldn't afford to keep three maids, but the house was of a size that couldn't be run with less than three. Even as it was, nothing really got done as it should have been done. Everything looked old and shabby, except for her bedroom and the drawing-room.

In the kitchen there were just worn linoleum, shapeless wicker chairs, an ancient kitchen stove, and all the utensils were worn out and the implements, like the brooms and brushes, were always losing their hairs, and nothing ever got replaced. I'm not surprised they advertised for temporary maids. They knew they wouldn't keep them for any time.

I stayed for three months and the only good I got from it was that it was there I invented my famous kipper savoury. It was funny the way this happened. One morning we had kippers for breakfast, and Mrs Bernard, who always had her breakfast in bed, didn't eat hers. When Ethel brought the tray down I threw the kipper into the pig bucket under the sink. But when Mr Bernard came down to give the orders he said, 'Cook, Madam would like you to make her a savoury for dinner tonight using that kipper that she left from breakfast.' My heart sank. I didn't dare say I'd thrown it away because if I had it would have ruined the day for both of them, and I didn't see why I should ruin someone's day over a kipper. So I just said, 'Oh yes, Sir, that'll be all right.' As soon as he'd gone upstairs I rushed to the pig bucket and I fished the kipper out. It was covered in tea leaves and some other nasty bits and pieces. So I rinsed it under the tap. Unfortunately as I rinsed, I was washing up at the time, it fell into my bowl of washing-up water and soap suds. So I fished it out again and hastily gave it another rinse, and I kept smelling it to see if the soap had gone. At last I thought it had. Then the problem was what to do with it to make sure it didn't taste of soap suds. Anyway I got all the flesh off and pounded it well in the pestle and mortar, and I used that good old stand-by, Escoffier sauce. It's a marvellous thing for disguising the flavour of something you don't want noticed. I sent it up well garnished and decorated, and to my surprise Mrs Bernard sent the parlourmaid down with a compliment. She said, 'Tell cook that's the most delicious savoury we've ever eaten.' I thought, 'That's it, girl. When you want real flavours stir things around in the pig bucket first.'

As you can imagine I hadn't been there long before I realized I'd got all the knowledge I was ever likely to get from them. So I left. The next job that I took was with a Lord and Lady Downall in Chelsea.

The contrast was fantastic. They were the most thoughtful and kind people I'd ever met, ever since I started in domestic service. Unfortunately *they*'d advertised for a temporary because they really needed one. Their own cook was in hospital and was only going to be away three months. They were so pleasant and unassuming in their contact with us that I think for the first time since I started work, I lost the feeling that we were a race apart, and that the gap between us and them was unbridgeable. They spoke to us in exactly the same way that they would speak to people of their own society.

For instance we were all called by our Christian names. And it was the first place that I'd been in where the people above – 'Them' – called you by your Christian name.

And the servants' hall was an absolute revelation to me. This one was comfortably furnished and it had a colour scheme to it. We had comfortable armchairs, a carpet on the floor, a standard lamp, and other small lamps around, pictures and ornaments. Things that you could tell were bought specially for us, not cast-offs from their rooms. Things that really matched instead of a room full of bits from the conservatory, bits from the drawing-room, and bits from the dining-room. The whole room was welcoming, so that when you had spare time you felt you could really relax even though you were still on duty.

We all had a colour scheme in our bedrooms, mine was green. I had a green carpet, a green eiderdown, and green blankets with satin bindings, and it was absolutely fantastic – a bedside lamp and a table.

Everything was done to make you feel that they really cared about you. All Lady Downall's servants had been with her for many years, and none of them had any intention of leaving.

As I've said, the reason I was there was because her own

cook was in hospital. And when she was ready to leave the hospital she was to be sent away to convalesce for a month at Lady Downall's own expense. To be taken care of for a whole month! Such things were a revelation to me.

And when it was the servants' birthdays they all had lovely presents, not print dresses, black stockings, and caps and things like that, but real presents. Things that they wouldn't have thought of buying themselves. Just to show you how good they were, my birthday came round six weeks after I got there, and *I* got a present. I hadn't told Lady Downall, she must have found out for herself, and she bought me beautiful silk underwear, the sort of thing I'd never been able to buy. Yet I'd only been there six weeks and she knew I was only going to stay three months, but it didn't make any difference.

It could have been that they were the real aristocracy. I think the name was very old.

Lord Downall had been something in India, like so many of the people I'd worked for. He must have been a big pot then. I never did find out what he did or had been. He was a very tall man, six foot three, extremely aristocratic-looking. He had eyes that sort of could see right inside you.

I remember the first time I met him. I happened to pass him on the stairs, and he stopped, and he said to me, 'Oh,' he said, 'are you our new cook?' and I said, 'Yes, Sir,' you know, colouring up like a beetroot, and he said, 'Well, I hope you'll be happy here. You'll find it's a very happy house.' And he was right, it was. The parlourmaid said to me, 'You ought to be here at Christmas. We have a simply wonderful time at

Christmas,' she said. 'We have our own tree and our own presents, all put round the tree,' she said, 'none of this business of having to go up there and parade in front of them. They're all put there overnight,' she said. 'We can go to a theatre during the month of January, any theatre that you choose, and you don't have to go together, you can take your own friend.'

I didn't wonder that Lady Downall never had a servant problem. There the servants really cared about their employers. If anyone had said that to me before I'd have said, 'Oh, that's my eye, no one cares about the people they work for. You work for them and you do the best you can because they're paying you, and because you like to make a good job, but you can't care about them.'

I got four pounds a month there too. You know I didn't wish their poor cook any harm, but I couldn't help hoping that she'd get complications and be away for a year or so. It's terrible, isn't it, to be like that, but I was so happy there.

And it was so pleasant when Lady Downall came down in the mornings; she'd say, 'Good morning, Margaret. Have you any suggestions for lunch?' in a pleasant tone of voice. Or, 'Oh Margaret, as there'll be such a large dinner party we'll have a cold lunch today. That'll give you more time for the preparation tonight.' Consideration, you see. A rare quality.

This gave me the incentive to cook as well and better than I had done. One of my specialities was soufflés. I used to make marvellous soufflés, I had a light hand in those days. Either savoury ones, or sweet ones. But I could never do much with them on those kitchen ranges. Either they got too hot and the soufflé shot up like mad before the centre was cooked, or else it never rose at all. I'd battled for so many years with kitchen ranges that I got a thing about them and used to look on them as my bitterest enemy. But there I had a gas stove and I was fine.

Every night when I went to bed there I used to pore over Mrs Beeton's cookery book. That was the book we all used in those days. I'd pick out a recipe and study it well so that when Lady Downall said next day, 'Have you any suggestions?' I could produce this recipe, sort of casual like, as though it had been a thing I'd done often. I used to work it out in my imagination until the dish was absolute perfection. In my mind that is, not always on the table. Still that happens to all cooks, we all plan things, but they don't always quite work out as we hope they will. Lady Downall used to appreciate any suggestions, and once she said to me, 'You know, I'm very fond indeed of old Aggie' (that was her real cook) 'and she's been with us for years, she started as kitchen maid in my mother's house, but it has been a very pleasant change having all these different things that you know how to do.'

Little did she know I'd sat up half the night before, learning them.

Lady Downall loved going to the Caledonian Market. It's closed now, but at that time it was thriving in Camden Town. She used to love wandering around looking at the genuine antiques, well, that's what they told you they were; genuine antiques. We used to take it in turn to go with her, and great fun it was. The chauffeur used to bring the car round about ten o'clock. I sat in front with him.

He was a very handsome man, not that I could do much about it because Lady Downall could see if you were laughing too much or anything. Anyway, the fact that he was handsome couldn't mean that much because he was already snaffled. He was married and had two children.

We used to wander around the market, and Lady Downall would pick out any items that she fancied and that she thought were good. She never bargained for them because she said immediately she opened her mouth she put her foot in it. She meant that if she asked about the price they knew that she'd got money, and they put their prices up accordingly. So if she saw anything she fancied, she would get whoever she had taken with her to go up and ask the price, and bargain for it.

I remember once while she was looking to see what *she* fancied, I was wandering around to see if there was anything I fancied, and I noticed on one stall a very large blue pot with a handle each side. I thought to myself, that would be just fine for my mother's aspidistra – everyone had an aspidistra in those days. So I approached the stall-holder in what I thought was a nonchalant manner; mind you, they know perfectly well you've got your eye on something, they weren't born yesterday. But I looked at everything but this pot, and I thought I was being very clever. At last I said to him, 'How much is that blue pot?' so he said, 'Oh, ten bob to you,' so I said, 'How much to anyone else, half a crown I suppose? I'll give you five shillings for it.' So he said, 'Five bob? You must be joking. Anyway, what do you want it for?' I told him I wanted it for my mother's aspidistra. 'Good idea,' he said, 'and when she's finished using it for that, she can knock one handle off and stick it under her bed! Two things for the price of one. You've got a good ten bob's worth there, haven't you?' I blushed like a beetroot, and beat a hasty retreat. I never went near that stall again!

23

ALL TOO quickly those three months passed. Perhaps flushed with my success at Lady Downall's I decided I'd try one more temporary job.

I got a place near Victoria Station. It was one of those grim, tall, rather shabby houses outside, with an interior to match. It was one of those 'I'm here for ever' kind of houses.

Here again we were underfed and underlodged. For the first and last time in my life I slept on chaff. The mattress was made of chaff, and laid on lathes, you know, not on a spring at all. As I moved in the night it rustled as though I was a horse turning over. Even at home we had flock beds that you could shake up and make comfortable.

I didn't sleep a wink on my first night, and when I got up in the morning I was determined to complain about the bed. But at ten o'clock when my employer, Mrs Hunter-Jones her name was (Hunter-Jones, hyphenated you know, you must always sound the two together), when she appeared she looked so formidable that all my resolutions to moan about it faded away completely. I just hadn't got the pluck to say a word. It's terrible to be a coward like that but one look at her face finished me. I comforted myself with the thought that I wasn't serving a life sentence, I had only gone there as a temporary, and temporary I now decided it was going to be.

The housemaid and the parlourmaid, they'd been there two years, but as their ages were sixty-three and sixty-five it wasn't easy for them to find other employment. Conditions were beginning to get a little bit better – not that people had suddenly changed and become more humane, but there were now more occupations for women to choose from, and naturally if there was other work they could do instead of domestic service they did it. So there was some competition and this meant providing better conditions. But at the ages of sixty- three and sixty-five domestic service was the *only* thing left to do.

For these two poor old things years of spinsterhood and working in other people's houses had made their hands bent, their faces all craggy, and their dispositions extremely foul. And the appearance of these blighted specimens of woman-hood plus that of the formidable Mrs Hunter-Jones made me determined to leave at the carlicst opportunity. You see all the time I was thinking I might get married, that was my main object in life, and every new job I got I thought some-body might come along, perhaps one of the tradesmen might be all right, and that would be that.

But I could see that this house was a dead duck from that point of view straight away, and the idea of getting experience as a temporary wasn't going to work either because Mr and

Mrs Hunter-Jones did no entertaining at all, and the plain-ness of the food was only equalled by the scarcity of it. So with no pleasure in cooking, no company but those two old drears, and a house that was as quiet as a mausoleum, I was very depressed.

Even if you've got a mistress who's disagreeable, if the other servants are young and lively you can extract some humour from the place even if it's only making a combined attack on her upstairs. We used to give them a sort of kitchen psycho-analysis, Freud wasn't in it. Mind you I reckoned we knew more about their sex life than he'd ever have dis-covered.

But that subject would have been out even if my gaunt companions could have discussed it. It's my confident opinion that the old dear could never have indulged; she hadn't any children and a look at her husband would have confirmed my view. He was a trophy, if the truth was known, and he might just as well have hung on the wall with the other antlers for all the use he could have been.

But not only was there no congenial company in this house, there was nowhere to sit and relax. There wasn't even a servants' hall. You just sat in the kitchen surrounded by the 'Ideal' boiler, the gas stove, the kitchen table, and the dresser. So I took to going out of an evening.

I had a friend, she only lived about ten minutes' walk away, who was also in service. I used to go out and see her about half past eight, but I was always in before ten o'clock. It didn't hurt anyone at all. But it didn't please those other two old servants. I know they were sour, but you wouldn't have thought they would have moaned about it because after all it didn't affect them. But the thing was *they* couldn't get out, so why should I be able to?

So after I'd been out a few nights they informed Mrs Hunter-Jones. This information was a great shock to her. She had never heard of such a thing as a servant going out above the stipulated time for her outings, so I had to listen to a long lecture, and demands as to why I wanted to go out of an evening. She said, 'You have every Sunday evening and one other evening free.' 'Yes, Madam,' I replied, 'but when I finish work there's nowhere comfortable to sit.' So she said, 'Oh well, other cooks have sat in the kitchen, why cannot you? You're certainly not free to go out whenever you feel like it.'

I thought about this and I thought about these two old spinsters. It didn't really make me dislike them because I could see that their lives were unhappy.

Their names were Violet and Lily, names which probably suited them some forty years ago, but it certainly didn't go at all well with their appearance or their dispositions now.

On one of the rare occasions when we all got chummy together they'd told me that they'd worked as a parlourmaid and a housemaid for twenty-five years in the same house for one lady, a childless widow. According to Lily and Violet, this lady had promised them that if they stayed with her until she died she'd leave them an annuity, enough money for them to leave domestic service and set up a flat together. Mind you, I thought they were muggins not to have seen the proof. Anyway, when the old lady did die it was found she hadn't made a will at all, and all the money went to her next-of-kin, her nephew. He just sold the house, and all poor Violet and Lily got was three months' wages, and then he thought he was being very generous to them, because nothing stipulated that he should give them anything.

So you can imagine after twenty-five years in one job, and what they thought was coming at the end of it, then to be dismissed with three months' wages. You can't wonder that they were grim, can you?

Mind you, it happened in a lot of cases. It was a way of keeping servants when you were getting old. But it's hopeless to trust in people like that. I wouldn't have believed a word.

The trouble was that they were convinced that their madam had really left them the money and that the nephew had done them out of it. I tried to explain to them about wills and solicitors and things, but they didn't want to believe me. Well, nobody likes to think that they've been caught for a sucker, do they? But it made me understand why they were so sour and everything.

It was only too evident they would never get anything from Mrs Hunter-Jones. She underpaid them anyway because she knew that they'd have difficulty getting a job anywhere else.

Still I didn't feel that by staying in the house I could alleviate their lot in any way. There'd just be three disgruntled people instead of two. So I gave Mrs Hunter-Jones a month's notice. It was a very unpleasant business working out my notice in that house. A month is a long time when people are unpleasant to you, and the two old dears, although I didn't make things any worse for them, resented that I could get out, that I'd got a future, and that they hadn't. They'd only got the past and that hadn't been too good.

My main worry was about my reference, because I sensed that Mrs Hunter-Jones wouldn't give me a good one in spite of the fact that I came to her with a wonderful recommendation from Lady Downall. I tried to get a written one from her so that I could read her opinion of me, and then perhaps I could have done something about it. But she wouldn't give me one, she said she never reckoned to do anything like that.

It was with some considerable trepidation that I gave the next prospective employer Mrs Hunter-Jones' telephone number. I knew they wouldn't meet each other because I had decided that I would work in Brighton for a while, so at least I knew that they wouldn't get together and have a good natter over me.

The job I went after was in The Drive which at that time was a very palatial road indeed. I was interviewed by a Mrs Bishop. I took great pains to tell her I'd only been temporary at Mrs Hunter-Jones', but she said that she would ring her up and would I call back the next day to see what the verdict was.

When I went she said, 'What a peculiar person your last employer is. When I telephoned her for a reference she said, "Well, I think Margaret Langley could cook if she was ever in to cook, but as she expects to be out morning, afternoon, and evening, she never has the time."' That reference would have been damning in the ordinary way but it turned out that Mrs Bishop had an odd way of life which made it difficult for her to get and keep a staff.

So in spite of Mrs Hunter-Jones' efforts she engaged me as a cook at a wage of fifty-two pounds a year. This was very good money indeed because this was not temporary, it was a permanent job.

You may think I'm going on about this reference business. But it was most frightfully important then. People were frightened that you might steal things or that you might be working 'inside' for a gang of thieves. They wanted to know all the ins and outs about you. Mind you, they never gave you a reference about themselves, which I used to think you had a right to; whether you had to work like a slave, whether they kept late hours, whether they were mean and selfish, whether they treated you like dirt; nothing like that, but they wanted to know all about you. And if you hadn't got a good reference from your last place it was useless to explain that you'd been in domestic service since you were fifteen years old, that there were many other people to whom they could apply, and that the reason that this reference wasn't a good one was because in your last place you dared to speak up about conditions of employment. Employers didn't want to hear that kind of thing. That was bolshevism. 'How dare one of the lower classes criticize the upper classes!' Girls like me who they considered came from poverty-stricken homes should be glad to work in a large house with food and warmth. To them upstairs, any home was better than the one that you lived in with your parents. It was mutiny if you said in your last place you didn't have this or that – it must have been better than what you've been used to. And as for domestic servants having aspirations to rise above the basement, such a thing was incredible to them.

Even Lady Downall was the same in some respects. I remember asking her if I could borrow a book from her library to read, and I can see now the surprised look on her face. She said, 'Yes, of course, certainly you can, Margaret,' adding, 'but I didn't know you read.' They knew that you breathed and you slept and you worked, but they didn't know that you *read*. Such a thing was beyond comprehension. They thought that in your spare time you sat and gazed into space, or looked at *Peg's Paper* or the *Crimson Circle*. You could almost see them reporting you to their friends. 'Margaret's a good cook, but unfortunately she reads. Books, you know.'

24

THE BISHOPS' house was a large, four-storeyed, detached building with the usual basement, and a back stairs for the servants.

Mrs Bishop was an absolute revelation to me. I had been used to solid superficial respectability, with 'Them' upstairs. But what a change she was. She was Italian by birth, nearly sixty years old, but made-up to look about thirty, and from the back view that's the age she looked. She had her face enamelled, I don't quite know what they did with it, but she never gave a hearty laugh, she just tittered so that it never cracked. She didn't move the muscles of her face. Her hair was dyed, and hair-dyeing in those days hadn't reached the perfection it has now, so that each subsequent dye was never the same colour as the last, and the head became patchy. I couldn't take my eyes off her when we first met. She had a figure slim like a young girl's. That was unusual in those days. People weren't figure-conscious, nobody thought of dieting. They merrily consumed three-course lunches, and five- or six-course dinners every day, and 'hang your figure'. She had an attractive husky voice. I thought she had a sore throat when she interviewed me. She was very proud of this voice, she said, 'It's just like Tallulah Bankhead's, you know.' Tallulah Bankhead was all the vogue at that time.

As well as the house they had a flat in London. They spent from Tuesday afternoon to Friday afternoon there. This meant that, although we had free time in the week, we never had a weekend to ourselves. This was the reason she had difficulty getting maids because they like their free days at weekends, especially if they happen to be courting. But it didn't worry me, I hadn't got a young man yet.

From Friday evening until Monday morning the house used to be packed with visitors, some were young business people, a lot were hangers-on of the film and theatre world, nobody of any class at all, always plenty of young men of a variety of nationalities. Mrs Bishop was very very fond of young men. None of us ever had half an hour we could call our own at weekends. I didn't mind at all, at least there was some life, even if I was getting it second hand.

In this somewhat bizarre household I used to have to go and get my orders while Mrs Bishop was in the bath. I was horrified at first because I'd never seen a nude figure, not even a woman, before. It was amazing, after a couple of weeks I got quite used to it, and I'd sit on the edge of the bath, while she used to tell me what she wanted.

One morning at ten o'clock I went to the bathroom. I'd got so used to going there I just used to knock and walk in without waiting for an answer. On this particular morning, to my horror, instead of seeing a very flat, nude, white body lying there, there was a huge, black, hairy one, standing up in the bath. It was an Italian. Well, it was the first time I'd ever seen a full-scale appendage in my life. And after having had a look at it I could quite see why Adam rushed to get a fig leaf! I would have too if I'd discovered I had an object like that! The shock! It took me about a week to get over this thing. Mind you, he didn't think anything of me seeing him at all. He told Madam afterwards that he'd like to come down and apologize to me. Thank heaven he didn't. After seeing him in the nude I couldn't possibly have seen him clothed. I should have been visualizing it all the time.

I remember the other maids, they wanted to know about it in detail, and everything. They said, 'I bet you rushed out,' 'I bet you had a good look.' Things like that had more importance in those days. Anyway, from then on I never went in without knocking and waiting to make sure it was Mrs Bishop who answered.

Young men were Mrs Bishop's life. They say life begins at forty, well she must have had twenty years of hard living. Mind you, she wasn't unattractive, her face was skilfully made up and we always had the blinds at half-mast. It gave her subdued light, and that helped.

She used to have some furious rows with these young men and I'd know that, when I saw her the next morning, I'd be in for a tearful session. She'd give me the same old routine over and over again, I must have heard it more than a dozen times. 'Oh, you know, Margaret,' she said, 'I was married straight from the convent, when I was seventeen years old, and I never saw Mr Bishop until I stood before the altar with him. I never had a chance to live when I was young, I was married to a man ten years older than me and I saw nothing of the world at all, and now it's too late.' Well, naturally, I had to agree with her. She didn't want my opinion, she just wanted my sympathy. I couldn't see that she'd made such a bad bargain, she had a lovely house, servants, jewels, and a life of ease; I mean if that wasn't living, it was a bloody good imitation. I'd have married Old Nick himself for the sort of life she had.

Mr Bishop was a different kettle of fish altogether. I think he was of German origin and had changed his name during the war. He had a very placid temperament. Of course, they lived entirely separate lives, she slept on one floor, the second floor, he was on the floor above and they had very little to do with each other. They went up to London together and they came back together, but they weren't married in the true sense of the word when I knew them; that was finished.

I liked him. He certainly had a sense of humour. While they were up in London we used to take the run of the house; use their sitting-room, play all their records, and I used to bang out tunes on the piano. One day there I caught my hand in the car rack and nearly broke my thumb. I had to be taken to the doctor's and have it bandaged. When I passed Mr Bishop the next day he said to me, 'How's your thumb getting along, cook?' and I said, 'Oh it's all right, Sir. It's a bit difficult to work with.' He said, 'Yes, and a bit difficult to play the piano, too, isn't it?' Someone must have told him what we did when they weren't there, but he said it with a twinkle. He didn't mind.

Still after all, this was mild stuff compared with what he was putting up with from Mrs Bishop. He turned a blind eye to that too. I heard that twice she had tried to commit suicide or staged a suicide by taking too many pills or something, and that one of the sons was a 'ticket of leave man' in Australia, as they called them: he was sent two pounds a week to keep him out there. I think he'd forged his father's name to a cheque. So he'd had his troubles in his time and wasn't looking for any more. They weren't of course what you could call the gentry.

But it was lively, you see. Every now and again when she had some Italian friends Mrs Bishop would come down to the kitchen and say, did I mind if they came down and made some special Italian dishes? I didn't mind because they were nearly always young people. Mind you, they made a hell of a mess and used to leave the kitchen in a filthy state; it didn't occur to them to do the washing-up. But I used to watch them and get all the pointers that I could. So although I couldn't say I was working for the 'quality', I couldn't care less. I got my money, had a gay, amusing life, and that was all that mattered to me.

One of these young men who was her favourite longer than anyone else was one of these Italians. Proper ice-cream man. He used to walk round with a little monkey on his shoulder, I used to be terrified. Mrs Bishop provided him with money; he was what you call a gigolo. He wasn't a day over twenty-five, and with her being sixty she probably didn't provide him with much else. So if he could find one of the young maids to have a little interlude with, he would. He'd come down to the kitchen with his foul monkey on his shoulder and he'd try to get you in conversation. He'd start off about food and that kind of thing, and go on to, 'Have you got a boyfriend?' I don't know why they ask you that. Then he'd edge round the table towards you, and I would keep edging farther and farther away, because I knew perfectly well that whatever his intentions were, they certainly weren't honourable. He never got anywhere with me. It just wasn't worth your while wasting your time on impossibles, all your efforts were needed to allure the possibles, the ones who might have good intentions.

I read in the paper the other day that the surplus of young men to girls in England today between the ages of sixteen and twenty-one is fifty-six thousand. It makes me see red. Because then in Brighton, there were five girls to every young man, so you can just imagine what a fight you had to have to get one and keep him. And we never had a free weekend, which was the only time a young man had got any money. By the time we met them they were dead broke, anyway. And if you said you were in domestic service it was still the same old story, you could see their faces change. The less polite ones used to say, 'Oh, skivvies!' and clear off, and leave you cold.

I remember one night Hilda, the parlourmaid, and I went to a dance. Hilda used to stuff her young men up with the idea that she was a secretary. This particular night we collected two naval officers. Of all the snooty fellows in the world, officers from the Royal Navy are the snootiest. I don't know what rank they were, probably the lowest that they could be, consistent with being officers. They were mean as well as snooty because they brought us back on the bus; no taxis. I never pretended to be anything else but the cook because it was always my fate to get a bit of supper for them. I thought that perhaps my way to a man was through his stomach. We used to take them in to the kitchen, you see; we weren't supposed to, but you've got to make up for not having weekends off. Just after we got in Hilda went upstairs to the lavatory and her officer came up to me and said, 'She's not a secretary.' I said, 'Well, she's whatever she says she is,' to cover up for her. 'Well, she's certainly not a secretary, she's the parlour-maid.' I said, 'How do you know?' He said, 'I took her into that place where there's a sink' (he meant the butler's pantry) 'and before she'd let me lay a finger on her she washed up the silver.' You see, she didn't think, she was so used to never letting the silver lie around dirty she had to wash it up. Well, no secretary would have done that, of course. Mind you no officer and a gentleman would have mentioned it. Poor Hilda never joined that branch of the Navy.

Still she had aspirations.

Anyway, life wasn't too hard there for me, there was an odd-job man to do the boiler and the front steps and the boots and shoes. The kitchen floor there was very good, it was paved with smooth red tiles and all you had to do was just wipe them over with a damp cloth. The usual enormous dresser that we always had was fitted with glass cupboards so that nothing got dusty. And there was a telephone in the kitchen.

After that previous place with Mrs Hunter-Jones, it was a great pleasure to be able to cook things like salmon steaks, and jugged hare, and to make real mayonnaise, instead of white sauce. We had things like sirloins and saddles, and I had the opportunity to practise and to learn cooking.

Although I was now quite expert, it was a good job I had never taken up any other part of domestic service like being a parlourmaid and waiting at table. I only had one experience of it and that was enough. One evening Mrs Bishop was giving a dinner party and Hilda was taken ill and couldn't wait at table. Mrs Bishop came rushing down to me to ask if I could come in between the courses and help hand things round. The housemaid was to do the silver serving, and I was to hand the vegetables round. I knew I would suffer agonies of embarrassment. You can just imagine coming up from the heat of the kitchen with a face like a peony and wearing a print dress into the bargain. When I arrived in the dining-room Mrs Bishop announced to the company at large, 'This is my cook.' Well, of course, everybody gaped at me, which didn't help, I felt like exhibit A. One of the vegetables was tiny little new potatoes, they looked very attractive in the dish on the silver salver, with mint and butter sauce – piping hot they were too. The first guest I had to serve was an attractive Frenchwoman. Well, I was so nervous my hand started shaking like a leaf – the dish shot down the salver and all these marble-sized new potatoes shot all down her front and her lap. She jumped up and let out a stream of French words I couldn't understand. Then I saw that one of the pota-toes had got lodged in her cleavage – so I tried to get it out with the serving spoon. The silly thing didn't keep still – it must have been burning her – anyway, instead of getting it out I squashed it against her breast. She flung the spoon out of my hand and screamed, 'Coshon, coshon' about half a dozen times. Talk about Oliver Twist, but she didn't ask for more. I fled downstairs.

About a week later when I thought the excitement had died down, I asked Mrs Bishop what this word 'coshon' meant. I thought it must have been something terrible. She said, 'Oh well,' she said, 'it's just a French word that means the same as damn does in English.' It was some years later that I looked it up in a French dictionary, it was spelt C.O.C.H.O.N., I found, and it means you're a pig or a swine. I didn't mind – she got the potatoes. I didn't.

Occasionally during the week Mr Bishop would come down from London. He had a girlfriend I think, in Brighton somewhere, we never saw her but we always assumed that was what he came for. He would always telephone to let us know that he was on his way so that he never caught us in any embarrassing situations. If he ever wanted dinner we never had to worry, he always had the same thing; giblet soup, we always had giblets because there were always chickens in the house; grilled sprats; and stewed pig's trotters. He used to pick up the old trotter and suck away at it. It was the same meal every time, that's what he liked, didn't want anything else.

If we were going dancing we didn't have to give it up, because this was supposed to be our free time. We used to arrange his dinner between us, the housemaid, the parlourmaid, and me. One of us would get on with his dinner while the other one would be getting ready for the dance, so sometimes he got a different person serving each course. Hilda would take in the giblet soup, then she rushed to change, so then the housemaid would go in with the grilled sprats, and then she would tear off, and I would rush up with the trotters. He never seemed to mind.

It was after I had been there some months I discovered that he had a most peculiar aberration. If he came down to the house on his own, he'd always ring the bell in his bedroom at about half past eleven at night, after we'd gone to bed. It rang upstairs on the landing outside the bedrooms, and Hilda or Iris, the housemaid, would slip on a dressing- gown and go down to his room. Then he'd ask them to bring him a whisky and soda, or a jug of water, or even a book that he'd left in the library. I said to Hilda one night, 'Why does he always wait until we've all got in bed before he rings that bell?' So she said, 'It's because he likes to see us in hair curlers.' I said, astonished, 'What do you mean?' She said, 'He likes to see us in hair curlers.' People in those days didn't have hair rollers like nowadays, they were all those dinky steel curlers, and we did our hair up every night in them because it was the fashion to have a mass of frizz, and the bigger you could make it stick out the better it was, you see. So I said, 'You're joking.' 'No, it's the truth,' she said. I said, 'Well, what does he do then when you go in wearing these curlers?' So she said, 'Well, he doesn't really do anything much. He asks us to take off our hair nets and then he fingers the curlers in our hair, you see.' I just couldn't believe it, it seemed pointless, stupid. I said, 'Is that all? He feels your hair curlers?' She said, 'Yes, that's all he does. And he's always happy and pleased when he does it,' she said. She just sat on the edge of his bed and he just felt her hair curlers, and that's all. Well, it struck me then, and it does now, as a most peculiar way of getting pleasure. It just didn't make sense, I mean whoever heard of anyone wanting to see anyone in hair curlers, never mind about feeling them? But Hilda and Iris did quite well from this peculiarity of his, because they used to get cosmetics or boxes of chocolates or stockings each time.

I could have got them as well if I liked. He wouldn't have cared who answered the bell at all so long as you went in your dressing-gown and your hair curlers, but I would never go. Not that I cared whether or not he saw me in hair curlers; I wouldn't let a young man see me, it would be absolute death to a romance and a possible home-provider, but it wouldn't have mattered about him. No, the reason I wouldn't go was because it was yet another demonstration of servants' inferiority. You see he wouldn't have dreamt of asking guests in the house if he could feel their hair curlers. But servants, they should be quite happy in his view because they got presents for doing it. But Hilda and Iris wouldn't agree with me over this; they said, 'Well, what does it matter, it doesn't do us any harm and we get something out of it.' I tried to make them see this, because they had aspirations, not that that got them anywhere. But Iris said, 'So we *are* servants, aren't we?' she said. 'And anything we can get given us for doing nothing at all is so much to the good.' And Hilda she said, 'I get quite a kick out of it, and when I'm waiting at table,' she said, 'and when Mr Bishop is sitting there talking so high-falutin' to his guests,' she said, 'I often feel like slipping a hair curler on his plate!' But I never heard of such a peculiar aberration in my life as hair curlers. I wonder what was the cause of it? Something tied up with his youth I expect, perhaps his mother had them or something.

25

ABOUT THIS time I thought I'd managed to snaffle a permanent young man; as you must have gathered, it was no easy task at all with so few opportunities around. This particular one was a window cleaner. When he used to come to clean the windows I'd ask him down to the kitchen and give him tea and cakes made by me, do myself up, and try my hardest to make an impression. They say the way to a man's heart is through his stomach, but believe me, it's mighty hard going at times, some of them have got pretty tough stomachs.

Anyway, this fellow, George his name was, had been taking me out for three months. Three whole months. It seemed a lifetime to me, quite long enough for me to consider him as a possible husband. But he had his faults and his worst fault was his meanness. Oh, he was a shocker for being mean!

When we went to the pictures he'd buy a quarter pound of chocolates, supposedly for me to eat in the cinema, then he'd hold them in his hand or on his lap, and proceed to gobble them up himself. I soon learned. Directly we sat down our arms used to swing like pendulums and within three minutes the chocolates had gone, the bag thrown under the seat, and we'd settle down to watch the picture.

Another mean streak was the way he passed all the pubs. That was the biggest failing of the lot. Pubs in those days were places you couldn't go into on your own, or even with another girl. If you did, even if you went in with another girl, you got a bad reputation. Everyone felt that you were easy meat, and they treated you that way too. The fact that you'd rather have a drink than a cup of tea was nothing to do with it. It just wasn't done. My mother and father used to like to go out at night and have a drink. They didn't drink much, perhaps they'd have two half-pints of beer or bitter each. It was strong then, and much cheaper because it was stronger. If you had two half-pints you felt the effects; now you can drink enough to blow you out like a balloon and you get home feeling flat as a pancake. If my mother and father wanted to go to the pub they took me with them. You weren't supposed to go in at fourteen, which was when I first started, but then I was always an enormous size and looked well over my age. I drank lemonade at first, then I progressed to shandy, and from there to bitter, and I got used to going in the pub. It wasn't so much for the drink, it was for the life.

Pubs in those days had life. A pub now is only one degree removed from a morgue, isn't it? Nobody speaks to anyone, there's no life or gaiety. Especially now that they're all made into cocktail-lounge type of places. The other day we went into a pub and there was a man humming to himself. He'd had a few drinks, but he was doing no harm, just being happy. Twice the manager came round and told him to stop, and the third time they ejected him. You mustn't enjoy pubs. I used to go into one on a Saturday night with my Mum and Dad before I even went into service. It would be crammed with people, you'd stand there holding your glass right up close to your chest, but you felt happy and it was lively, it was life. That's how I started drinking. I liked the life of the pubs, and I still do. I'd rather go in a pub and have a drink than go anywhere. Luckily, my husband feels the same. (Yes, I got one in the end.) So if we've got any money we whoop it up, if not we just have a couple of beers.

Leaving aside the life you get in a pub, there was another reason that I resented George not taking me there and that's the effect drinks have on you. I used to feel amorous after a couple or so and so did any young man. Any fellow I met who had a face like the back of a bus and who I wouldn't have looked twice at if I'd have been stone-cold sober, looked like Rudolph Valentino after a beer or so. Mind you, I had to be careful not to have too many, there was a borderline, you wanted enough so that they would kiss you and make a fuss of you and so that you could leave them thinking that next time it might be all right to go a bit further, but you didn't want them dashing at you like madmen the very first time they took you home. After all's said and done, you've only got one lot of goods and if you're going to distribute them to all and sundry you haven't got anything worth keeping when the real one comes along! Anyway, every time we got to a pub this George would say to me, 'Would you like a drink?' so I'd say, 'Well, if you would, I would,' then he'd say, 'Well, if you would,' and then I'd say, 'Not unless you would,' and by this time we'd passed the pub and I never did get him inside. I didn't like to look too eager because after all, I was thinking about George as a permanent institution, and I didn't like it to look as if all I thought about was rushing into a pub.

So after a month or two of going out regular; just going to the pictures, the cheapest seats, gobbling a quarter of sweets between us, and never going in a pub, I very reluctantly decided that George would have to have his cards. After all, if a man doesn't spend much on you when you're not married to him, it's a sure thing he's not going to afterwards. If he's not going to take you into a pub when he's already out with you, you can't see him leaving the fireside to go, can you?

When I look back on it now, I just made the efforts to keep him, and put myself out that way because the selection was so poor. When all's said and done, he was a wretched little specimen; he wasn't even as tall as me, and he had no conversation of any kind. He made these model things, model aeroplanes. He told me he had a marvellous collection. Can't you imagine it, a lot of old dust-harbourers they are, you can't do anything with them, and they clutter up the place. I bet somebody's got him now, and cursing him and his flipping aeroplanes. But the interest I used to show in them! I'd say, 'Oh marvellous, can you really make them? I'd love to see a model,' and when he brought one round I stood cooing over it when I couldn't really give twopence for it. The lies you had to tell men to make out that you were interested in them, simply because there was no selection. Girls nowadays if they don't like what a fellow does or what he looks like, they tell him to run after his tail. But not then, no fear you didn't.

Of course, there were some old men about, there always seem to be, and they tell you they're as young as they feel. That's all very well but if they look about ninety it does make a differ-ence, doesn't it? Some of them don't feel all that good either.

I stayed a year with Mrs Bishop. By this time I thought I really ought to get a job where there were more servants and I could have a kitchen maid. So I answered an advertisement in the *Morning Post*; I thought I'd go back to London again.

The house was in Montpelier Square, Knightsbridge. They were Dutch people, bankers, very wealthy, solid, and respectable. He looked just how I envisaged a Dutch banker should look; tremendous corporation, with a gold watch-chain across it.

It was in this house that I saw the change in the status of domestic servants. In other places I'd noticed what must have been the beginnings, but here I found a complete change. Here we really counted as part of the household.

Including the lady's maid, there were seven servants, and we each had a bedroom of our own. And very comfortable rooms they were, and our tastes were consulted. I was asked if there was anything I wanted changed, if I had enough clothes on the bed, if I wanted any more lights in the room, and that kind of thing. It was obvious that they really did want you, and appreciated you being there.

The kitchen was furnished with every appliance that was then known, and although it was still in the basement, it was light and airy, painted white, none of this chocolate brown half up the walls, and green the rest. In the scullery the sink was white enamel, not one of those cement affairs, and aluminium saucepans, which was a change from either iron or copper.

Everything had been bought especially for the staff, none of that 'this will do for the basement'. All our uniforms were provided free. I'd always had to buy all my own uniforms before, the parlourmaid, the housemaid, and the kitchen maid all had striped print dresses, and they were allowed to choose what colour they liked, any shade, pink, or green, or blue. As the cook I was allowed to choose my own colour scheme and style. I had various patterns shown to me. It was all so different.

Madam was very strict. Everything had to be just right, but then she'd paid for it. Meals had to be served absolutely to time, and every dish cooked to perfection. But now I felt she had the right to expect it. She had shown she cared for us. It was up to us to care for them.

Some of the meals she used to plan herself, others I used to work out; sometimes a whole menu, which I'd never been used to doing. I did make some mistakes at first. There were so many things that I'd not done before, or even seen done. But I had old Mother Beeton to rely on. I don't think she ever failed anyone; she'd got recipes for everything under the sun. I know people laugh today about how it says, 'Take twelve eggs and a pint of cream' but of course in those days you did take twelve eggs and a pint of cream.

Having a kitchen maid was quite a help of course, but I wasn't really a lot of good with her because I had such strong recollections of the terrible time when I was in that position and I was determined that I'd never be that harsh when I was a cook. But I found it was quite true what that old harridan of a Mrs Bowchard used to say; that you've got to go around nagging at the kitchen maid.

This one I had there, unless you went for her all the time she didn't bother, and I couldn't be strict enough. I wasn't used to being in a position of authority, I couldn't order her to do something. I'd ask her to and if she was a long time doing it I'd set to and do it myself. Well, that's not the right training for a girl, really and truly. Still there it was, I just couldn't go around nagging at her, saying she was no good, that she'd got to pull her socks up and being generally foul. For one thing it wasn't my nature and for another it seemed just as quick to do it myself. But it wasn't good training for her. I think I failed her.

Madam didn't fail me. At first I found it hard to believe in her interest and concern. I mean after years of poor food, poor surroundings I'd become convinced nothing short of a bloody revolution would get better conditions for domestic workers. Yet after I'd been there a few weeks I realized that Madam really wanted us to be satisfied with our jobs. It's not that she loved the lower classes, she didn't, but she believed that a contented staff made for a well-run household, which it did. Because servants that feel they're being put upon can make it hard in the house in various ways like not rushing to answer the bell, looking sullen, dumb insolence, and petty irritations to make up for what you're not getting. Not there they didn't. As I say Madam didn't love us, we didn't want her to, we wanted what we got; being well paid and doing a good job in return.

I became very proficient as a cook there and I know my efforts were appreciated not only by those upstairs but by the staff, in particular by the butler, Mr Kite.

He was a man about fifty years old, and he'd been in domestic service since he was thirteen; he started as a page-boy and worked his way up. His first place was a country house where the staff included six footmen, two stewards and still-room maids, six housemaids, a chef, an under-chef, four kitchen helpers, and fourteen gardeners; a tremendous establishment! The outside staff lived in cottages on the estate, but the inside staff had the whole top part of the house to themselves. Mind you the men were rigidly segregated from the women, and if one of the men servants was ever found anywhere in the women's section after they had retired for the night, he was instantly dismissed without a reference.

I asked Mr Kite what it was like working in those conditions, and he said, 'Oh, they were real gentry'. 'In what way were they different from our employers here, then?' I asked. Mr Kite said, 'Well, they were so far above the servants that they literally didn't see them. I remember one evening when I'd risen to be a footman, I was waiting at the dinner table after the ladies had retired and the port was being circulated, and the gentlemen were talking about a very scandalous rumour that involved royalty, and they were all adding their quota to the rumour. One of the guests remarked, "We must be careful that nobody overhears us," to which the host replied, "How could they overhear us? We're alone here," and at that time there were three footmen in the room. But we must have been invisible. So that's how much above us they were, literally to them we weren't there.'

One thing I used to envy the people upstairs for was the way they spoke. I used to wish with all my heart that I could speak with their cultured voices. I said to Mr Kite once, 'You know, if only we could speak in the way they do it wouldn't matter if we hadn't got twopence in our pockets, we could walk into the Ritz and as soon as we opened our mouths the waiters would rush to show us to a table; whereas like we are now, if we went in with fifty pounds and asked for a table the only place they would show us to would be the door.'

But Mr Kite was a bit prosy; he sort of mixed with the people above and he got, like so many did, to be like them in lots of ways. He used to bring out platitudes as though they were pearls of wisdom. He really liked being a butler; he used to say, 'I wouldn't change places with any man, there's no shame in honest toil.' I don't know what he meant by *honest* toil, there's a lot of dishonest things being done, but I'm sure toil isn't one of them! Then he'd say, 'There's only two things in life that a man needs; comfort and love.'

Madam supplied all his comfort, I often wondered if I should supply the love. Not that he ever asked me to do so, but I dare say that propinquity and my cooking would have brought him up to scratch if I'd set my heart on having him as a husband. But that would have meant staying in domestic service for ever; a prospect that I couldn't bear to contemplate. Anyway, this was the time I realized my lifelong ambition, I did get married from this place, and it was my last permanent job in service.

192

26

LOOKING BACK on my years in domestic service I've often wondered why the status of our work was so low. Why we were all derogatively labelled 'skivvy'. Perhaps it was the intimate nature of our work, I often used to think that was it, the waiting hand and foot on, and almost spoon-feeding people who were quite capable of looking after themselves. In some ways we weren't much better off than serfs, inasmuch as our whole life was regulated by our employers; the hours we worked, the clothes we wore – definitely the clothes we wore at work, and to some extent the clothes we wore when we went out. Even our very scanty free time was overshadowed by the thought that we 'mustn't be in later than ten o'clock'. We weren't free in any way. So maybe that was the reason why the work and those that did it were looked down on, because we were, as it were, bound to our employers.

The employers always claimed that the training they gave you stood you in good stead when you left and married and had a family of your own. When I left domestic service I took with me the knowledge of how to cook an elaborate seven-course dinner and an enormous inferiority complex; I can't say that I found those an asset to my married life.

My husband was a milkman and he earned three pounds five shillings a week, out of which he gave me three pounds, so the ability to cook a seven-course dinner was no help at all. I promptly had to unlearn all the elaborate cooking I had done and fall back on the sort of cooking that my mother did when she brought us up. And all the pleasure I had in cooking disappeared in having to do that sort of cooking.

Mind you, when I first got married I used to do a lot of fancy dishes. I thought that my husband would like it. I used to go to a lot of trouble, with cheaper cuts of meat of course. It involved a lot of work, and when it was over my husband would say, 'Not bad, old girl, but I'd just as soon have fish and chips.' That soon knocked the gilt off the gingerbread to my mind.

Well, every art requires appreciation, doesn't it? I mean people who paint, sculpt, or write books want an audience, that's the reason they're doing it for, and it's the same when you're a cook. You need somebody who savours it, not one who just says, 'Oh, it's not bad.'

Anyway I soon got rid of the seven-course-dinner complex, but the inferiority complex took me far longer to eradicate. I tried. At that time psychiatry and psychology and all that ballyhoo were beginning to be the big thing, and there were no end of books published about how to avoid blushing and what to do about an inferiority complex; so I got one, thinking I might find out what to do about mine. Not only did I read books about it, but I went to classes where I discovered that the complex manifests itself in two forms; either you're timid or you're aggressive. I'd got the latter form. I can assure you it was a far from endearing trait, and it did nothing towards my ambition of 'how to make friends and influence people'! With no money, not good-looking, and very aggressive, you make very few friends and you influence nobody at all. I came to the conclusion that aggression only achieved results when it was allied to beauty or power. Well, I had neither of these desirable traits, so common sense should have taken over from there and convinced me that my position in life was just to be a sort of downtrodden housewife, one of the great army of housewives who've got aspirations, but never manage to do anything about it.

As well as books I had advice from people – it's amazing the amount of people that are always so lavish with their advice, isn't it? It would be, 'What you need is to have a family', or 'You need to educate yourself', or 'What you need is to travel'. Well, as the first of these exhortations was the easiest to accomplish I decided to go in for that. And it certainly occupied my time because I had three children in five years. Three boys. I got quite blasé about it.

I remember when the last one arrived it was a Sunday. Incidentally, all my three children were born on Sundays, I don't know if that means anything or not. My husband went to fetch the midwife, who was just going to church, and was far from pleased about it, though how she thought you could possibly regulate when they were going to come, I don't know. Anyway, the sight of her gloomy face didn't help me at all – having a baby isn't a picnic at the best of times. When it arrived she said, 'Oh what a pity it's another boy.' So I said, 'Well, I don't care if it's a blooming monkey so long as it's got here at last!' She looked at me in shocked amazement and said, 'You know, I look upon every child I deliver as a flower sent down from above to be planted in the earth's soil.' This kind of talk from someone who had produced no flowers at all – she was a spinster – made me say, 'What about all the seed that falls on stony ground?'

I took a very prosaic view of the whole proceeding, because when I was a child I'd lived in a street where most babies were born as a result of Saturday night revels. They were all known as 'beer babies'.

When Albert and I decided to get married naturally I wanted to leave service straight away. After all's said and done, all my working years had been building up to the fact that by getting married I could get away from it with all possible speed and rapidity. So when the date was set I gave a month's notice.

This time I had a perfectly legitimate reason for doing so and Madam was very pleasant about it. It was a funny thing that although none of them really liked you to leave if you were going to another job, if you left to get married it was a totally different thing. It was acceptable and it was respectable.

And yet the business of getting a young man was not respectable, and one's employers tended to degrade any relationship. It seemed to me one was expected to find husbands under a gooseberry bush. Their daughters were debs, and they could meet young men at balls, dances, and private parties, but if any of the servants had boyfriends they were known as 'followers'. I think 'followers' is a degrading term, it brings to your mind people slinking through back streets, not seeing the light of day, with any young man that cares for you. Why should you have to do that? Why should the fact that you're a servant and in love be wrong when the whole deb set-up was manufactured to bring their daughters together with young men? They could have said, 'If you have a young man you're interested in, you can ask him in to the servants' hall when you've finished your work.' But no, you had to slink up the area steps and meet him on the corner of the road on some pretext like going to post a letter. And on your night out when you came back you couldn't stand at the top of the area steps with him or bring him down to say goodnight to him. He wasn't a young man, he was a 'follower'. They made you feel that there was something intrinsically bad in having a member of the opposite sex interested in you at all.

We decided to get married in a registry office. We hadn't got much money, and Albert and I didn't think much of all the pomp and ceremony. It was a quiet affair. I got all the usual inquisitive remarks. Such things as, 'You're getting married to get out of service', and, 'Are you really in love?' I wasn't madly in love, but I cared about him, which I thought was a good basis to get married on.

In view of the fact that my husband only earned three

pounds five a week, of which I had three, you might wonder why I didn't go out to work. Women simply didn't then. Working-class husbands bitterly resented the very thought that their wives should have to work outside the home. It seemed to cast a slur on the husband and implied that he wasn't capable of keeping you. If a man was unemployed, well that was a different thing. Then you had to.

Our first home was in Chelsea and there was a woman living in the basement next door to us who was married to a Russian, a Mrs Balkonsky, her name was; her husband was of course Boris. She had five children, and she got about the same money as I did. She was an extremely good milliner, an occupation that she could have followed in her own home, and supplemented the family income. Yet her husband was so against her doing any work or making any money apart from what he gave her, that she wasn't allowed to.

Mind you, I didn't want to go out to work. The time never hung on my hands at all, I was only too glad to have nothing to do for a while. Although I was a feminist and stuck up for the rights of women, it didn't go that far. I asserted an independence as regards the running of the home, I wasn't subservient in any way to my husband. I considered that he received good value for the money he gave me in every way; in the physical relationship, in the running of the home, in the social relationships too, and I considered that I wasn't under any obligation to him at all.

In any case the only kind of work that I knew how to do well was cooking and to do that would have meant going out at night and doing dinners. Well, I don't think that the wife going to work at night is a very good basis for a marriage relationship.

I wanted to make a success of marriage as I wanted to make a success of other things in life. And so much of my time had been spent thinking about getting out of service that it was a long while before I felt that home life wasn't enough, and by then I had collected a family of three children, so that any aspirations I had had to go by the board for the time being. Looking after three children is a fulltime job to me at any rate, because I was a mother in the full sense of the word, I think.

As I've said, after we got married we lived in what we considered was the best part of London, Chelsea. We paid fifteen shillings a week for a bed-sitting-room, with a minute little kitchen. We had the first child there. But naturally as the family increased, one room and kitchen wasn't enough so we had to move. We went in turn to Willesden, Harlesden, and Kilburn. They're very dreary, dingy places with houses to match the kind of locality.

I had three children in the first five years of my marriage and by then – Albert was still a milkman – money was getting a bit tight.

When our eldest child was about five years old I happened to be out one day and 1 met one of the maids who I'd been in service with. She told me that the people she was working for were at their wits' end because the cook was away and they'd got to give a dinner party. She said, 'Why don't you come in and cook the dinner for them?' I said, 'I couldn't, I haven't done that sort of cooking for years.' 'You'll pick it up again straight away, you can't forget that kind of thing. Why don't you try?' So I went home and spoke to Albert about it. I put it to him. It would mean at least ten shillings or a guinea for doing it, and the money would be very handy for the children. So he agreed and I did it.

I made quite a good job of it too, and after it was over the lady of the house came down and asked me if I would like her to recommend me to her friends. I said 'Yes'. From time to time people that she knew would write to me and ask me if I could come and do a dinner; sometimes for six, sometimes as many as twelve, in which case they would have some dishes in from outside as well. When it was a small dinner I got half a guinea, but for an elaborate one I earned two guineas, and when you consider that my husband was only getting about four pounds a week even then, two guineas was a lot of money indeed. And I quite enjoyed these little expeditions. Apart from the money it gave me an insight into a different kind of life. People were so different, so friendly. They'd be in and out of the kitchen talking to you as though you were one of them. In domestic work things had certainly changed.

27

THIS WAY of life passed pleasantly enough until 1942 when my husband was called up. Albert was conscripted into the Royal Air Force, so I decided that I'd move back down to Hove.

I didn't want to stay in London in wartime with three young boys, so I wrote to my parents to see if they could get me a house. It was quite easy to get houses in Hove at that time because a lot of people had left. They didn't like the hit-and-run raids they were having there. They got me a six-roomed house for a pound a week. It was marvellous, the first house we'd had since we'd been married. The most we'd ever lived in before was three rooms and a share of lavatory.

I remember one place we had at Kilburn, we had to go downstairs and walk through someone's kitchen to get to the lavatory. All through the summer the man used to sit right outside the lavatory door on a deckchair, and it was most embarrassing to ask him to move. I'm sure that's where I first suffered with constipation!

Now everything would be my own, I thought. I was in

clover. You can imagine what our stuff looked like in it, because we only had enough for three rooms. It had to be spread all around. I just had one bed in each bedroom, nothing on the floor, but I didn't care.

All the boys got on well in Hove; they all went to the same elementary school at first, and then they passed the examinations to get to the grammar school. While this was a great joy, it was also a terrible worry. With three young boys to look after on my own I couldn't go out to work, and the separation allowance that I got at that time was very poor indeed.

It wasn't until I'd written goodness knows how many letters to the Education Authorities that I managed to get more money. But I found great difficulty in managing even so, and each time Albert got a promotion – he was eventually made up to corporal – we didn't benefit, because out of his increased money the government docked my allowance. So there was no incentive for him to try to get further.

I couldn't make the boys' clothes now. If they'd been girls I could have, but boys have got to look the same as everybody else. You can't send them to school in home-made suits.

I remember one terrible occasion, the only time in my life when I had to apply for charity. They only had one pair of shoes each and although when my husband was home he used to mend them, he had been posted overseas. I was at my wits' end as to how to get them repaired. So I went down to the Soldiers', Sailors', and Airmen's Association who sent me over to the Council. It was something too terrible for words. You need a hide like a rhinoceros, it seemed to me, to ask them for anything. Some people were used to getting all and sundry. They never turned a hair. But this was the first time I had ever asked for anything. I went in very nervous with a face as red as a beetroot. I felt like a pauper. 'Why do you want shoes for them? Why haven't they got shoes?' I said, 'They've only got one pair.' 'Why don't you get them mended?' they asked. 'I can get them mended,' I said, 'but in the meantime they won't be able to go to school. They've got no others.' After this kind of talk they returned me to the Soldiers', Sailors', and Airmen's place. I went back to them and I said, 'They said it comes under your jurisdiction,' and they said, 'It doesn't, not to supply shoes. You go back to the Council and start again.' When I went back and through the whole process again, they grudgingly gave me some forms. They don't give you money and they don't give you shoes, they give you forms to take to a special shop in Hove.

They wouldn't let you have shoes, you had to have boots, charity boots. My sons had never worn boots before. I never entered fully into how much they must have felt it. I was so obsessed with how I felt, I never investigated their feelings. Going to school wearing boots, and everyone knowing that they're charity boots because they were a special kind.

When my boys went to this grammar school, it was still a fee-paying school. So naturally the parents of the boys that were there were far better off financially than we were. A lot of them had been to preparatory schools. And they had money. Some of the boys had a pound a week for pocket money. A pound a week! I couldn't give mine a shilling. I remember when I had a bit of trouble with one of them – he drew a moustache on the headmaster's photo – the headmaster saying to me that it was all poppycock their feeling inferior because they hadn't got money. 'I came up the hard way,' he said, 'I only got to a grammar school on scholarship level, and I only had sixpence a week pocket money.' But times had altered. People had more money then.

Another terrible thing was that if you had an income of under five pounds a week you were entitled to free dinners. Well, there was no one else in any of their classes that had free dinners, and each new term the master would say, 'Stand up those who want tickets for dinners.' Well, you just imagine how you would feel if you're the only child in the class whose parents can't afford to pay for your dinners. I didn't fully understand it myself at the time. If I had realized the situation I wouldn't have been ambitious to get them to a grammar school, I really wouldn't. I used to write to the master in advance, I knew which one they would have, and say, 'Will you please not say out loud, "Who is going to have a free school dinner?".' I admit they did take notice then, and they didn't do it.

Another thing that I didn't realize was sport. Cricket for instance. I couldn't buy cricket flannels or cricket boots. I ran up football shorts for them, but I couldn't afford the journeys for away matches. I thought, it doesn't matter, they're getting a good education, that's what matters. But those other things did matter.

I think that one can be too ambitious. You educate them, you send them into a social community of which they can't be one. People have the same herd instinct as animals. There's only got to be one that's different and they kick hell out of him.

28

WITH THIS struggle on I decided to go out to work. I decided to do housework again. I couldn't take on cooking because there wasn't a lot of work for cooks in wartime. It had to be housework. It was very poorly paid at that time. When I first started I got tenpence an hour. It seems fantastic now when you think about it. I suppose everyone must have been getting the same otherwise I'm sure I would have asked for more.

I worked for a vicar, which was jolly hard work. You know what vicarages are; there's the day for the boy scouts, the day for the girl guides, the day for the Women's Institute, the Mothers' Union, and of course these old vicarages are not labour-saving places. They were planned with a house full of servants in mind. Still I enjoyed it there. The money was bad, but there were perks; left-over food, and when there was a jumble sale the vicar's wife always used to let me pick out anything I wanted first. She'd say, 'Just give a few coppers and take your choice,' and many a decent suit or jersey I got for the boys before the horde came in.

I stayed at the vicarage job for some time, and then one day I was chatting to a friend who was also doing domestic work and she told me she was getting is 1s 3d an hour; the rate had gone up fivepence an hour in a comparatively short time. Well, there's only one reason for doing that kind of work, money, so I started to look round for another job.

The first thing that amazed me was the difference that I found after so many years. Large houses that were once opulently furnished and had had a large staff were now reduced to no staff at all; just someone coming in for a few hours daily. Much of their lovely stuff had gone; they had had to sell it to pay their income tax.

Most of these ladies were very elderly and they accepted this change in their status with fortitude. Some of them used to talk to me about their changed circumstances and their vanished possessions. I remember one house where I worked, I used to go there two mornings a week. All they had left of their silver was a large tray, one of those which a whole tea set is carried on, and one day when I was polishing this, Mrs Jackson, a very elderly lady, said to me, 'Ah, Margaret, when the silver service stood on that tray, and when the butler carried it into the drawing-room, it used to look a picture of safety and security,' she said. 'We never thought that our way of life would change.'

I couldn't help feeling sorry for them, even though judged by my income they were still fairly well off. It's much harder to be poor, isn't it, when for years you've had money rolling in, than if you've never had money at all; and then to come down to doing such a lot of their own work at their age. It's easy to turn to when you're young, you're resilient.

Mind you, the funny part was that even though now they could only afford dailies, some of them still retained their old autocratic ways. They used bitterly to complain about the sordidness of life, they were very fond of saying that, that everything was 'sordid'. And their favourite was, 'The working class are aping their betters', the betters being them of course, and 'The country is being run by a collection of nobodies and is going down the drain'.

One of the ladies I worked for was a Mrs Rutherford-Smith. One day she said to me, 'Margaret, you're a very good worker, and I like you, but you've got one failing and I hope you won't be offended when I tell you what that failing is. You never call me "Madam".' And then she added, 'You know, Margaret, if I was talking to the Queen I should say "Madam" to her.' I wanted to reply, 'Well, there's only one Queen but there's thousands of Mrs Smiths!'

Mrs Rutherford-Smith and those like her missed all those little attentions that used to be their prerogative, the hat-raising, the deference from tradesmen, and the being waited on by well-trained servants.

Many of the people for whom I was a daily were old and lonely, and I was the only person who provided them with contact with life outside. This seemed strange because many of them lived in flats, and you'd think that living in a block of flats you'd be in a sort of microcosm of life. But it just isn't so. I've worked in half a dozen such blocks and I've never met a person either going in or coming out. Everyone seemed to be isolated in their own little cell. They needed to live in them as they were easy to run. But it was a very lonely life for them.

Some who had adopted a philosophical view talked to you as though you were one of themselves, but others felt that they were really doing a great kindness in sitting down with you and being on equal terms with you. They thought it was very odd that a daily should show any signs of intelligence.

There was a Mrs Swob that I worked for. I shouldn't really call her name 'Swob' – it was spelt Schwab, and she pronounced it 'Swayb'; that's how she liked it pronounced, but much to her fury most people pronounced it Swob.

This Mrs Schwab's house was filled with antiques, terrible old dust-collectors, especially some round mirrors that she had, with convoluted gilt frames, and she showed no signs of pleasure when I knocked one of the knobs off one of these frames. 'You must treat things better, Margaret,' she said. 'Don't you love good objects?' 'No, I don't, Mrs Schwab,' I said. 'To me they're just material things; I have an affinity with G. K. Chesterton who wrote about the malignity of inanimate objects,' I said, 'and I think they are malign because they take up so much of my time, dusting, polishing, and cleaning them. Look at that vase,' I said, 'that you say is worth a hundred pounds, if that was to drop on the floor and break it would just be three or four worthless bits of china.' That set her back on her heels for a few seconds. 'I didn't know you read, Margaret,' she said. 'I read a lot of course.' She was one of those, whatever you did, she did it, only ten times more.

I was talking about films once. 'Oh yes, I could have been a film star,' she said, 'I wanted to be but at that time I was going out with the man who is now my husband. He wouldn't let me. Everyone was most disappointed.' You'd be amazed all the rubbish I had to listen to, they ladled it all out, and you had to look suitably impressed. You're working for them and you want your money, and if it wasn't them it would be somebody else. They employ you to be a captive audience. Still, while you're listening you're not working.

This Mrs Schwab had one of the most infuriating habits; every time I went she used to say to me, 'When you scrub the bathroom, Margaret, don't forget the corners.' This gained her less than nothing. From then on I never used the scrubbing-brush, I just threw the soap round the floor.

The last straw there was when I was sweeping the balcony. One morning she said to me, 'Oh' don't sweep the dust that way, sweep it the other way.' Well, did you ever hear such drivel? I collected my wages. I hadn't got the nerve to tell her I wasn't coming any more because instinctively I felt she would let loose a flood of invective, she looked that type to me. I wrote a very posh letter, I thought it was, anyway, to the effect that 'it must be as irritating to her to feel that she had to keep telling me how to do things, as it was galling for me to have to listen to her'.

You didn't have to worry about references on a daily job. You just said you'd never been out before, or that the people you last worked for had died. As a matter of fact the last people I worked for had all died. I don't know whether there is any sinister connexion, but they have.

I can't help thinking that people who were once wealthy and now have to live on a fixed income are worse off than ordinary working-class people, working-class people's incomes do rise to meet the cost of living. They can ask for a rise, and go on strike if they don't get it, or they get a cost-of-living bonus. But people who are living on fixed incomes like these old ladies have got to keep on trying to keep up some sort of show. A place like Hove is full of these decayed gentlewomen who are struggling to make ends meet. And in spite of the kind of idiosyncrasies I've mentioned, they do a marvellous job, because they're trying to cope with a way of life that their upbringing gave them no preparation for at all. I've been amazed at the resilience and zest for life of some of these old ladies.

29

IT WAS when my youngest son was going to grammar school and my eldest was preparing for the university that I realized we had nothing in common to talk about except the weather. They would come home and discuss history, astronomy, French, and all those kind of things, some of which meant nothing to me. I'd never tried to keep up with the Joneses, but I determined to have a shot at keeping up with the boys.

First of all I thought about taking a correspondence course. But apart from the expense, you're on your own doing a correspondence course; if you don't feel like working there's no one to urge you on, you're not in rivalry with anyone and it doesn't matter how long you take.

Then one of my boys' history masters told me about a course of lectures given by Professor Bruce, Extra-Mural Professor from Oxford. They weren't expensive, I think it was only a shilling a time, or cheaper if you took the whole lot, twenty-four of them. I took the lot.

It was fascinating to me this course of lectures. He must

have been a brilliant teacher because the lessons were in the evening from half past seven to half past nine, with a break in between for a cup of coffee, but often with the discussion that used to go on afterwards it was eleven o'clock before I got away, and eleven thirty before I got home. My husband used to say, 'I don't know what kind of education you're getting that keeps you out till half past eleven.'

But it was a real eye-opener for me, I'd always thought history was a dry thing, a succession of dates and things like that.

Then I started going to evening classes in philosophy, history, and literature. The only thing that really beat me was this metaphysical philosophy. You know when you first start anything, you want to be all high-hat. You don't want to go to the same things that everyone else goes to, you want to come out with some high-falutin' name, so I signed on for metaphysical philosophy.

I never knew what it was all about. All I could understand was it was something to do with being a hedonist, or some such thing. After six evenings I decided that it wasn't for me. But that was the only subject where I didn't stick the course out.

Where has it all taken me? Well, I passed my 'O' levels at the age of fifty-eight, and I'm now taking the Advance levels which I hope to get before I'm sixty. People say to me, 'I can't understand you doing it.'

I think it springs from the beginnings. All life is bound up together, isn't it? I liked school, I won a scholarship which I couldn't afford to take; I went into domestic service. I was dissatisfied and all this dissatisfaction was worked out in my attitudes to the environments of domestic service. If I'd been something else I should have been militant against that life, I expect.

When I got married, I had the boys and became a mother pure and simple. Then when they were off my hands it came out again.

People say, 'I suppose you got bored with life', but it wasn't as sudden as that. The seeds are in you and although it may take ten, twenty, or forty years, eventually you can do what you wanted to do at the beginning.

Would I have been happier if I'd been able to do what I wanted when I was young? I might have been. I'm not one of those who pretend that because you're poor there's something wonderful about it. I'd love to be rich. There's nothing particularly beautiful about being poor, having the wrong sort of clothes, and not being able to go to the right sort of places. I don't particularly envy rich people but I don't blame them. They try and hang on to their money, and if I had it I'd hang on to it too. Those people who say the rich should share what they've got are talking a lot of my eye and Betty Martin; it's only because they haven't got it they think that way. I wouldn't reckon to share mine around.

Looking back on what I've said it may seem as if I was very embittered with my life in domestic service. Bitterness does come to the fore because it was the strong feeling I had; and the experiences are the ones that stay in my mind now.

I know it's all dead and gone. Things like that don't happen now. But I think it's worth not forgetting that they did happen.

But we did have happy times and I did enjoy life. Remember, I'd never been used to a lot of freedom.

Domestic service does give an insight and perhaps an inspiration for a better kind of life. You do think about the way they lived and maybe unbeknown to yourself you try to emulate it. The social graces may not mean very much but they do help you to ease your way through life.

So despite what it may sound like, I'm not embittered about having had to go into domestic service. I do often wonder what would have happened if I could have realized my ambition and been a teacher, but I'm happy now, and as my knowledge increases and my reading widens, I look forward to a happy future.

Climbing the Stairs

To my husband, with love

Introduction

IT'S DIFFICULT FOR people to realize the social and financial changes that have taken place since the 1920s — it seems such a short time ago.

When I tell people what it was like when I went into service in 1923, at first they say, 'How awful for you.' Then it suddenly strikes them that it wasn't very long ago, and they think you're exaggerating, that it wasn't like that, that either you had very bad places to work in or that you've made it out to be a lot worse than it was. But in fact there have been vast changes since then.

I think what people fail to understand is that although the status of domestic servants has really risen so dramatically, the real reason for the change is the scarcity of domestic servants nowadays. If they were ten a penny as they used to be they'd be treated in the same way as we were. This goes for other workers, too. I don't think people have changed; it's events that have altered their attitudes.

When I went into service the very name 'service' meant

that you'd said goodbye to all personal freedom – the same as it did for men in the Army, the Navy and the Air Force. Like domestic service, these services used to be filled from the ranks of the uneducated and untrained.

Then there were few jobs open to ill-educated girls. Chances for women were coming, I know, but they were for women who'd had an education – whose parents had either been enlightened and had seen that they were educated as well as the boys, or for women who from the moment that they could get hold of their own money had made sure that they educated themselves.

Most of the people I worked for sprang from the middle classes who, when they acquired wealth and rose in the world, adopted all the social standards of the upper classes.

And the upper classes regarded the state of the poor as inevitable. We were always with them and so long as you didn't attempt to rise in the world – so long as you knew the state you'd been called to – they were even prepared to be gracious and benevolent towards you. So long as they knew that you knew that they were being gracious and benevolent.

I think that they had the same feelings about servants then as wealthy people have now about their possessions – their homes, their cars and all the gadgets that make life worth living. These things need looking after. They don't want them to wear out too quickly, but if they go wrong or become tiresome they can be replaced.

Servants were not real people with minds and feelings. They were possessions.

Since my book *Below Stairs* was published I've had a number of letters from people who were irate that I wrote in the way I did. They said that their mothers always looked after the servants. A number of older people have said also that they thought about their servants' comfort and saw that they had a nice room.

Yes, I agree; perhaps they did. But they still looked on their servants as their possessions. The servants must never have a life of their own. The employers were entitled to say to their servants, 'Oh, what did you do on your day off? Where did you go? Who did you go out with?' And to expect a truthful reply. But if you were to say to *them*, 'And what did you do when you were out last night? Did you have a good evening?' they would have been horrified. You couldn't ask such a thing; you had no right.

When I was reading history for my 'A' levels recently I discovered that even Disraeli, and he was supposed to have been a Liberal, said that there were two nations. And he meant the rich and the poor.

Well there were two nations when I was fifteen, and now I'm sixty-one I still think that there are two nations in this country, even though things are so much better. Just give us a period of high unemployment and you'll see what I mean.

Another great change that there's been is in fashions. When I first went into domestic service, there weren't the facilities that there are now to buy cheap, but good, ready-made clothes.

Now a lot of the well-to-do openly boast that they buy

things from Marks & Spencer or shops like that – buy them ready-made. It's quite the done thing nowadays. But it wasn't the done thing in those days.

Then they had everything made for them. We used to make our own (and they looked like it), because bought ready-made clothes were so expensive.

Of course we used to try to copy the styles of the rich and the people that we worked for. And I often used to think that it was we servants who really changed the fashions. Because as soon as we copied or made anything that looked remotely like what they were wearing upstairs they would discard it and get their dressmaker to design something else. Probably we flattered ourselves; perhaps they would have discarded it in any case.

Mind you, this gap that there was was also something to do with being young, because no matter whatever your status in life then, whether you were working, middle, or upper class, no young people were of any importance.

We were never known as teenagers. We were just young – too young to know anything about business or politics or even living our own lives. All we were expected to do was to keep quiet, take advice and let those who had experience and know-how get on with it.

It didn't just apply to the lower classes. It applied to the well-to-do just the same. Young people's opinions were not consulted and weren't expected to be given either without being asked for. They were learning, and when you're learning you can't advise because you don't know. And that applied to all strata of society.

Nowadays everything's geared to young people. Vast sums are made by firms like the clothing, cosmetics, records, and magazine manufacturers. They make fortunes out of young people. So if these firms are basing their commercial structure on supplying young people with the material things – and if the Government is spending great sums in providing the facilities and opportunities for education – then we shouldn't be surprised at the type of young people that results.

It's no good us crying 'enough, enough' when youth gets up and tells us how they want to see the world run. Because we've made them like that. We've made them important.

But when I look back on my life – although the working-class people of my generation had to work hard for a living – I don't envy young people at all today.

It may seem that they've got everything – material things and freedom to live their lives in the way they want to – but they've also got the urge and the anxiety of wanting to improve the world; as for us, we only wanted to improve ourselves.

Margaret Powell, 1970

1

I was three days in my first place in London before I had
a chance to go out. I arrived there on a Wednesday and
as a Wednesday was to be my one afternoon and evening
off in the week obviously I didn't get it that week, so my
first time out was on the Sunday. I was allowed from three
o'clock till ten o'clock every other Sunday, but that first
day it took me so long to do all the washing up that I didn't
get away until four.

I'd had a letter from my mother the day before – the Saturday. Mother must have sat down and written it the minute
I left home, saying that I was to be very careful indeed;
everybody knew what London was like. Not actually stating
anything definite – kind of innuendoes. Anybody would
have thought I was some sort of raving beauty and that
every man who looked at me was going to make advances.
Instead, what I was in those days was fattish, on the plain
side with big hands and bigger feet, and with these poor
ingredients I didn't know how to make the best of myself – I

don't think many working girls did. At the end of her letter my mother put 'and don't talk to any strangers'. Well, since I didn't know a soul in London if I didn't talk to strangers I wouldn't talk to anyone. So it looked as if I would have to be dumb for the rest of my stay.

Anyway there I was, all ready at four o'clock to go out and I was mad to go and see Hyde Park because it was a place I had read about with its soapbox orators and the guardsmen in their red coats walking around. I asked the cook what number bus to get on because I didn't want to look like some provincial hick that had just come up to London and didn't know anything. I was going to ask for Hyde Park, hand over the right money and look as if I knew it all.

I got on the bus that she told me and I went upstairs right to the front so that I could see everything. I sat there for ages looking all round and very soon it struck me that the buildings were much the same kind that you might see anywhere. But of course being as they were in London I thought, oh well, they must be marvellous.

No conductor took my fare. One came up several times but he never reached the front of the bus. I sat on and on looking. I thought it seemed a long way but I had no idea where things were. Then I could see that we were in a very seedy neighbourhood: dirty little shops, a very slummy place – far more slummy than some of the places around my home.

Before I could do anything about it the conductor came up and said, 'This is the terminus.' So I said, 'I haven't seen Hyde Park yet.' And he said, 'No, you bloody well won't see it on this bus either. You're going in the wrong direction.' 'But this is the right number,' I said. 'Yes,' he said, 'this is the right number but you're going the wrong way. You got on on the wrong side of the road.' 'Well, why didn't you come up and get my fare – why didn't you tell me?' So he said, 'You try being a conductor on a ruddy London bus, and see if you're going to tell people who don't know where they're going where they should be going.'

I got off the bus very crestfallen and not knowing what to do at all. So he said to me, 'Where did you want to go?' I told him I wanted to go to Hyde Park and also that it was my first time in London. So he said, 'What are you going to do now, then?' He thought for a moment. 'I'll tell you what,' he says. 'We'll be going back in twenty minutes. We're going over the café to have a cup of tea and that – why don't you come over with us.' Well, I wouldn't have dreamed of doing a thing like that at home. Not only might someone you know see you but, I mean, it just wasn't done. But after all was said and done I'd gone to London to have an adventurous life so I thought, 'Well, here goes,' and walked over to the café with him and the bus driver.

It was obviously a working men's café full of lorry drivers and bus crews. I was the only member of my sex but nobody seemed to show any surprise at seeing me, so I assumed that they often took women in there.

The bus conductor – I found out that his name was Perce – said, 'Well, sit down.' And we did, at a table that was covered in American cloth and innumerable flies, and he went to get cups of tea for us. That tea! It was so black. What they did was to stick soda in the tea urn – it's a well known trick at these working-class cafés – to get all the colour out of the leaves and make it look strong. And he brought us cakes about the size of tennis balls and the same consistency, too.

Anyway we got talking and this Perce – of course his real name was Percival – told me he lived at a place called the Elephant and Castle. So I said, 'How did it get that name?' 'Oh, well,' he said, 'originally it was called The Castle after the pub there but the landlord's wife got so fat drinking all the stock that they called it The Elephant and Castle.' Green though I was I didn't believe a word of it but I dutifully laughed.

The bus driver, Bert, was a mournful, cadaverous-looking creature and he spoke in such a resigned tone of voice that you felt he'd eaten life's troubled apple, core and all, and all that was left for him was a gradual descent to the grave. Part of his trouble was that he suffered from gastric ulcers. These he told me were rife among bus drivers because of the shift work and the irregular hours they had to do. This and the fact that they couldn't stop the bus often enough to empty their bladders. So they got these gastric ulcers. He reckoned they should have been paid danger money. He may have been right but it's my opinion they got their ulcers from drinking that black tea and eating all those rub-bery cakes.

Anyway when I'd got to know him a bit more I found he was a non-stop talker. He showed me photos he'd had taken when he was young and healthy. Apparently he used to go boxing on a Saturday night to earn himself a bit – in the boxing booths, and he told me he'd won twelve fights in a row and used to be called the 'Wapping Wonder'.

I was absolutely fascinated at the thought that this elderly man – this one-time 'Wapping Wonder' – was interested enough in me to tell me his life history. I began to think that there must be more in me than I knew about.

But afterwards the bus conductor, Perce, deflated my ego. When Bert went to that place reserved exclusively to men he said, 'Don't take a bit of notice of what he says because he tells everybody that old tale. I've heard it hundreds of times. He couldn't knock the skin off a rice pudding. All he ever talks about is bladders and boxing.'

Then Perce asked me why I wanted to go to Hyde Park. So I said, 'I just want to look at it.' 'No,' he said, 'you must have a reason.' 'Well,' I said, 'when you live down where I do you read about Hyde Park. Surely it's one of the sights of London, isn't it?' 'Well, I've never bothered to go there,' he said, 'and I live here.' 'Yes,' I said, 'it's just like the seaside. The residents never bother to go down on the beach and sit on the stones – it's only the trippers and visitors that do that.' 'Well,' he said, 'don't go into Hyde Park of a night on your own, it's full of prostitutes.' 'Oh,' I said, 'is it?' And far from damping my ardour I thought that was marvellous – I wanted to have a good look at them.

I'd visualized them as very alluring types of women, mysterious-looking – rather like Pola Negri the vamp who was all the rage on the films at that time. So I thought I must go and see them. 'Yes,' says Perce. 'Dressed up in all their finery on the broadwalk there. And woe betide if anyone tries to get on their pitch.' 'Well, what do they look like?' I said. 'Oh, they dress in muslins and things like that.' 'Oh,' I said, 'like Greek soldiers that wear those kind of ballet skirts.' Then Perce said, 'They might look like that but I wouldn't want to get in a fight with them. My father was in Greece during the war and he was always telling us tales about the Greek soldiers, how tough and virile they are. "Yes," he used to say, "it's more than starch that keeps those ballet skirts up."'

The implication was lost on me but everybody roared so I laughed too. After all he was providing me with refreshments even if they weren't light refreshments. Anyway I wanted a free ride back and I got one. I went upstairs again and this Perce kept running up and chatting to me and then he made a date to meet me on my next night off.

So there on my first time out in London after months and months without a boyfriend in my own home town I'd met one and made a date with him.

Mind you, until Perce had told me what a line-shooter Bert the driver was I'd found little to choose between them. In spite of his age and appearance I'd rather fancied myself going out as the girlfriend of the Wapping Wonder. But I never could abide line-shooters. I'd had a belly-full listening to George when I was kitchenmaid at my first place in Brighton.

2

GEORGE WAS THE chauffeur-gardener at the place where I first went into service in Hove and he was somewhat of a character. He hadn't always been in domestic service, which makes a difference because a man who's been in domestic service all his life – say, from the time he was fourteen – starting off as a hall boy, boot boy, page boy, or what have you and working his way up to under-footman and butler – is quite a different person from a man who's done different work and then comes into domestic service later.

Men who've been in service all their life – I wouldn't like to say they were effeminate – but they have a much quieter, gentler way of talking and they're nicer in their appearance and the way they do things. And I'm not using the word nice as a compliment here.

This George, he'd spent years in Australia which in those days was probably a far rougher country than it is now. And not only that, he'd been in the Outback, on a sheep farm. Later he was in Sydney but most of the time he was on this sheep farm, and he was always talking about the life out there. How it wasn't riddled with class distinction, how out there Jack was as good as his master. None of this 'yes sir, no sir, very good sir' and 'bloody hell how are you today sir' and bloody kow-towing just to earn a living.

Sometimes Mr Wade the butler would say, 'Well, why do you do it? If you don't like it why don't you leave and do something else?' But George was getting on and it wasn't easy to get a job in those days. George ignored him anyway. 'I tell you,' he said, 'my boss on the sheep farm, he could have bought this bloody Rev' (meaning the Reverend who we worked for) 'he could have bought this bloody Rev up ten times over, and yet at mealtimes we all sat down at the same table – boss and workers on the farm – and the boss's wife and daughter waited on us and brought us our food round and everything. Can you imagine that kind of thing going on here?'

Of course you couldn't. But it was only money that made the boss different from George and the other men on the sheep farm. And working in the Outback I shouldn't have thought that there were any grades of service. They were just workers, even the boss himself.

Maybe they had a nice home. According to George it was the last word in luxury but I can't see that it could have all the refinements that you got here. The nearest neighbour was about fifty miles away so they had to make their own life. There couldn't have been dinner parties, balls, operas and the kind of things that the well-to-do had over here. So obviously they did all mix together because otherwise it would be the boss and his wife isolated from everybody.

But you couldn't make George see that. He said we were all riddled with bloody class here. He's like a lot of people who've lived abroad and come back. The places they've left are always better. Everywhere's marvellous where they're not.

Between George and Mr Wade, the butler, there was always a sort of a feud going on. I think it was partly jealousy because being the only two men in the house they vied for attention from the servants.

Mr Wade used to think that George's manner and his speech were crude and vulgar while George thought that Mr Wade with his soft voice and his lily-white hands was no sort of a man at all. He used to say, 'Fancy having to bath and dress that old bugger upstairs. What kind of job is that for a man?'

I'd defend Mr Wade. 'Well, you drive him around don't you?' 'Oh,' he said, 'that's different.' 'And I've seen you tuck him in the back like you were tucking up a baby.' I couldn't say too much as I was only a kitchenmaid.

Then he'd say, 'Wade's no kind of a man at all. No wonder he never got married. He probably could never have performed if he had.'

I wasn't really sure what performed meant, but everybody laughed so I presumed it was something a bit on the obscene side.

George's idea of being a man was to swear and spit and intersperse words with 'bloody this' and 'bloody that' and make dirty jokes out of anything. And between him and Mr Wade there was a gulf that could never be crossed.

After one of these 'I love Australia' conversations Mr Wade asked George in a very lofty tone of voice why, if he liked Australia so much, did he ever leave it? George then gave us some long yarn about that he never would have left it but that the boss's daughter fell in love with him and as he didn't want to settle down at that time he thought he'd better leave and so he went to Sydney.

Of course the truth of the matter probably was that he started pestering the boss's daughter and the boss didn't like it, because no matter how democratic the boss was, if he was as wealthy as George made out he was, I daresay he had other ideas for his daughter than that she should marry one of his sheep men.

But anyway that was George's story. So he lit out for Sydney. Then he went off delirious about Sydney and what a marvellous place it was. He said, 'That's the place for men. They keep women in their place in Sydney. None of this bloody taking them out to the pub with you like they do over here. There aren't any pubs where bloody women can go.' And that suited George down to the ground.

'Mind you,' he said, 'the pubs are only open till six o'clock in the evening so you all knock off work at five and you make a bee-line for the pub. You swill all you can, and then you stagger home or if you can't get home you stagger to the gutter and you lie down there.' George thought it was a marvellous life.

Then he told us that while he was in Sydney he married

a widow about ten years older than he was and that her late husband had left her a lot of money. And I'm not even guessing when I say that he married her for her money. Then he persuaded her to come back to England with him.

Now he hadn't got a picture of this wife of his – we never did know her name. In fact he said very little about her. He used to go off at great length about the other women he could have married out in Australia; when he did speak about her he never had a kind word to say for her except that the only good thing she ever did in the world was to leave it.

He'd say, 'She was such a cold-hearted old bitch. She used to dole out her favours as though they were diamonds.' And he'd add, 'She was no bloody good in bed anyway and before she'd let me in with her I always had to wash and shave and clean my teeth. And what the hell's that got to do with * * * * * * *.' I use asterisks to denote my meaning because people make such a fuss about that word as though it was a new sort of vice, but the word and the deed were in use when I was young, I can assure you. In fact I never heard it called anything else.

Then he went on, 'And she made me do all the bloody work in bed. Wore me out she did.' So cook said, 'Is it still worn out, George?' She could say things like that, you see. She had a nerve. So he said, 'Oh no, I reckon I could bring it up to scratch if the occasion arose.'

Then Mr Wade said, 'I shouldn't think the occasion will ever arise.' George got so furious over this that he said, 'I'm still a man, you know. I bet if it were a contest I could beat you any day of the week.' And an argument started. But neither of them was given the opportunity to prove it. This was the vain kind of boasting you get from men.

The real reason why George used to get so livid about his wife was because when she died instead of him getting the money – the money he'd married her for – it went to her two grown-up sons. It was in trust for them and he never got a penny. So for the most part of the time George had a grieving hatred of his wife.

But once a month on his weekend off he used to go on a real bender. He'd go to the local pub and he'd order a half-pint of cider to be served in a pint glass and into this he used to tip two double whiskies and two white ports. And this was his starter. Then he would steadily drink white ports for the whole weekend.

He'd come back in on the Sunday night reeling about, and he would get maudlin.

All drinkers vary. Some people get very merry. I do. It's always worth anybody's while to buy me alcohol because they get good value for their money. I get livelier and livelier. My husband gets very quiet. Others get aggressive, which is no good at all. But old George used to get maudlin.

He'd come in, walking on the balls of his feet to keep his balance, and the tears would be streaming down his cheeks. And then he'd start a long monologue about his dear departed wife. He'd say, 'Oh, she was a lovely woman, a lovely woman. I should never have persuaded her to come back to this bloody country. She would still have been alive now if we'd stayed in Australia. This bloody country

236

is enough to kill anybody. Do you know when she was ill I looked after her like a mother. I waited on her hand and foot. And I could have saved her if they hadn't carted her off to hospital. They killed her. They killed her in that bloody hospital. All of them bloody bed baths – that's what did it. Removing the natural juices that covered her body. Bloody water.

'But,' he said, 'I tried to save her. That last few days before she died when they had the screens around her I used to go up with a bottle of whisky. And when the nurses weren't looking I'd pull back the covers and rub her all over with it. To try and put back some of the warmth that bloody water had taken away.

'Yes,' he said, 'I worshipped every hair on that woman's body.'

Then he'd burst out crying and he'd sob himself to sleep while we tiptoed upstairs wondering how many hairs she had and how much worship George would have to have done on them.

3

GEORGE MAY HAVE loved Australia, but it wasn't until many years later that I finally went abroad myself, with my husband Albert.

The day that I heard we'd won fifty pounds on the football pools I thought that the millennium had arrived. We'd never seen fifty pounds in our lives before nor even anything like that amount.

Well, of course, straight away we started talking about what we were going to do with it. When you suddenly realize you've got fifty pounds and the largest sum you've ever had before is about ten pounds then you think that it's going to do a wonderful lot of things. First of all we thought we'd refurnish the house. We settled on things that would have come to five hundred pounds at least.

Then I said, 'Oh, I don't know. I like the place as it is.'

Then we decided we'd all have new clothes and then that idea faded out.

And then I said, 'We haven't had a holiday in years. Let's have a holiday with it.'

A holiday to me and my husband meant going somewhere in England. So we started to consider places. We didn't want to go to another seaside place, living as we did at Hove. And we didn't want to go to the country because I can't bear the country.

I don't like all those static things – the trees and fields and I don't really like animals. I wouldn't walk through a field if there was even one cow in it, never mind a herd. Have you ever noticed the way cows look at you – as if they can see right through and they don't like what they see? Scornful-like. And then they start ambling towards you. They might be going to be friendly but it's a bit too late if they get right up and you find they're not, isn't it? I don't dislike pigs, but with these factory farms it's not like the days when farmers used to let you walk around and scratch the pigs. Nowadays farming's done on such a big scale that they don't want strangers walking around.

There there are the country pubs. Everyone makes such a thing about country pubs. When you go into one every face looks up at you and you get a vista of blank faces turning towards you. They know you're a stranger to the place and they want to keep you feeling that way. You walk to the bar thinking you're a kind of leper.

The country's very nice if you like being next to nature but I hate nature.

Some people say what interesting faces country people

have got; what thinkers they must be. But I know what they're thinking. You've only got to look at the expression on their faces to know what they're thinking – bugger all. Or nothing worth thinking about, like the crops, the farm and is it going to rain and looking up at the sky and musing about it. Of course it's going to rain. It always does in the country. At any rate it does when I'm there. And another thing they're thinking is – what the devil are you doing down there? What are you after? Thoroughly suspicious they are. And even if I don't know what they're thinking I don't want to know. I don't go for a holiday to sit and wonder what people are thinking. I go to enjoy myself.

The alternative was to go to a big town like Bristol, London, or Edinburgh.

I like big towns because you're anonymous there. I like to be anonymous. I don't want the spotlight on me. Well, I didn't then; I don't mind it so much now. In any case I hadn't got many clothes to wear and not much money so I wanted to be anonymous.

I like to be in a crowd so that nobody notices you from the rest. I feel at home in a crowd and I feel at home amongst all the things that are made by man. I like everything that's machine made and man made. I like shops. I like cars. I like the new lighting that they've installed. I like everything that's mechanically made. I like things that have all been made with somebody's brain, by man's ingenuity, and it increases the stature of man to me – because after all's said and done we're only midgets here and we've only got a very short tenure of life on earth, so I think that anything that anyone's done to enhance life here is interesting and worthwhile. People keep saying that in spite of all these inventions people are no happier, but how can they tell? They don't know how happy people were that are dead and gone.

Anyway, while we were still wondering about what town to go to I had the marvellous idea of going abroad.

Of course Albert wasn't keen because he doesn't like changes. He likes things to go on in the same old way, and the very thought of going abroad, different food, different people and you can't speak a word of the language – and no country's like England. I could see these thoughts going round in his mind. I mean there's not another country in the world that's as good as ours.

It was the same when he joined the RAF during the war. He didn't fancy travelling all over the world. As it turned out he didn't have to. All the time he was in the Service he only saw one aeroplane – and that was on a scrap heap. He was in the RAF for four years – never got off the ground, and never got any farther than Yorkshire.

He had a marvellous job there. He used to go out and pick up matchsticks and barely did a stroke in the whole of the four years. Four years' rest it was. When they got tired of doing nothing they used to shovel the coal from one heap and put it in another heap.

But he'd heard about abroad – that it was the land of vice and the food was terrible. That they ate snails and slugs. That it was uncivilized and that the people all wore little grass skirts. He wasn't at all happy about the idea.

Anyway I sent to several travel companies for their brochures – you know the sort of things. They'd pictures of
glamorous people in the most beautiful clothes and others
lying about on the beaches with a lovely sun tan. It never
rains in any of those brochures and there's never a word
about what you do if it does.

One or two of the holidays we thought were marvellous
but then we found out that they wanted about five hundred
pounds for those. There really wasn't a lot of choice. We
only had the fifty pounds from the pools though we thought
we might scrape up another ten pounds – that was as much
as we could do in the time available to us. So after we'd got
through the brochures about three times we finally settled
on a holiday that was twenty-four pounds each for ten days.

For that we would have five days in a place on the very
tip of Holland so that we could make trips into Germany
and Luxembourg and Belgium and we would have four
days in Paris. This sounded a good bargain so we paid the
deposit and then we tried to save up as much as we could.

We didn't go out anywhere. We became practically tee-
totallers. Believe me I wouldn't want a holiday every year
if you'd got to be a teetotaller to have it. A lot of people
do that. They save up their money so that they can have
one big fling. I daresay we could have had a much better
holiday that way, but just imagine being miserable for fifty
weeks so that you can have two weeks' holiday. Then perhaps it rains all the time or the holiday doesn't go, like jelly
that never sets.

In any case I think that if you've had a miserable fifty

weeks you've probably lost the capacity to enjoy yourself. But we didn't mind too much because we'd got this lump sum and we felt it wasn't too long to wait and that we were going to do something entirely different.

We felt really adventurous. Talk about Captain Cook and his voyage round the world or Christopher Columbus discovering America – the thought of Mr and Mrs Powell going abroad knocked them into a cocked hat. We were quite the big noises in our neighbourhood.

On the great day we had to be at Liverpool Street Station at eight o'clock in the morning. This meant we had to put up for the night in London and that was nearly disastrous. It cost three pounds ten for the two of us. We thought it was ruinous – absolute robbery. We had to do it because we couldn't get to Liverpool Street at eight o'clock otherwise.

We got there about quarter past seven – all eager and agog. We had a terrible job finding our party. We thought our party would be the only party. We didn't realize that we were a very small cog in a large wheel and that there were lots of other parties – much bigger parties – parties going on things with names like The Hook Continental. We didn't do anything like that. We had just an ordinary old train down to Harwich.

Finally we found our party and we got on the train. And then we met the courier. Oh, what a charming man that courier was! Of course we didn't realize then that charm was his stock-in-trade, that it was a façade and there was nothing behind it, just all charm.

He spoke to us individually and held my hand. He was a

very handsome man – I felt quite thrilled. I felt more thrilled too because incidentally the others were rather elderly – I think I was about the youngest, or looked the youngest anyway. And I was certainly the liveliest. And he sat down and held my hand. (It was a long time since any man had held my hand apart from my husband and that was old hat.) He gazed into my eyes and I felt he really cared about me. I didn't intend to throw my cap over the windmill or anything – not that the opportunity ever arose. He told us various funny little anecdotes about other trips he'd been on and things like that. You know how charming people can talk. If you try to analyse it it's all so light that it just goes away in a puff of smoke but when they're telling it to you it seems so interesting. And he was good-looking, too, which made all the difference because after all if he'd had a face like the back of a bus charm wouldn't have got him anywhere. But with charm and good looks and that lovely public-school accent . . .

Now there's a swindle for you – that public-school accent that takes you in to start with. It gets you anywhere – if you haven't got two pennies to rub together that public-school accent sees you through.

As he moved from table to table on the train everybody was saying, 'Oh, isn't he a charming man!' We were properly taken in by him.

Then he told us not to buy anything on the Continent without telling him.

'You're bound to want to bring back a piece of jewellery or some perfume,' he said. 'If you want anything just let me know and I'll tell you the shops to go to and mention my name and you'll get it cheaper.'

We swallowed this because you think, what would he tell you it for if it wasn't true? We found out later.

We eventually reached Harwich and got on the boat to go across to the Hook of Holland. The sea was rough and it was a terrible boat. There was nowhere to sit and you couldn't even get a place to hang over the side and be sick. At last I found somewhere and just lay there hoping to die.

Albert was fine – never turned a hair. And what particularly grieved me was him coming back from the bar saying, 'Do you know how much whiskies cost in there? About a third of what we pay at home and it's a bigger measure.'

What a time to choose to say a thing like that when I was calling for the angel of death. I felt so ill and every time I went to the lavatory to be sick they'd just let me be sick and then turfed me out again.

It was a horrible boat – not enough room, no chairs, no nothing. Mind you, even if it had been comfortable I couldn't have enjoyed it.

The funny thing was when we eventually got to the Hook of Holland I felt as right as rain again. It amazed me that Albert wasn't disturbed at all because he wasn't any more used to it than I was. He said it was because he's got a placid disposition that it didn't upset him, that because I'm always so eager and excited and never keep calm it happened to me.

Anyway when we arrived at the port there was a coach

waiting to take us across to this place on the very other side of Holland where we were staying – Walkenberg.

About halfway across we stopped at a place where our courier had an arrangement – where we could get coffee and cakes cheaper. So we all piled out of the coach like a flock of sheep with him at the head of us. We must have looked a very motley collection buffeted by the storm at sea. And most of us were elderly, what I call good elderly people. You could tell that never in their lives had they deviated from the straight and narrow. In we went and Albert and I had two cakes and a cup of coffee each – and we paid in francs.

I couldn't work it out there and then but when we got back in that coach I did and I said to Albert, 'Do you know what that cost us for two cups of coffee and four cakes? It cost us twelve and six. Good God, if that's the kind of place where he's got an arrangement I shudder to think what it's going to cost us anywhere where he hasn't.'

We got to Walkenberg and the hotel where we were going to stay at eleven o'clock that night. And the brochure had said that when we reached there a warm welcome would await us. Not only did no warm welcome await us – no kind of welcome at all awaited us. There was simply nobody there. Empty hotel.

We were stuck down one end of the dining-room and the courier plonked forms in front of us which we had to fill in and sign. We never saw the proprietors. And Albert and I weren't even in the hotel – we were in an annexe on the other side of the road. At the time we couldn't have cared less. We were so excited about being abroad we didn't mind where we slept.

But it just shows what kind of party we were with – they all went to bed. They come abroad and on the very first night there they go to bed at eleven o'clock – just because they are used to doing it. Well, we didn't.

We went and found our room and put our things in and went off down the sort of main street and found a place where people were sitting outside and we sat there drinking beer until two o'clock in the morning. Although we were so tired we had to prop our eyes open, we were determined to be able to say that we were drinking beer there at two o'clock in the morning. Fancy the others going to bed. Aren't the English people terrible? They've got no daring in them.

All right the beer was horrible stuff like – well, it's like water compared with English beer. I agree they've got wines that we haven't got and it's cheaper but their beer's no good at all. And Albert's a beer drinker. During the course of our holiday he got so fed up with not having a decent beer that he asked for a Guinness. He only did it once. They charged him eight and six for a glass of Guinness. They said they had to import it. No wonder nobody ever gets drunk over there because although the places are open all day you could drink that beer till you floated in it and it wouldn't do anything for you.

Still we made out we were living it up. We wrote back most glowing accounts of sitting outside this place drinking beer at two o'clock in the morning. We were frozen to death. It was cold and the beer was weak but we didn't write about that.

That was our first night there.

The idea of course of staying at this place at the very tip of Holland was to make coach trips into Germany, Luxembourg, and Belgium. And that was another stupid thing in the brochure. You had to write and say just where you'd like to sit in the coach. I chose two numbers in the middle. Well, when the coach arrived at the hotel it was already half filled with people from another tour and they weren't going to shift for us. We just had to sit where we could. And didn't some of the others moan. Albert and I didn't because we didn't really care that much. It was only a small thing.

This first day we went into Germany and the brochure said, 'Germany with its lovely castles and a trip down the Rhine – a visit to the Drachenfels and Cologne with its wonderful cathedral.' And we had a packed lunch. Oh, those packed lunches! Salami sausage, strong salami-sausage sandwiches and an orange – and we got the same every day. I couldn't eat the salami and I couldn't even eat the bread because it was so tainted with garlic.

So off we set on our coach ride and the first stop was what they called the Drachenfels. It's seven hills in a row supposed to look like a dragon. Well honestly you'd have to be as blind as a bat to ever think it looked anything like a dragon. It didn't compare with our South Downs. Just seven little lumps. The top one was very high admittedly but I couldn't see a dragon anywhere. When we got there there was a little railway that ran up to the top of this highest lump and the courier said we were all going to go up in it.

So I said, 'I'm not.'

Now on these tours they can't bear you to deviate. It worries the couriers. You've got to be the same as everybody else. By the look on his face I could see that I worried our courier.

'Oh, I couldn't go up there – absolutely impossible – it's too high,' I said.

'Oh,' he said, 'it doesn't leave the ground.'

'I hope not,' I said, 'for other people's sakes.'

He said, 'The views up there are marvellous.'

I said, 'They wouldn't be any good to me, I couldn't look at them.'

I simply refused to go. He didn't like it but he had to put up with it in the end.

So Albert and I wandered through the town on our own. And I think that was the best part of the holiday. We found a lovely little German beer garden where there was a man playing one of these xylophone things with hammers and we hadn't been there above ten minutes when he started playing English tunes. And there was dancing. It was very lively.

In the interval this man that was playing came over to us and said, 'You're English, aren't you?'

Of course we lapped this up. It gave us a feeling of prestige. So we ordered him a drink and he joined us.

He said, 'You know I can tell almost anybody's nationality now. I've been playing in this beer garden for the last twenty years.'

So I asked, 'How is it you speak English so well?'

And he said, 'Oh, I was a prisoner of war in England.'

This was in the 1914–18 War.

He chatted with us a bit. When he left I said to Albert, 'What a charming man.'

'Yes, charming thirst, too,' said Albert. 'Do you know he ordered four beers while he was sitting here and all on us.'

We were certainly paying for our experiences. Still I expect he felt we owed him something, he having been a prisoner of war.

Eventually we went back and joined the coach. Then we drove to Cologne. By the time we got there, with what I'd drunk in the beer garden I was only thinking of one thing and that was the loo.

There we were in Cologne. There was that lovely cathedral and there was the ladies' lavatory not far from it. And there were dozens of coaches – all queuing for the loo. It took me twenty minutes to get in and out and we were only allowed half an hour in the city. Talk about see Naples and die. I tore into the cathedral, looked at some gold plate and tore out again. That was Cologne for me apart from the loo.

Then we came to the Rhine. Well, the brochure had said a trip down the Rhine. We just went across in the ferry. That was our trip down the Rhine. As we went across we could see one or two castles – but what a swindle.

A mortifying thing about going in and out of these various countries was that the customs men come in and collect your passport. Yon know what passport photos are like – mine was absolutely hideous. It made me look an ugly ninety. Yet they look at it, look at you and then hand it back, so you're forced to the conclusion that it really looks like you. Very mortifying.

Anyway we got back about ten o'clock, had a hot meal which was good and Albert and I went out on the town again.

The next day was another one of these coach trips. You've got to be in the very best of health when you go on a holiday like ours because they're absolute endurance tests. We went to Luxembourg which they had said was a charming little country. I admit it was very pretty. I enjoyed it there until the courier had the idea of taking us down into a grotto.

I don't know if you've ever been in one of these underground grottoes – shocking things they are. You go down to the bowels of the earth on an iron spiral staircase and the last bit of it is slippery and slimy. I fell the last four steps into the mud at the bottom. It's dark down there and there's an underground river. You get taken in a boat on this river but you can't see a thing. And I was worried about my clothes, wondering how muddy I was, which I couldn't see down there. I think grottoes are very much over-rated things and it stank to high heaven. Well, you can imagine it, can't you? I mean it's been there since time immemorial. Everybody says 'Oo' and 'Ah' – I've never seen anything so daft. I mean you might as well put the light out and sit in your own room. At least you could sit in comfort, couldn't you?

The next day we went into Belgium which wasn't

interesting at all because they took us to Brussels, and I didn't think much of Brussels. It seemed such a dirty town to me. Apart from that there was nothing special about it at all.

Then we had one day at leisure in Walkenberg – getting our strength up as it were for the trip to Paris. This we were both looking forward to. The very name Paris conjures up images and does things for you.

The hotel we stayed in there was a good one. Mind you there was trouble from some of the party who didn't like being on the top floor. I almost felt sorry for the courier when he said to me, 'You know, it doesn't matter what party you go with, you always get people who moan and groan the entire time. You'd think that they were on a luxury tour the way they go on.' Though incidentally I noticed that at mealtimes the courier always sat at a separate table on his own and he never had the same kind of food as we did. He did far better. He was on a luxury tour by comparison.

The next day we went out shopping in the morning. Albert was going to buy me some perfume – something he'd never bought me in his life – and he asked the courier whether he had an arrangement. He had – and he directed us. Albert bought me a little tiny bottle of scent. Two guineas it cost. And when we got back to England I found we could have bought it here for forty-five shillings. Three bob we saved – on the carriage I suppose. I don't see where the arrangement came in. Let's face it, the only thing was, never in this world would Albert ordinarily have spent two guineas on perfume for me. So at least I got it, and it was marvellous. I used to use it very sparingly, a spot at a time. I hadn't used half the bottle before the scent went out of it. It doesn't always pay to be too careful.

Of course we wanted to go to a nightclub. Some people that I was doing for at home had said that we should go to the *Folies Bergère*.

'Don't pay for a seat,' they said, 'you can stand at the back for the equivalent of ten shillings and it's just as good because not only are you near the bar but you can see everything that's going on.'

So I told this to the courier.

'Oh, no,' he said 'you'll never get in the *Folies Bergère*, you have to book months ahead to get in there.'

We should really have gone and found out for ourselves, but we didn't. We thought, he must know doing these trips every year.

Then this courier said, 'I've got a better idea. I've got an arrangement with a nightclub called Eve' (and the way he said Eve made it sound ever so salacious) 'and for two pounds ten each you can sit at a proper table and share a bottle of champagne between four of you.'

We hesitated. Five pounds for two of us seemed an awful lot of money. But then to go to Paris and not be able to say you've been to a nightclub? After all, to us they seemed the main feature of Paris life. So I said, 'Oh let's do it. That'll be our last big expenditure. Let's go.'

Albert was keener than I was. Naturally it would be more interesting for a man than a woman. I couldn't see what there was going to be in it for me. If there were any turns on I wouldn't understand the language. But Albert wanted to go back and say that he'd seen a bit of nudity, so we decided to go and we gave the courier our money. When I look back and think of the money that man made I could pass out. I must admit we had taxis there – though we had to make our own way back. I'm certain he wanted to make sure we got there.

When we got inside the place it was so small. There were only two rows of tables and a bar at the back, but by the time we'd paid two pounds ten each we couldn't afford to buy any more drink anyway. Four of us sat at a table with a tepid bottle of champagne in the middle. I'd had champagne when I was in domestic service and I knew what it should taste like. This stuff was absolute rubbish. We sat there sipping it and then the first turn, if you could call it a turn, came on.

It was twelve girls nude from the waist up with very fancy dresses below the waist. There were gasps from most of the men. One man belonging to our party went as red as a beetroot. Albert sat there all nonchalant looking as though he saw such things every day. He didn't. You've never seen such a collection in all your life. Talk about twelve raving beauties – they must have gone out on the highways and byways and scoured the lot in. They were short and fat and tall and thin. And the shapes of them! Some had appendages that looked like deflated balloons – others had got them about the size of footballs which looked as though they'd blown them up before they came on the stage. Some had got such a little that you couldn't tell what sex they were; they might have been men for all we knew. And they didn't do a thing – they just kept walking round and round. There was a notice up saying 'Do Not Touch The Girls'. Even Albert said, 'Good God I'd have died before I would have touched one of them with a barge-pole.' If I tell you that Albert was bored to tears in less than five minutes you can understand what they were like.

Then came a sort of quick-patter act. Some people laughed – presumably they were French and understood what was being said. We didn't understand a word.

Then the girls came on again with different dresses from the waist down – paraded round again with their inane giggles. I said to Albert, 'Have you ever seen the female sex looking like that?' He said he hadn't and I believed him. Of course it was nothing to me – it was like bread and bread. I spent the time studying those who had pimples and where they had them.

We were there an hour. Just turns interspersed with these girls. It was dreadful. When we got up and went we left by the back stairs and as we passed a paybox I saw that we could have gone in and stood for the equivalent of twelve and six. When I told all the others they were furious and they ostracized the courier for the rest of the trip. We didn't. We wrote it down to experience. We put ourselves in his position. If we were taking a pack of greenhorns around we'd have had to have had very good characters not to have made a bit out of them.

Anyway apart from that we enjoyed Paris hugely. We

saw the Louvre, the Palace of Versailles, all those kind of places – and Paris is a beautiful and interesting city. We'd wander around on our own then sit outside the cafés watching life go by.

Twice at our hotel they served us with something like meatballs, tasty but mysterious. I was intrigued with them. And I've always been a bit pushing. I'd read in the papers about Lady So and So or the Duchess of Something or Other being abroad and coming back with the most marvellous recipes. They'd been down to the kitchen and the chef had given them these recipes which they printed.

So I said to Albert, 'I've a good mind to ask for the recipe of these meatballs.'

He said, 'I wouldn't bother. I don't want any of them when we get back home.'

'Well,' I said, 'neither do I but I just want to go back with some sort of recipe.'

So I said to the waiter – he spoke perfect English – 'Will you please ask the chef for the recipe for me?' in a nice sort of way. I thought that he might even invite me down in the kitchen.

The next day I inquired of him, 'Did you ask the chef how these meatballs are made?'

He said, 'Yes, I did, and the chef said, "God knows, I don't." '

I expect they were like those resurrection pies that the cook used to make us sometimes when I was in service. All the bits of meat that you thought had long departed this life would appear again with a pastry crust on and we used to call it resurrection pie. But did I feel deflated by that waiter. Talk about *entente cordiale*.

On the way back home we were booked to have lunch at Antwerp at a luxury hotel. And it was a luxurious place, not a bit like the hotels we'd stayed in.

We arrived at Antwerp an hour before lunch and we wandered around the town; we were then to meet in this hotel. As we went up the steps we felt like the poor relations, we'd hardly any money left by that time. It was a huge palatial entrance with a grand staircase all thickly carpeted. I was dying to go to the lavatory and I said to Albert, 'I wonder where it is?'

He said, 'Ask somebody.'

It was the sort of place where you imagined the people that went there didn't go to the lavatory.

And I said, 'Oh, I haven't got the nerve to.'

Eventually I discovered it was downstairs. You've never seen such toilets. I suppose all posh hotels are like it. It was lovely there. You didn't have to put money in and there was a whole row of basins, gold-plated taps and a separate towel at each basin. So I washed my hands. And then from nowhere sprang an old harridan holding a plate and I looked at this plate and there was nothing less than the equivalent of half a crown in it. Of course I hadn't the nerve to give her less. I should have stuck it out but she looked so intimidating.

The general run of toilets in France are something too terrible for words. They may be better now – since de Gaulle, I mean. But I'd never seen anything like the sanitary arrangements. Those awful ones they have in the street where the men's legs show below and their head and shoulders above, and you can visualize what the middle's doing. I think they're revolting.

We were on a tram once and I could see a man sort of leaning on his elbow in one of them – for all the world as though he was there to have a rest. And we went in a café on our own the first day and when I went to the toilet I stood outside waiting and a man came out. Embarrassed? I went the colour of a beetroot. Then another one I went into was just two toilets and a sort of half-tiled wall and I discovered there were three men sitting with their backs to me. They've got no reticence at all. Talk about all friends together. The funny thing is that after you've been there a couple of days – you keep drinking that awful beer that runs through you – you don't take a bit of notice. It just shows what a thin veneer civilization has really.

After lunch at this posh hotel we set off for home. The trip back wasn't too bad. It was smooth. But I still couldn't enjoy a cheap whisky because after we'd bought some cigarettes and some wine to take back, we'd nothing left. By the time we got to Liverpool Street Station we were a sorry-looking lot.

In the brochure there was something about the friends we were going to make and I'd had visions of exchanging addresses and writing to these friends and keeping in touch. Instead of that – not only was nobody speaking to the courier – they weren't even speaking to each other.

When we got back home I said to Albert, 'Let's have another look at this brochure and go through the things that weren't as they said they would be.' But as we read it again we saw in very small print at the bottom 'Turn to the back page'. So we turned to the back page. There again in very small print was written 'On this tour the agents exercise the right to make any alterations that circumstances may demand'. So that it had just been that in our case the circumstances had been very demanding.

4

TO SAY THAT I was surprised to get a date after being in London barely a week is to put it mildly. I couldn't believe my good fortune. Surely, I'd thought, there must be more of a scarcity of females up in London than there is down in Hove. And not only that – I'd got a date with a man who had a regular job. A bus conductor.

My mother was always on to me about the merits of getting a young man who had a regular job. 'It doesn't matter how small the wages are,' she said, 'so long as it comes along regularly every Saturday.' My poor old mum must have felt it with Dad's irregular work. Some weeks there was no money at all. She often used to say to me, 'If only I could be sure of two pounds a week I'd be in heaven.' So there was I, in heaven, too.

As I've explained, my afternoon and evening out was on Wednesday, except of course if they happened to have a dinner party on that night. If they had, you were expected to give it up. You weren't expected to have made plans so it couldn't matter to you whether you had Wednesday, Thursday or any other day.

Anyway this Wednesday was all right and I met my Percival. He'd told me he liked to be called Percival. I thought both Perce and Percival were terrible names, but after all beggars can't be choosers.

When I met him he told me he was going to take me to his mother's to tea. Well, if he'd told me he was taking me to the Ritz I couldn't have been more astounded. I mean in our circles you were never taken to tea to a boy's house unless you'd been going steady with him for a long time. To be taken to tea to his mother's house was tantamount to being engaged to him. This put the wind up me properly. It was going to be an ordeal meeting Perce's mum. It hadn't happened to me before. I'd never been out with a boy long enough ever to get round to that stage. But I knew girls who had and they'd told me how they'd had to run the gauntlet. They said it was something that required the strongest nerves.

Anyway to Percival's home we went to meet his mother – or 'Ma' as he called her. I'd never have dared call her Ma even if she'd become my mother-in-law, which she never did. I'd never have dared call her anything but Mrs Tait, which was her name.

She was about five feet nothing in size but in strength of character I reckon she was about ten feet tall. I was overwhelmed by her. There was no sign of a husband and at first I wondered what had happened to him – whether he'd departed this life or what. But she told me a very mysterious story how one day he went off to visit some relatives. He took nothing with him because he was only going for the day – no money and no clothes – and was never heard of again. He never came back. He never even visited the relatives. So I said to her, 'Whatever did you do, Mrs Tait – did you notify the police?' 'Oh, yes,' she said. 'But you must have nearly gone mad with worry,' I said. 'No,' she said, 'it was the Lord's will.' See, she was one of those who when anything happened it was the Lord's will. She asked me how old I was and as I'd already put two years on my age and told Perce that I was eighteen I had to tell her the same.

During the course of the tea I discovered that she'd had three sons, triplets, and she'd called them Lancelot, Tristram, and Percival which was the one I'd got – this Percival. She'd got the names out of a book called *Morte d'Arthur*, which she'd found on a second-hand bookstall when she was pregnant. At that time I'd never even heard of the book, but later when I did I found it was the last book I'd have read when I was pregnant. I never heard such rubbish. Tales of knightly chivalry when you're lugging around a stomach the size of a pumpkin. I always was large when I was pregnant and after all she was carrying triplets.

Also, I couldn't help feeling that the names Lancelot, Tristram, and Percival were unfortunate names to have to go to school with. Percival told me that they were shortened to Lance, Tris, and Perce so I suppose they got away with it. But when I was at school there was a girl in our class named Cecilia who didn't. Then we had an Anastasia and her mother said to the teacher that she didn't want her name shortened; she was to be called by the whole name. We did just that and she had a hell of a time. You know how cruel children can be. I was glad my name was ordinary. Nobody wanted to be different then – not at the kind of school I went to anyway.

After we'd had tea this Mrs Tait subjected me to such an interrogation as to my antecedents that I felt she'd missed her vocation. She should have been a member of the Spanish Inquisition. It was so ridiculous too, as it was the very first time I'd ever been there and it was quite likely I wouldn't go again. I couldn't understand at first why Perce didn't put his oar in and tell her to shut up. Then of course I realized that he was over thirty years old and he must have got used to it. By his age he'd probably brought a number of girls home to be inspected and rejected.

I discovered that Lancelot and Tristram had escaped their mother's clutches, for which I didn't blame them. One had gone to Canada and one had gone to Australia and they'd both been gone about ten years. During this time they were writing letters home saying how much they missed their mother or so she said, but neither of them had made the trip back. So I could see by all this interrogation and all this talk that she was determined not to lose Perce and I suppose you couldn't really blame her. She'd got no husband and only that one son to keep her, so life would have been difficult for her without him. Yes, it would have had to have been a very determined girl that would stick to Perce if she'd been got at by his mother every time he took her home.

Much to my relief, at about half past six Perce suggested

that we go out. Just him and me. We were to have gone to the films but when we got outside he suggested we went to a dance instead. Well, I wasn't too keen on going to a dance. I had to be in by ten o'clock which would mean leaving about half past nine, but he said he didn't want to be late because he'd got an early shift, so off we went.

It was a small suburban hall, not a bit like the Palais de Danses that you get now. Just a large bare room with a few fancy shades hanging down and a three- or four-piece band right at the end. The floor was smothered with some kind of powder stuff. It was the kind of place where they held meetings and socials through the week, not a proper dance hall. It only cost one and three to go in and although it was still only seven o'clock there were already a lot of people there.

Most of the girls were dressed up. Some had got knee-length dresses and some had got what were fashionable at that time, dresses hanging down longer at the back than at the front. And they wore very light flesh-coloured stockings which were all the go too in those days.

The men hadn't bothered at all. They were mostly in Oxford bags – trousers about two foot wide at the bottoms. To me they seemed a very weedy-looking lot, but as I'd gone with a partner I could afford to be critical.

Of course like all dance halls at the time there were a lot more girls than boys and there were none of these courtly gestures of a boy escorting you back to your seat. No, they just left you bang in the middle of the floor and went and congregated at one end while you made your own way back to sit and become a wallflower again.

I couldn't help thinking how pretty and sophisticated the London girls looked in comparison to those from my home town. Some of them had got Eton crops which were coming into fashion at that time. My sister used to have an Eton crop but you've got to have the right face for it. With my kind of features if I'd had an Eton crop I'd have just looked like a hard-boiled egg with a top knot.

After a time Perce went off to get me a cup of coffee, and while he was gone a young man came up and asked me to dance. Well, I thought, here goes. I'm not bound to Perce. After all he hadn't bought me body and soul for one and three which was all he'd spent so far. So I got up to dance with this fellow.

'I haven't seen you here before,' he said. 'No,' I said, 'it's my first time.' 'Are you with anyone?' he said. 'Yes, I've come with a boyfriend.' He turned a bit pale at this. 'Won't he mind you dancing with me?' 'Why should he mind?' I said. 'Oh,' he said, 'that just shows you're a stranger here. When you come with a boyfriend you don't get up and dance with someone else.' I'd seen quite a few girls dancing with more than one partner and I said so. 'Ah,' he said, 'but they all know each other or else they're related. No complete stranger who comes with a boyfriend ever dances with anyone else. What will you do if he's annoyed?' I said, 'What will you do?' He swallowed hard and then said, 'I shan't do anything – I'm off. You see I'm known here.' And he left me in the middle of the floor.

Anyway just at that moment Perce came back. He'd seen what had happened and his face was black as thunder.

I felt as though I'd been caught in some sort of orgy. He said, 'Never you do that again. I'm known here and it makes me look bloody silly when I bring a girl and I leave her for a minute and she dances with somebody else.'

Now who'd have thought there was all that ridiculous protocol? All this 'I'm known here'. What a funny way of going on. I thought about my mother and how she'd said that London dance halls were dens of vice. Well, I thought, she should come and see this one. Talk about the height of respectability. And if this was London, the city of sin, it looked as if I was going to leave it as unsullied as when I came to it.

Anyway, eventually Perce calmed down. He even saw me to my bus. But I remember thinking on my way home – this isn't going to last much longer, and in short supply though men were I can't say it worried me. Still, before Perce and I parted we'd arranged another meeting for the following Wednesday – a proper glutton for punishment I was.

5

LITTLE DID I think when I'd agreed to meet Percival that Wednesday that this included his Ma once again. Apparently every Wednesday evening when he was on early shift they went together to a Meeting. I soon found out that going to a meeting meant going to a sort of church thing for an hour and that they belonged to a strict rigid religious sect called 'The Ruth Elders'. I'd never heard of it before, nor have I ever heard of it since. But according to his Ma it was a breakaway from the Evangelical Church. They'd done away with all forms of ceremony, no infant baptisms, no stained-glass windows and no ceremonial robes or anything like that.

I didn't see how I could get out of going. I thought perhaps it was another test to see if I would be a fit companion to go out with her son. I mean, I'd already had the interrogation about my antecedents the first time and I thought – oh well, this is the second round.

Mind you, I'd already made up my mind that nothing on

earth would induce me to see his Ma again because I knew that it was becoming a sort of tug-of-war and I wasn't going to join battle. If he wanted his Ma more than he wanted me well then that was that as far as I was concerned. I didn't really care.

So we went to this hall where The Ruth Elders met and most decidedly she never exaggerated when she said that they went in for stark simplicity.

It was just a bare hall – cold as charity, wooden floors with hard wooden benches and lit by a gas light. There were about thirty people there and much to my relief we sat down in the back row.

Everyone was old. Apart from me Perce was the youngest by far. They had a pastor though I don't know if you would call him a pastor. I call him a pastor for want of a better word, but he didn't wear any dog collar or cassock and surplice or anything like that at all. He was just dressed in a dark suit.

He said a little prayer to start with and we all had to kneel down on this wooden floor. I was thinking about my silk stockings all the time. Then he gave about a ten-minute sermon promising us that hell and damnation would follow for anybody who deviated from the straight and narrow path. I remember looking around at the congregation and thinking that such a chance would be a damned fine thing for any of them.

After the sermon there was silence for about a couple of minutes and then all of a sudden to my amazement, and to my horror too, some woman got up and started declaiming loudly about the sins that she'd committed since she'd been there last.

Talk about audience participation. One after another they all got up and started shrieking out in a loud voice of all their wickednesses. And these sins were the silliest things. Like they'd taken too much pride in their appearance or they had a ha'penny too much given them in change and they hadn't gone back to the shop with it. And one of them had lost her temper at home. The last female that stood up – she got into such a frenzy, I thought she was going to throw a fit.

Looking back on it I suppose all this bursting forth was a kind of outlet for their repressed sexual emotions which no doubt they never gave rein to at home or elsewhere.

There she was ranting and raving and thrusting her arms towards the pastor. I said to myself – steady, girl, here it comes: the big sin of the week. Then came the awful truth. One morning she felt so tired she didn't get up and make her husband's breakfast. Well, I ask you. Omission it might be – sin never. It was all so piddling.

Then, after calling for a few minutes' more silence, the pastor said that if there were any troubled souls there, would they come up to him for advice, and he'd lay his hands on them.

Well search me, if I'd had all the troubles in the world nothing would have induced me to have gone up and let him lay his hands on me. I mean, all right if he'd been one of those intense, spiritual-looking aesthetic priests, but a portly, smug-faced man that looked as if he'd just left the mayoral banquet – nothing would have induced me to have gone up there. In any case they'd have all passed out if I'd have told them my sins, and even mine weren't that bad. That was the end of The Ruth Elders.

Then Perce said, would I like to go round to the working men's club with him? I'd never been to a working men's club before and I had no idea what it was like so I agreed. This was going to be another first and last for me.

Oh, what dumps they are! Maybe they're not now but they were then. It was another bare room with nothing in it at all. No carpet, no rugs, no nice tables. Talk about a boost to the male ego. Everything was there for men but nothing for females at all. Men had got billiard tables, card tables, and darts but all the women did was just stick up at one end of the room. It was a working men's club but never mind about the working men's wives or their girlfriends.

When we got there Perce dumped me at the women's end while he went off to play billiards. This after the prayer meeting was not my idea of going out with a young man.

Yet none of the other women seemed to mind about being down there, with their boyfriends and husbands up the other end all clubbing together. Some were knitting and some were just talking. They tried to be friendly, I've got to give them their due. They asked me what I did so I said I was in domestic service and they said, 'Oh, a skivvy!' Not nasty at all; it was just their name for domestic servants, but you could tell by the tone they said it in that none of them would ever be seen dead in service, for which I didn't blame them.

One of them worked in a fried fish and chip shop. She needn't have bothered to tell me that because you could smell it a mile off. One of them took rather a fancy to me. She was a woman of about thirty-five – not married – a barmaid. Violet her name was. She said to me, 'I wouldn't stick that life. Why don't you take a barmaid's job?'

Why? My mum and dad would've gone stark raving mad if I'd ever written home and told them I was a barmaid. They'd have been up post haste to rescue me. All right. Nowadays barmaids have got a certain status. Pubs are nothing like the riotous places they were in the old days, and half of them have been made into these cocktail-lounge things. But then a barmaid was a low job. There weren't many of them – mostly there were barmen.

I remember when Mum and Dad used to get me to go round on a Saturday dinnertime to get half a pint of Burton from the bottle and jug department. It was right next door to the public bar and the language of the barmaid in there was worse than any bargee or labourer that I've ever heard.

This Violet, she said it was a lovely life – jolly and lively. I daresay it was, but I couldn't help thinking to myself that men don't marry barmaids. She was an example. She was thirty-five and she wasn't married and she was already beginning to go off, as you might say. Oh no, being a barmaid wasn't for me.

After I'd been there for about an hour Perce brought me over a cup of tea and then he said that they were going up to the pub for an hour to have a drink. Naturally I thought we were all going too. So I got up and he sort of hissed at me under his breath and said, 'No, not you. You stay here.'

I was infuriated at this. Stuck there with all these women while he went out to the pub. So I said, 'I'm certainly not stopping here' – hissing at him too under my breath. And he hissed, 'Do you want to make me look a bloody fool in front of all my mates?' Well, what could I do. I just had to let him go. But what an idea of enjoyment.

My mum would never let my dad go out without her and I don't blame her in the least. When you get married to a man you never want to let him go out without you because once he starts that he'll do it for ever. When a woman gets married it's her whole life – the man is her life. But to a man marriage is just another part of his life because he's still doing exactly the same sort of work that he did before he got married. And he's still got all his pals and he doesn't want to give them up. So you've got to keep a tight rein on them.

I remember when I first got married Albert, my husband, and I had always gone out together. Then I had the first baby. And when the baby was about a fortnight old Albert said, 'I think I'll go over the road and have a drink.' I said, 'Well, all right, I'll come too.' So he said, 'What about the baby?' 'It's your baby as much as mine,' I said, 'and if you can leave it so can I.' I wasn't having any of that kind of lark.

Anyway Perce and the rest of the men poured out over to the pub and of course no sooner had they gone than a sexual conversation started, and amongst these females it was too terrible for words.

The married women went into great length and detail. The act of sex might have been a private act physically but it certainly wasn't private verbally. I'd never heard such things in my life. And the jokes they were telling.

Mind you, it did make a change from The Ruth Elders. But doesn't that show you the duplicity of people? That Perce must have known the kind of things that went on in the club.

They say that women are complex creatures, but believe me you can't beat a man when he wants to put one over on you. This was one of my first lessons but I have had many others since.

After a bit this Violet got me on one side and said, 'I wouldn't waste any time on that Perce if I were you, because you'll never get him away from his mother.' She said, 'He's been coming to this club for the last eight or nine years and he often brings a girl but they never last long.'

I knew it was true that you wouldn't get him away from his mother. You couldn't really blame her because there's nothing stronger than the maternal instinct. They don't think that they're distorting their son's life – that they're making them not a real man. He had a feeling for his mother that he shouldn't have had. I don't mean to say that they had an incestuous relationship. Of course they didn't, but a man who's been living with his mother alone year after year, he'd be simply no good as a husband.

To start with you can never measure up to their mother. And then they're not the kind of men that are interested in sex because if they were they wouldn't have tied themselves to their mother in the first place. The fact is that the maternal relationship is so big that they haven't got enough left for anyone else. I mean, even if you went all out and got them it'd be more like living with your brother than a husband.

So there was Violet telling me all this, but I already knew as much myself.

She said, 'The only time that you can ever get his kind up to scratch is if you get them half canned or if you put in all the spade work yourself. In any case,' she said, 'the end result isn't worth bothering about.'

So with her advice and my own experience I decided that night was the parting of the ways for me and Perce. What with his mother fixation, his 'men only' drinking and his Ruth Elders – even if I'd ever got him to the altar, which I doubt – I'd have had a scratchy sort of married life. For people mixed up with these strict religious sects the word sex is taboo and the deed of the four-letter word is something too terrible for them to contemplate.

6

THOUGH I WASN'T impressed by the working men's clubs, I have always been a fan of pubs. You might say that I've known three generations of pubs. There's pubs I knew when I was a child, there's the pubs I knew in my early married life in London and elsewhere, and there's the pubs that exist now. And the differences are vast.

When I was a child, it was true to say that for the middle and upper classes the Englishman's home was his castle, but for the working-class man the pub was his castle. It was a place where no do-gooders had the right or the courage to come as they did to one's home where, for the sake of the charity they distributed, you had to listen to them and pretend that you believed in what they were telling you. Once you got in a pub you, metaphorically speaking, drew up the draw-bridge and there you were – lord of all you surveyed. And what you surveyed was lively, warm, and happy. It might have only been a superficial atmosphere and it could be quick to change. It often did, ending up in a free-for-all fight, but even those were enjoyable. After all that's part of a castle's life, isn't it – fighting?

When I was about seven or eight I often used to go into the pub on a Saturday dinnertime to get my mum and dad half a pint of Burton. The bottle and jug department used to be right next door to the public bar and the people who were in it were the kind of people that I saw every day of the week – people who lived round us – but you'd never have thought they were the same people. As I looked through they seemed to have changed their characters completely. The way they spoke and the way they laughed – they had come alive.

Kids used to be allowed in the bottle and jug department – it didn't matter how young you were. I think there was just some peculiar rule whereby it didn't matter about your age if you got it in a jug but you couldn't have it in a bottle with a screw top. Why – I don't know. Whether they thought you might drink it out of the bottle – but I should have thought it more likely that you'd do that with a jug. Mind you, I never drank any of my mum and dad's half-pint of Burton – if I had my life wouldn't have been worth a tinker's cuss. Dad used to measure it out – to him it was liquid gold – and if there was short measure I had to go back with it. When you could only afford half a pint you saw that you got it. Then it used to be measured out fairly between Mum and him.

The life that used to go on in the pubs was as good as a variety show. Some nights my mum and dad used to let us stand at the doors and we'd be fascinated by it all. Publicans allowed hawkers to go in selling matches, bootlaces, toys, scurrilous ditties, and a sure cure for the clap. Not that we knew what the clap was then, but it used to sell well – the cure I mean.

In our pub there used to be a man: on a Saturday night somebody would buy him a pint of beer and he used to balance it on his head while he slowly undressed as far as the waist, and if he could get everything off without spilling it he could drink it for free. And sometimes after this he'd try dressing again for another wager but it was much harder and many a time he upset it and it'd go to waste.

I know a lot of people used to think it terrible leaving kids outside a pub. But my parents were very good. They wouldn't leave us there when it was freezing cold. If they could see we were getting fed up they'd bring us biscuits or a bottle of lemonade between us. But generally we didn't worry; there was so much going on. Today I don't like to see it – but only because I reckon the kids might die with boredom.

There was another man who used to come in who said he had a performing flea. He used to call this flea Algernon and he'd hold a matchbox in his hand, then open it a bit, and say, 'Would you like to see Algernon do a somersault?' And then he'd talk to this flea and say, 'Come on, Algernon, show them how clever you are. There, did you see him do it?' And then back to the box again and he'd say, 'Would you like to see Algernon do a double somersault? Come on Algernon, alley oop.' Then he'd lose Algernon and he'd cry, 'Oh, he's lost. Algernon's lost. He's fallen in love – I think with you, miss, or you, sir.' But nobody got panicky;

nobody worried about a flea loose because fleas along with flies were the thing that you had in your home. For fleas, as I've said, we used Keatings powder and for flies those terrible sticky things you hung from the ceiling. My mother used to put one up sometimes on a Saturday dinnertime and by Sunday there wouldn't be one space left – they'd be two or three deep, you know, and it was horrible if you hit it with your head. So nobody worried that Algernon was roaming. Then he'd say, 'Look lady, he's on your coat.' And he'd go to pick him off her coat and he'd lose him again. And then it would be, 'There he is on the wall.' And everybody would stand gaping, their eyes going all round the walls. But the thing was, there never was a flea – it was an imaginary Algernon. But there would be the customers following imaginary Algernon, until at last it struck the landlord what money he was losing because while they were looking they weren't buying any beer. So eventually either the customers would buy the man beer to console him for the loss of Algernon or the publican would eject him.

Another person we used to watch was an old man who stood outside holding his hand out with a ha'penny in it waiting for someone to add to it. Perhaps when someone went in they wouldn't contribute but when they came out they were feeling far more mellow so they'd cough up.

Then he'd dart into the pub – have a drink – then come out again – put his hand in his pocket for another ha'penny and start once more.

Sometimes this happy jolly atmosphere would change and instead of the sort of friendly swearing a hard note would creep in and it would be swearing in earnest – and then the fighting would start. But the publicans didn't mind. There weren't many barmaids, mainly barmen – great hefty fellows who also acted as chuckers-out. We'd stand away from the doors and out the troublemakers would come, thrown on to the pavement covered in sawdust and beer. We used to think it was marvellous – as good as going to the pictures – and free too.

Some twenty to thirty years after this, when I was married and Albert and I used to go into pubs, they were different. Or at any rate they seemed different. Most of them had three bars – public, private, and saloon – and people seemed to keep to their particular definition. The type of customer was different or dressed different. In the public bar would be the working class. Working class, that is, who never dressed up at any time, never changed and wanted the bar to be just spit and sawdust, darts and dominoes. Then in the private bar would be the kind of people who didn't want to go in the public bar where the language and the people were too strong and salty for them, but nevertheless didn't want to mix with what they thought were the snooty ones in the saloon. The saloon bar was a mixture. You'd get the working-class people who when they'd finished their work would dress themselves up and go there as well as the well-to-do who used it as a matter of course. We used to go in the private bar during the week because it was cheaper, but at a weekend we dressed ourselves up and always went in the saloon. It was a sort of class and dress consciousness.

Although they weren't the same kind of places they were still friendly and cheerful. Full of people, especially at weekends, and they'd still got the mahogany and mirrors and brass beer handles – the impedimenta of a pub. Barmaids were in the ascendancy, and to have a barmaid instead of a barman made a vast difference. They were bright, cheerful girls, often peroxided or hennaed which was all the go in those days, and with the beer or spirits they dispensed a fund of good humour. They'd listen to you; if you had a hard-luck tale, they'd be sympathetic, or if you told them a bawdy story they'd screech with laughter. They were all things to all people and they added sort of another dimension to the pub.

I don't know how they stood socially. It sounds terrible to compare them to prostitutes – they weren't of course – but just as there is a type of man who likes prostitutes and prefers them to anyone else, so there was a type of man who liked barmaids. But never in a million years would they ever have dreamt of marrying them. They loved them, called them 'sweetheart', told them things they'd never have told their wives, shared their business troubles, their office jokes, and you know how obscene office jokes are, laughed with them and teased them and often bought them presents. They treated them I suppose as a wealthy man might his kept woman, and they expected the same things from her, except of course the sex bit, but marry them – never.

Christmas in the local used to be like the old childhood Christmases. The decorations, Christmas trees and a spontaneous kind of gaiety. The landlady would come round with the gin bottle for the ladies, and the landlord would dispense free beer to the men. In the local Albert and I used in Chelsea it was a mixed kind of pub – rich and poor – but all knew each other, and although Albert and I didn't join any of the large parties it wasn't because we wouldn't have been welcome. It was just that we didn't accept from people drinks that we couldn't afford to return. And people respected that. But you could talk to anyone in there. You didn't feel ostracized because you weren't in a position to buy a round. And the talk was interesting and friendly. You could either pass the time of day or have half an hour's intelligent conversation – so that for very little money you could have an enjoyable social evening.

I suppose pubs really started to change after the last war, and that change is now almost complete. Occasionally you'll come across one of those pubs that's still got the glass, the mahogany and a whiff of the old atmosphere, but you are made to feel an alien – an unwelcome stranger. I suppose the landlord doesn't want you because the pub might become popular. Then he'd have to employ staff, the brewers would raise the rent, he'd lose the regulars he's used to and the way of life that suits him. And the customers think on the same lines. They've seen what's happened in other pubs and they don't want it to happen there – and who's to blame them.

I think that television was the beginning of the end of pubs as we knew them, as television has been the death of so many things. I remember when it first came in how the pubs tried installing television in the bar. That was an absolute disaster. If you've ever been into a pub in the early days of television you'd know what I mean. The bar would be full of people all watching. And apart from the noise of whatever programme was on, it would be as silent as the tomb. You'd go in and ask for your drink in a whisper. And if you didn't want to watch the thing, which we didn't, you'd start a *sotto voce* conversation. Then the heads would flash round and shh you like snakes. Oh, it made a real jolly evening out. It didn't take long for publicans to realize that installing television was no answer to this falling trade, because the people watching television spent very little money and the people that didn't want to watch were so bored that they gave up coming into the pubs. And that I think was the beginning because people lost the habit. This doesn't apply in the City and the West End of London. There, pubs are lovely places to go to, particularly at dinnertime. You get food, drink, and conversation. No, it's the provinces that seem to have given up trying.

Some people blame the decline of pubs on the influence of women. I don't agree of course. To my mind the presence of women has done away with a lot of drunkenness. Whereas men on their own didn't care how they got – the kind of disgusting condition men can get into left on their own, over-indulging in foul jokes and things like that – when they've got a woman with them or near them they've got to not only moderate their language, they've got to moderate their drinking too. Because the money's got to do for two people instead of one. No, I think women add a great deal to pubs. Surely a pub is a place for social intercourse. Well, if it's only going to be exclusively for men, they've got very little conversation, because men are inherently lazy about using their brains. They're not interested in talking about anything but their work, dirty stories, what girl they've been out with or what girl they hope to go out with, and what they're going to do to her when they get her out. Women have changed this. So I think they've done a lot for pubs.

In any case with the equality of the sexes rearing its ugly head, as men put it, why shouldn't women share in the social life? When you marry a man you don't expect that your domain is going to be just the home, do you? An example of what it used to be like is this. About eight o'clock at night the man says, 'Well, I'm off to have a drink. Cheerio. I shan't be late. Have my supper ready for me when they close.' What the devil did he think you were? He could've waited till the cows came home for his supper as far as I was concerned. And when he came back he'd have found I was out too. That's what so many working-class wives had to put up with. They were nothing but unpaid housekeepers. I wasn't and I never intended to be.

What I think has changed pubs, and what may eventually almost destroy them, is 'nationalization'. Because that is what is happening. They're being 'nationalized' by financiers.

Instead of having any number of local breweries, family concerns, owning a few pubs in a small area – we've now got four or five industrial giants run by accountants and computers from boot-box blocks of offices dictating what the public will drink. The pubs are managed for them by the faceless civil servants they now choose as landlords, tenants, or managers.

In the days of the small brewers they knew about local tastes and interests. They studied their customers. If it was thought that something was wrong with the beer the brewer would come round and find out what. I'm willing to bet that half the people who brew the stuff now have never tasted it in their lives.

And the way they decorate and furnish places! They look clinical, like something out of the Ideal Home Exhibition. But pubs aren't homes or they shouldn't be. You come out of your home for new surroundings and what do you find? Thick carpets, soft armchairs, a sort of cocktail-lounge effect. And the breweries say that's what the customers want. How do they know? Did they ask them? And if the customers want that why aren't they there to use it? A lot of people – people like my husband and me – feel out of place in these cocktail-lounge kind of places. But you've got to go there because they've done away with the private bar and you've only got two grades now – public bar and this kind of phoney set-up.

Then they haven't got the drinks you want. My husband likes drinking beer – mild beer. And they don't serve it except in the public bar. And when you ask you can see them thinking, 'What are you doing in here then if you can't afford expensive drinks?'

It's not just television. Maybe it's because in an affluent society people don't need what we do – the support and company of other people as a sort of prop in our leisure time. Perhaps money does that for you. Makes you independent. But if that's what being rich means, I don't want it. I still need to depend on people for my enjoyment.

It was strange how packed the pubs used to be during the war – and I don't think this was just because we had to have the alcohol. In a time of adversity we wanted the feeling of togetherness. It's a pity that it takes a war to give us this kind of unity with each other.

7

GLADYS WAS THE under-housemaid at my first place in London. She was a year older than me and although she wasn't what you'd call a pretty girl she had loads of personality. I used to look forward to our Sundays off together. Every other Sunday we got and we always started by going out to tea.

We used to go to rather posh places where they had all gold paint and plaster cupids and marble pillars, and for the price of a pot of tea and two or three cakes you could really feel that you were living it up. We'd sit there and there'd be well-dressed people all around us with their high-faluting talk. And wooing young men would have their girls there.

Personally I could never see why people wanted to do their courting in restaurants. I think there's nothing less conducive to love than seeing people opposite you chewing all the time. I never could understand this mania that English people have for eating out. Either the food is so wonderful when you eat out that you're not in the least bit interested in your partner, or else you're so interested in him that you aren't taking a bit of notice to what you eat.

When I was trying to get a young man I'd never go eating because the way some young men eat – shovelling away at their food, chewing with their mouths wide open – you can't help thinking, 'Heavens above, would I have to sit opposite that every day of my life if we got married?' So it's best not to know.

All men have got defects, we know that, but you don't want them paraded in front of you before you've taken them on, do you? After you're married you can do your best to eradicate the defects but you can't start eradicating before you've got your man up the aisle.

Then there's the kind of man who always props a news-paper in front of him. Of course you can't see him eating but you want a man to talk to you.

The whole art of spending a married life together is not just popping up to bed. Your husband should be able to talk to you. Perhaps when you've been married years you don't worry so much, but when you first get married you visual-ize dainty food, a nice tablecloth and the man sitting there and talking to you about interesting things. Of course it's all in your mind. It doesn't really materialize, but that's what you think it's going to be.

So I don't think eating goes with courting.

Drinking is another thing altogether. You go into a pub or a lounge and you have a glass of wine with a stem to it and you sit there holding the stem and you gaze into each other's eyes over this glass of wine. You can really feel romantic like that. Love and wine go together but love and food don't.

Mind you, you never found any young men in those kind of teashops because no unattached males ever went there. You'd find them in Lyons if you wanted to pick up a couple, but never if you went in those kind of semi-posh places.

Still we had to give up the chase some time, didn't we? We couldn't devote our whole lives to looking for men.

One particular Sunday we decided that we'd go to the Trocadero. It was a place that we'd only been in once before and we'd found it too expensive for us. It was the height of luxury. They had very deep carpets and beautiful subdued lights, and there was a band that played sweet and low music.

One of Gladys's uncles had just got a job there as a trolley waiter and we thought we might get things a bit cheaper so we decided to chance it.

It really was marvellous.

They served tea in silver-plated teapots and instead of knives to cut your cake with you got those little forks with two prongs. I know it's daft but nevertheless you feel that you're really moving with the high-ups when you don't have a knife to eat your tea with.

The only thing was that Gladys's uncle struck a somewhat incongruous note in all these luxurious surroundings. I suppose it was because he was over sixty and he'd got flat feet, a very red nose and he'd a scraggy neck so his Adam's apple bobbled up and down in a very peculiar way the whole time he talked.

Still when he brought the trolley to us I'd never seen such lovely cakes in my life – and he whispered to Gladys, 'Have two for the price of one.' And we did this two or three times.

The beauty of the Trocadero was that you didn't have to hurry. In some of the teashops we went in we didn't like to linger because somebody might be wanting the table. But in there nobody seemed to bother. It was a sort of afternoon ritual. We sat there nearly two hours.

And these teapots that they gave you. You could get four cups of tea for each of you if you kept sticking the hot water in. Of course eventually it came out almost like pouring it straight out of the hot-water jug but that didn't matter. We got four cups each so we sat there sipping away and listening to the band.

And the toilets there! They were an absolute revelation. There were three of them and they were lovely ones. The walls stretched right up to the ceiling – not like those where there's no top or bottom. There were basins to wash your hands and as many towels as you wanted.

So we really had a wonderful afternoon at the Trocadero.

That evening Gladys suggested we went round to see her aunt – the wife of this uncle. They lived just off Ladbroke Grove.

It was a terrible place. A house with five floors if you included the basement, and there were three families living on every floor. Four rooms on each floor. One family had two rooms and the other rooms had one family each. The smell when you went in the passage was appalling. It was compounded of stale food, dirt, and the smell of sweaty humanity.

Mind you, Gladys never turned a hair. It could have been the roses of Picardy for all she knew. Maybe coming from Stepney as she did she was used to it.

I've seen some slummy places in my own home town but nothing to compare with that. You didn't dare put your hand on the banister – it was coated in filth. Each particular family was supposed to take turns doing their bits of the stairs down from one floor to another, but with three families on each floor there were quarrels as to whose turn it was and nothing ever got done.

Gladys's aunt lived on the top floor. All they had in the way of water was one small sink on the landing halfway up and that had to do for those two floors. So that there were six families using one tiny sink and one lavatory.

The contrast between this and the Trocadero!

I said to Gladys, 'Surely your uncle can afford a better place than this?' She said that he probably could if he stuck a job but he drank a lot, which accounted for his red nose. Apparently he was always drinking and losing his job and I suppose that was what they were reduced to. It was a terrible hole! I didn't know how anyone had the spirit to keep clean there.

Gladys's aunt had been in domestic service and she bitterly regretted ever leaving it. She'd loved the place where she worked. And she was delighted to have an audience of two who themselves were in service. She was on about Sir and Madam and Master Gerald and Miss Sarah. I thought it was absolutely stupid. After all those years still calling the people you worked for Sir and Madam and Master and Miss. It just shows you, doesn't it – there is a type of person who likes domestic service? They feel there's a certain prestige attached to serving the high and mighty.

While I was there she got out some newspaper cuttings about this Miss Sarah who was in the suffragette movement and I was interested in this.

This Miss Sarah wasn't one of the more militant ones – not like the Pankhurst woman. She didn't go around setting fire to churches, slashing valuable paintings or putting lighted paper through people's letter boxes. But there were a couple of newspaper photos of her. In one of them she'd got a policeman's helmet stuck on her head and in the other she was there with a lot of other women debagging a policeman.

I must say I was surprised because I hadn't realized that these suffragettes came from well-to-do homes. I couldn't think that people who'd got a comfortable home and didn't have to work could really feel there was anything they ought to fight for.

My mother was a very strong-minded woman – what you would call a militant woman – but she never bothered about the rights of women. So long as she'd got the vote in her home – and, believe me, she had – she couldn't care less about the political vote.

Some Sunday evenings Gladys and I used to go to Lyons Corner House which was a very lively place. The only snag was that we had to leave by half past nine and really it was only beginning to warm up then. We used to get there about eight o'clock. We'd choose the cheapest thing on the menu – egg on toast or sometimes beans on toast. And then we'd perhaps have a glass of shandy or if we were very daring and we weren't too hard up we'd have a glass of wine.

There used to be two women who went there regularly. We saw them every time we went. They were about thirty – very sophisticated type of women – hair cut very short. They used mascara, lipstick, and a dead-white powder. I suppose in a way they looked like clowns, but we didn't think so.

The most daring thing was that they used to smoke cigarettes. All right, Gladys used to have a puff now and then up in the bedroom that we shared. I'd keep cave and we'd open the window and flap a towel about if we thought anyone was coming. But to smoke in a public room – and not only that, they used long holders too, like Pola Negri on the pictures – we thought was the height of sophistication.

We used to try to get a seat near the band if we could because it gave a sort of cachet. Everyone tried to get there. It was an eight-piece outfit.

After we'd been going there about half a dozen times we got to know some of the players and we thought they were marvellous. They had a kind of uniform of black, very tight-fitting trousers with a red stripe down the side and red jackets with black facings. And we found them very attractive-looking indeed. And of course we were flattered that they took any notice of us.

Two of them in particular we had our eyes on. Fortunately

we didn't each have our eyes on the same one. Gladys was keen on the one who played the drums, and the one who played the piano I thought would do all right for me. That is if we ever managed to get out with these two remarkable young men.

One night they began calling out to us asking what tunes we'd like them to play – and that was something that sort of made you feel somebody.

I forget what sort of numbers were popular at that time or how we knew they were. I suppose the errand boys were our disc jockeys then, because whenever a hit tune came out all the errand boys would be riding about on their bicycles whistling it.

I used to like the soulful sentimental numbers like *You Were Meant For Me* – romantic things – not like these pop things they have now which seem to be full of hidden meanings. You don't know whether it's an exercise in sex or whether it's a song.

Anyway after we'd chosen a few tunes, a waiter came over with a note from one of them – I don't know whether it was the drummer or the pianist – asking if we could meet them one night.

Well, you can imagine Gladys and me; we were in a seventh heaven thinking that these beautiful bandsmen had actually invited us out. We sent back a note by the waiter saying that we'd meet them at five o'clock on the next Wednesday. We said five because that would give us extra time to do ourselves up and make ourselves look attractive.

And then Gladys said to me, 'On no account tell them that we're in domestic service.'

So I said, 'Well, they're bound to wonder what we do because we have to get in at half past nine.'

We sat there searching our brains. First of all we were secretaries to someone or other and we were doing night work or then we were looking after an art gallery at night.

I said, 'They won't believe anything like that at all, Gladys, so it's no use coming out with those cock and bull things.'

At last we settled on a story that we were cousins. We didn't like to say we were sisters because we were so unlike – and her mother was an invalid and we had to be back at half past nine because the person who looked after her wouldn't stay any later. It sounded a bit thin but it would do.

But after all this planning and scheming we got a horrible shock. There we stood on the corner where we'd arranged to meet at five o'clock and when they came in sight a couple of more insignificant-looking creatures you've never seen in your life.

In uniform and sitting down they looked marvellous but out of uniform and standing up they were simply ciphers. Both about five foot four. We towered above them. And they were wearing horrible flashy light-blue pinstripe suits, gingery-coloured shoes and trilby hats. You've never seen anything like it in your life.

I was horrified to think of all the work we'd put in night after night to get this couple to take us out.

Gladys whispered to me, 'Let's get them in the flicks as quick as we can so that nobody sees them.'

This we did. And while I was sitting there I couldn't help thinking of all the young men you read about. The favourite novelists at that time were Elinor Glyn, Ethel M. Dell and Charles Garvice. And I don't know where they found the type of men that they wrote about: the kind of he-men and yet chivalrous with a kind of power over the women so that they made them do what they wanted. I'd never then nor since met any men like it.

Mind you, all these wonderful lovers on the films Rudolph Valentino and Ramon Novarro – they were just pasteboard lovers, weren't they? I could never understand women raving and going mad about Rudolph Valentino and sending for his photo. In any case who wants a man that you've got to share with a load of other women?

I used to wish that you could find an Englishman who was a sheikh. And I used to think that with the shortage of men there was it would be nice if a man could have three wives like sheikhs did. You could all take it in turns to be number one wife, couldn't you? I wouldn't have minded waiting my turn at all. But Englishmen have got neither the inclination nor the stamina.

Later when I was married I used to think it would be fine for women to have two husbands because you really need two husbands. One to go out to work for you, to support you and keep a roof over your head, and one for pleasure, because the one that does all the work is too tired for pleasure.

Anyway, there I sat in the pictures getting some sort of pleasure by watching sheikhs because I knew that these two we'd got with us were no sheikhs. One and six to go into the pictures and a fourpenny ice-cream and that was the extent of what they were going to spend on us.

When we came out we separated. Gladys and I had agreed on this. We had a kind of code whereby if we'd got two young men who might be dangerous if they got us on our own we would never separate. When we used to go to Hyde Park and walk around with guardsmen there we'd never separate. Nothing would have induced me to be alone with a guardsman. I mean, they'd got no money to start with so you could be sure they were on the lookout for some pleasure that costs nothing.

But these couple of weeds – they didn't rate.

When we got outside my pianist steered me down a dark street. Nowadays of course you can't find a dark street. I don't wonder people do their courting in broad daylight – it's either that or not do it at all.

Well, we walked down this dark street and all of a sudden he stopped and started getting sort of het up – breathing heavily all over me just like a lot of other young men I'd had – puffing, panting, and pawing was about the extent of their repertoire. And it's so ridiculous, isn't it, because if you want someone to start patting and pawing you, you obviously have got to have some feeling for them? You've got to think that you'd like them to do it. But when you've met someone for the first time you can't have much feeling for them at all, so why should they think you have?

It just shows the colossal egotism of a man, doesn't it – that he thinks every woman he takes out wants him to drape himself round her neck and be affectionate to her? They don't even give you time to get to like them. And the last straw came when he suddenly burst out laughing.

'What are you laughing at?' I said.

'Oh,' he said, '1 can't help thinking of the girl I'd arranged to meet tonight. I wonder how long she waited for me?'

Well, I was simply livid. What a thing to say to me. That he'd arranged to meet another girl and then ditched her at the last minute.

Just at this time we'd come to an Underground station so I said, 'Do you mind excusing me for a minute – I want to go to the lavatory?'

I hated saying it because we never mentioned things like that.

He said, 'All right then.'

I said, 'You wait at the top of the steps. Don't move, will you? I shan't be long.'

So I went down – bought a ticket home and left him standing there. Just like his other girlfriend waiting. And I kept laughing in the train just as he had. Men!

8

THE ONLY TIME I nearly lost a girlfriend over a boyfriend was when Gladys and I shared one between us. We picked him up one Sunday afternoon in a Lyons' teashop; the place was so crowded that the only empty seat was next to us and he came up and said with a rather attractive accent, 'Could I please sit down at your table? It is the only place available.' From the way he spoke we could tell he was a foreigner.

Gladys, who was never at a loss where the opposite sex was concerned, got into conversation with him. We found out that his name was Jan de Beers and that he came from Amsterdam. He assured us that he was no relation to the diamond people of that name. He needn't have bothered, because what with his appearance, which was by no means smart, and the fact that all he was having was one bun and a cup of tea, we knew that already.

We were rather wary of foreigners, particularly Italians and Spanish, because we knew they came from very hot countries and the passion and heat went together. We felt they wouldn't respect English girls. I know it sounds trite now, the word Respect, but it was a word that was continually drummed into us so we took notice of it then. If we met foreigners from the more temperate climates like America, New Zealand, or Australia these were quite all right because obviously they were more affiliated to us. They had the same colour of skin as we had. In those days, as far as we were concerned, anyone who had got the same colour skin as we had got must be all right. Mind you, we thought Indians were all right because they had lovely coffee-coloured skins and there was always the chance that they might be sons of rajahs or princes or things.

Opposite the place where we were working the house had been taken over by the Government for Indian students; we never got any further than waving to them at night because of the caste system. They were educated enough to know that we were only servants and that it wasn't going to do their prestige any good to be seen out with people like us. Apart from his bun and cup of tea Gladys and I weren't surprised to find that this young man was no relation to the diamond people because we never found any young men who had got any money and we never expected to. For us it was enough that he was good-looking. He said he had been a steward on a ship that had gone backwards and forwards to and from South Africa but that the last time it had docked in Southampton he decided not to sign on again but to work in England for a while. I was a bit sceptical about this explanation because he seemed young to be a steward. I assumed that by the time you got to be a steward you would be at least twenty-five to thirty.

Anyway he went on to say that he was working in a factory on night shift, the nature of his work he was unable to explain for some reason or another. Gladys said, 'Is it secret work?'

'Well, no,' he said, 'it's not secret.' But he wouldn't explain what it was. He said his English wasn't good enough. Later on I suggested to Gladys that he was probably only a night watchman. She got annoyed with me when I said that so I knew that she had already begun to like him – she always got annoyed if you made any detrimental remarks about a fellow whom she had begun to like. Even if he had a face like the back of a bus and no money or education this meant nothing to Gladys if she took to him.

The moment Gladys met a young man she never failed to start weaving a romance around him. This I found strange considering how hard-headed she was and the fact that she came from Stepney; maybe Stepney was a place where you have got to weave romances and have a strong imagination because it was the only thing that enabled you to live there.

Anyway this Jan de Beers took us to the pictures that night. He sat in the middle and bought us identical boxes of chocolates and after that the three of us went out together about half a dozen times.

The occasion of the rift between Gladys and me was when she said that she was going to meet this Jan on her own one night. This meant I was to go out by myself. I was up in arms immediately, not because I had fallen for him but because I felt she was assuming that he would prefer to go out with her rather than me. And I couldn't see that he'd shown any inclination to do this.

Mind you there were the intervals when we each had to dive off to the loo and when I was gone he may have said something to her. I'll agree he never said anything to me when she had gone to the loo, but that doesn't mean to say he hadn't said anything to her to the effect that a twosome might be better than a threesome.

As regards looks there really wasn't much to choose between Gladys and me, as neither of us was particularly good-looking. The only thing was with Gladys coming from Stepney as she did she could usually produce some very colourful stories about her life down there. This Jan was a very sober and sedate young man; he neither drank nor smoked and he told us he was a member of the Dutch Reformed Church, which meant nothing to us, in fact Gladys shocked him because she said if the Church needed reforming there wasn't much hope for the congregation. But perhaps because he was such a very moral young man he used to lap up all these lurid tales that Gladys would tell about life in Stepney.

I used to think he was a spy compiling a book in secret about the social life of the working-class people in England: telling of the seamy side of life, and showing it wasn't such a land fit for heroes as everyone was led to believe.

However the funny thing about this fellow was that he didn't really understand what Gladys was saying. Although he thought her tales were dreadful and immoral they didn't have the same implications for him as they did for Gladys. For instance she used to tell about a woman who lived next door to where she did. This woman's husband was a deck hand and whenever he came home it seems he got her in the family way, but while he was away she took on another man and they used to sleep together in the same room as the children. Jan said, 'Oh, how awful,' and you could tell he was shocked. Gladys said, 'Yes, wasn't it, but you see they had no other rooms.' Jan thought it was awful them being immoral but Gladys thought it was only immoral because they were doing it in the same room as the children.

Anyway I reckon I must have made my feelings pretty plain about Gladys and him going out without me, because on our very next evening out she told me he was bringing a blind date for me.

I wasn't very pleased about that because my experience of blind dates was that you really needed to be blind to be seen out with one. With all the surplus females about any young man who couldn't get a girl by himself had something wrong with him. But I was wrong, for when we did meet my blind date he wasn't too bad. Charley his name was and he was an under-steward with the P&O line. This Jan was lodging in this Charley's house and Charley's mother was Jan's landlady.

When we met, Charley said we were all invited to a party because his mother had just got married again, the third time this was, and the party was in a large room in a pub. I wasn't too keen on parties as not only did you meet a lot of people you'd never met before and you fervently hoped you were never going to meet again, but whenever we went to a party we'd got to leave by nine-thirty just when things were warming up, which killed everything stone dead. Still we agreed to go. When we got there it was like all other parties, the usual seething mob of people meeting for the first time in what they think is a convivial atmosphere and feeling they've got to add their quota to it by drinking, laughing, singing, and talking, and putting on a complete change of personality from what they have in their own homes.

Anyway we were taken up and introduced to this Charley's mum and her third husband. I was astounded that she had ever been able to get one husband never mind three. I'd never in all my life seen such a fat woman; she must have weighed fully twenty stone. She'd got arms like legs of mutton, several double chins and great mounds of flesh in front. The appendages that nature had endowed her with were resting somewhere down on her waist. This was mainly because she wore nothing to stop them. In those days bras were never heard of for the working class; you wore a thing called a liberty bodice which was very much like a strait jacket. All it did was suppress the mass of flesh and make it flat, but if you didn't wear one at all, which she didn't, anything you had was left hanging around in all directions.

And yet all this massive weight was supported on the most slender pair of legs you have ever seen. She had lovely legs and she only took size four and a half in shoes so really if you just looked at her feet and legs, which was maybe all her husband intended to do, it wasn't too bad.

The new husband wasn't at all a bad-looking specimen. You couldn't help wondering what he saw in her, whatever induced him to marry this mountain of flesh. Leaving aside the physical difficulties of any amorous interludes, there was the fact that she had already got through two husbands. I'd be very suspicious of anyone who had got through two husbands.

The first one had succumbed to an attack of influenza and the second fell off a ladder. He was a window cleaner. Later on, after I had got to know Charley's mother a bit better, she showed me photos of her first two husbands. Unlike her third, they were certainly no oil paintings – a fact that she freely admitted.

The first one, Henry, had a very short upper lip like a rabbit. I've seen children like that and it looks quite attractive on them but when they're grown up it looks ludicrous. She said to me, 'Henry not only looked like a rabbit; he was like one in bed, too. Our first night together could have been a fiasco because on our honeymoon when we got to the boarding-house they were full up and the only way they could make room for us was to turn their children out and give us their room. Unfortunately the beds were bunk beds.' 'Still,' I said, innocently, 'even from bunk beds you could hold hands.' 'Oh,' she said, 'Nature had endowed him so generously that I held a lot more than that. Oh, yes,' she said, 'and we managed. Of course I wasn't as fat as I am now but I weighed all of fourteen stone even then.'

I decided it was time to change the subject. 'How did you meet your second husband?'

'It was very soon after Henry died, in fact I met Frank at the funeral. He was a friend of Henry's and he came round several times to console me for my loss. I've always been the sort of woman who must have a man around to cook and clean for; I'm lost without one. So we got married after four months. But then,' she added, 'I know that Henry would have wished it.'

You know, it's peculiar to me how many widows always seem to know just what their departed husbands would have wished for them. I knew a woman once who never listened to a word her husband said nor ever took his advice when he was alive, but once he had removed himself from this world (via a rapid descent from a cliff) based the rest of her life on what he would have said or thought. Being as she never gave him a chance to express any thoughts in life I wondered how she knew what his wishes were now he was dead. Anyway to get back to Charley's mum.

'How did you get on with Frank, your second husband?' I asked her. 'Ah,' she said, 'he was a sad disappointment to me. No go in him at all, no stamina. He was always on about what a friend Henry had been to him, how much he missed him and the comfort he felt in being in Henry's home amongst all the things he'd loved. I don't know whether he included me amongst the things Henry had loved. If he did, perhaps he felt he shouldn't show any enjoyment at using Henry's property. No,' she said, 'Frank was always so mournful, in some ways it was a happy release when he fell off that ladder cleaning windows.'

I don't know if she meant a happy release for her or

for Frank. I was interested to know how she would make out with her third husband but I got fed-up with waiting around for Charley to come back from his trips at sea. And so did Gladys because her Jan and my Charley teamed up on the same boat together and calmly sailed out of our lives. I mean it's all very well saying absence makes the heart grow fonder but it's got to be given a chance to get fond to start with. Otherwise it just makes the heart grow accustomed.

9

PHILOMENA KEMP WAS the parlourmaid in my first job in London. She was engaged to be married and her young man was named Fred Keatings.

One Sunday, on Philomena's afternoon off, it was raining cats and dogs so Mrs Bowchard, the cook, asked her what she was going to do. Philomena said, 'Well, I'm meeting Fred but I don't know what we shall do, it's raining so hard.' Neither of them wanted to spend money by going to the pictures or suchlike because they were saving up to get married. So Mrs Bowchard said, 'Well, bring him in, that'll pass the afternoon away and by the time you've had tea maybe the weather will have cleared up and you can go for a walk. That way it won't cost you anything.'

So in Fred came and we all sat down to tea. There were six of us altogether. Gladys the under-housemaid, Jack, our sort of handyman, the cook and me, and Philomena and her intended.

Philomena was busy making her trousseau. Everybody

made a trousseau in those days and you tried to have as many of everything as you possibly could. Philomena had bought no end of linen for her bottom drawer. Six of everything, sheets, pillowcases, towels, and she was making three of everything for underclothes. I don't know why three – one on, one off and one in the wash I suppose. Mind you, if you were well-to-do you had far more than three of everything.

Still, not only the rich had. I remember my mother telling me that when she was in service one of the maids had a dozen of everything. Calico of course they wore in those days. But, mind you, she'd been engaged for seven years, so I presume she had the time to make them. Philomena hadn't, so she was making do with three.

Crêpe de Chine was all the go in those days. There weren't things like nylon or tricel or any of the man-made fibres that there are today. *Crêpe de Chine* was a lovely silky material, and at this particular time Philomena was making a nightdress of it. It was an eau-de-nil colour – a very pale green – with a low neck. I remember how daring we thought it was. None of us except Jack, who was a widower, had ever been married and we didn't know anything about that kind of thing. She was sewing bows all down the back of it at intervals of about four inches which I thought was rather daft.

Philomena was the youngest of sixteen children. Her mother had worked through the alphabet and that's why she got such a peculiar name.

She had a photo of her mother in the bedroom that she

shared with the housemaid, and she was such a prim-looking little woman. You wouldn't have thought she'd had one child, let alone sixteen.

Mind you, people did look more prim in those days. No make-up, your hair done up in a bun and your clothes covering almost every portion of your anatomy. You were bound to look prim. Nowadays so much shows that almost everybody knows what they're buying before they even sample the goods in the marriage market.

Once I said to Philomena, 'Fancy your mother having sixteen children. She doesn't look the type.' She said her mother was so fertile that if she'd only kissed her father sixteen times in sixteen years she would have had sixteen children. I suppose she knew what she was talking about. She said her mother was a very religious woman and that she always read the Bible every night before she went to bed. She certainly needed to get strength from somewhere I reckon.

Anyway back to the kitchen.

After tea Philomena got on with her sewing while we sat around making ribald remarks about the low-necked nightdress. And then we chanted that little rhyme, 'Change the name and not the letter, change for worse and not for better.' Her name was Kemp and his was Keatings so she wasn't changing the letter; she was embroidering the initial K on everything. It's one of those ridiculous, old wives' tales but I partly believed it. When you are that age you believe anything.

While we were going on in this way Jack, the handy-man,

suddenly said, 'I well remember my wedding night.' So we all pricked our ears up expecting either some very sentimental recollection or some very erotic one, preferably the latter as far as I was concerned. And the others were, too, I expect because we didn't go much on sentiment in the servants' hall.

'Yes,' he said, 'we got married in a registry office. We had very little money and we couldn't afford a proper reception. We hadn't anywhere to live or any furniture, so we stayed on at my mum's. We had a bit of a "do" in Mum's front room and all the neighbours came in with crates of beer and bottles of wine and there was dancing and whatnot and about midnight I was blind drunk. I took my boots off and got into bed. I woke at about six and I suppose I was still fuddled from all the booze I'd had. I got out of bed, felt under it for my boots, put them on, crept downstairs in the dark the same as I'd done every morning, put the kettle on, made myself a cup of tea, picked up my sandwiches and went off to work. It wasn't until I'd been at work about an hour or two and saw all my mates grinning at me and then kept on hearing them say, "Old Jack he looks tired today, doesn't he? I wonder why Jackie looks so tired? He must be working too hard. You should take a holiday, Jack." Then it came to me that I'd got spliced the night before. Well, when dinnertime came I ran all the way home. I'd never got there so quick in my life and I had three lovely courses for my dinner.'

Well I didn't know whether to laugh or cry. It bore absolutely no resemblance to the lovely bridal nights that I read about in *Peg's Paper*, where the husband is so chivalrous to his bride that he carries her over the threshold and then they have a lovely candlelit dinner together. And then they go upstairs and the blushing bride goes into the bedroom, undresses on her own, puts on a lovely chiffon nightdress and sits up in bed with a bow in her hair and then a sort of veil is drawn over the rest of the proceedings. So old Jack's account of his wedding night was like nothing I'd ever heard before.

And Fred Keatings, he sat there quiet all the time. Never a glimmer of a smile while Jack told his story. He was such a sober, respectable young man. He sort of oozed sobriety from every pore and I could see that he took a very poor view of Jack.

Mind you, Jack knew that Fred Keatings didn't like him. He couldn't resist making sarcastic remarks to Fred. One thing that used to annoy Fred particularly was old Jack asking if he was related to *The* Keatings, the makers of the famous powder that killed bugs, fleas, and beetles.

For my part I wouldn't have minded a bit being related to The Keatings or having some shares in their concern because they must have sold gallons of their powder. I know in my own home, owing to the slummy places that my dad had to go, doing his painting and decorating, we always had enough fleas to fill a dozen circuses. My mother used to wage a perpetual war on them. She used to powder the bed with Keatings so that every time you made it a miniature sand storm went up.

Perhaps Fred had an aversion to fleas. But one look at

Fred and you knew that no self-respecting flea would ever bite him. He was such a poor specimen of humanity that he'd never provide a happy hunting ground. He was a wet, phlegmatic kind of person. You could never visualize him showing any kind of emotion let alone a passionate one. Yet Philomena used to say that he was very passionate, that she had to fight to keep him on the straight and narrow. But he certainly never showed any signs of that in the servants' hall.

He used to sit there drinking a cup of tea with his little finger sticking out at right angles and his hands were so pale they looked like white slugs to me. He used to make me shudder. And then there was the nicety of his speech and his obsequious manners. I suppose these were the result of his job. He was a shop assistant in a very large draper's stores and he'd been doing this kind of work from the time he left school. He started to work in a gentlemen's hatters as errand boy and he gradually worked his way up till he was a sort of chief shop assistant. His greatest ambition was to become a floor walker. Personally I thought it was a terrible ambition.

They don't seem to have floor walkers these days. I suppose the aisles are so full of people there wouldn't be enough room for a floor walker to manoeuvre. But in those days with less people around and less money around, it was more the well-to-do who patronized these kind of shops and I well remember the floor walkers in their frock coats – snootiest people imaginable, they seemed. But they were very discerning.

They could size up a customer the minute they saw one. The deference in their manner when greeting somebody who looked as though they hadn't a ha'penny to their name but they sensed came from a titled family! Whereas someone smart with probably a lot of money would only get slight attention. They graded their civility according to the aristocratic position of their customers.

To listen to Fred's conversation you would have thought that all the nobility and gentry came up to Fred's counter in preference to anybody else. He'd say, 'Who do you think I served this morning?' Nobody cared of course but you knew that you were going to hear just the same. 'Why,' he said, 'Lady Betty – now there's a real lady for you.' What an unreal one was I never did find out. 'She gave me such a sweet smile.' What were you supposed to say to that? Then he'd say, 'The Duke of Walton was in trouble over a tie for his young nephew, the Honourable Peter. The Duke is elderly, you know, and he doesn't know what young men like today.'

Well, I thought poor old Philomena.

Personally I felt that if he was the last man in the world I would never have married him though the time was to come, believe me, when if I could have got a Fred Keatings I would have been glad. I thought I'd had it. Once or twice I thought I was going to be on the shelf – for ever.

But nevertheless at that time when I was only sixteen I was full of hopes. I wasn't going to marry anyone like Fred Keatings. I could see Philomena, slippers all ready for him. 'Well, dear, what kind of day did you have today?' And there she'd have him trotting out about who he'd served and what they'd said and the sweet smiles they'd given him. Day after day and year after year it would go on till he got to be a floor walker. Then it would be ten times worse. That's what I thought at the time.

But alas for Philomena it wasn't to happen.

There they were, all set, introduced in the proper way – no picking up – making all her trousseau with her bottom drawer ready, and Fred Keatings with his eyes upon becoming a floor walker and a model of propriety. Yet they were never to marry.

A few days after our kitchen party Fred Keatings, that model of rectitude, was arrested for indecent exposure. And that was a heinous crime in those days.

Mind you, it happened to me once or twice and I always laughed. I just couldn't help it. It looked so funny. Nowadays they are given medical treatment but they didn't do things like that then. They just got put in prison. Fred was sent down for two years because it was discovered that it was his third offence.

And poor Philomena. She went right round the bend – off her head – and she had to be put into a mental home. Talk about losing your head for a man. Today people would probably take the thing in their stride and the wedding would have happened. But then of course it was a disgrace and anyone who was disgraced became a social outcast, an untouchable. It shows too the importance a girl attached to getting married, so that losing a boyfriend could send her out of her wits.

10

THE NANNIES I particularly remember were from the time when I was a kitchenmaid in London. The people I worked for had a married daughter with three children living with them, which meant having both a nanny and an under-nurse. We disliked all nannies, nurses and under-nurses because they were neither flesh, fowl, nor good red herrings as you might say. They were not the kind of people you worked for and they were not of the kind of *us*. They were sort of out in limbo. Perhaps this wasn't true of the under-nurse. She got the worst of both worlds – not rated by the nanny and we classed her as if she were, as she had to be with the nanny. Yet even nanny wasn't one of *them* because she had to work for her living. I suppose in fact nannies didn't have much of a life, but we thought they did, and we disliked them intensely in the kitchen because we had to prepare different meals for them.

The nurse would come down and tell the cook what menu she wanted, and cook would be awkward and bloody-minded because as far as the cook was concerned only one person should give orders and that was the madam. But if the nurse thought that the day's meals were unsuitable for the children she'd come down and say so and others would have to be cooked specially for them. Then when the nurse went upstairs cook would explode and I got the blast. No, we didn't like nannies.

But as I say the under-nurse really had a horrible time of it because she was stuck up there with only that nurse for company and she had to work hard. There was a day nursery and a night nursery; the under-nurse had to scrub both these out each day and when I say scrub I mean scrub, because in those days there was linoleum on the floor. She had to do the washing for the children, the napkins and the rougher stuff, while the nurse did the dainty things.

I hadn't been at that job long when another baby was due, which made it four children. Never in all my life had I seen such a carry-on about somebody having a baby. I wouldn't have believed people could have made all that fuss. To begin with there was a shuffling round of rooms because our nurse didn't take children from birth – so another nurse arrived, took her room, and ours had to sleep in with the under-nurse. And the room had to be redecorated which was another thing that annoyed our nurse because, as she said, it hadn't been redecorated for her who had been with the family for three years, so why should it be redecorated for someone who was only going to come for a month or two. I said to the cook, 'She'll reap the benefit when the nurse has gone, she'll go back into it.' I should have kept my mouth shut. The cook picked up the carving knife and made a gesture and uttered something too horrible to repeat.

Anyway two weeks before the baby was expected this nurse who took babies from birth was installed – so you can just imagine what it was like in the household: two nurses and an under-nurse, three kids and one on the way. That was when I made up my mind never to go to another place where they had children. With the hostility that there was between this new nurse and the old one, you could have cut the atmosphere with a knife. Yet they had to be outwardly polite. It was 'Good morning, Nurse' and 'What do you think of this, Nurse?' But the old nurse wouldn't let the new one do anything so she just sat around getting in the way, waiting for the baby to be born. And what with the fact that the baby was a week late as well – she was left hovering for three weeks. The only one that benefited was the under-nurse because our nurse joined forces with her against the other one, so for once in her life everything that she said and did was right. This changed of course as soon as the other nurse went.

Then after the baby was born, yet another nurse came – a wet nurse to feed the baby, you see. She had a month-old baby of her own but she came in several times a day to feed ours as well. I must say I found this procedure most peculiar at the time, but I didn't after I'd had my first baby because I had so much milk I used to chuck the stuff down the sink although I was feeding my baby. People talk now about how good these cans of food are. They start ramming them down the baby's neck when they're two months old and

317

they say how much healthier babies are for it. I had so much milk that I fed my first child until he was eleven months old and he never had anything else. It was so cheap and we were hard up, and it was clean and hygienic. I never had to bother about washing out bottles and as I say I had so much of it I often wished I knew another baby that I could have given it to. I didn't realize then that you could go up to a hospital with it and that they're always glad to accept it.

But this woman got paid for it. I used to wonder, did her own baby suffer? If somebody had to go short it obviously wasn't going to be the baby that she was being paid to feed. She only came for a month though – after that the baby was put on to one of these patent foods.

But during those weeks what with two nurses and an under-nurse and a wet nurse, absolute pandemonium reigned. I didn't help matters because one day I had to tell our nurse that the wet nurse had arrived.

So I said, 'Daisy's here.'

She said, 'Daisy?'

I said, 'Yes, you know, Daisy the cow, who comes to feed the baby.'

Talk about lese-majesty. She drew herself up to her full height. 'How dare you,' she said. 'Associating the sacred rights of motherhood with being a cow. It's nothing like being a cow at all. It's giving life to someone.'

She went on like that for about five minutes. I went down to the kitchen and told the cook, looking for sympathy.

'Serves you bloody well right,' she said.

I suppose it did.

Nowadays, as I say, mothers don't like feeding their babies. They think there's something distasteful about it. It's these damned little cans of food – that's what it is. If they had to do what we had to – put stuff through the sieve and mash it all up once we put the baby on solids, they'd feed them. I used to sigh for the days when I fed them myself and had no bother at all.

Then of course well-to-do ladies didn't feed their babies because it ruined their figures. It spoiled the shape of their bosoms. Perhaps it doesn't nowadays because of the bras they've invented. But I really don't believe that anyone can feed a baby, not for any length of time, and still have the same-shaped breasts afterwards.

And again at that time no well-to-do lady who went to a lot of social functions was going to be pestered with having to feed her baby every three to four hours. Why did they pay out money for nurses and under-nurses if they were going to be tied to the baby themselves?

The whole paraphernalia of their way of having a baby simply amazed me and Gladys. Her mother had had swarms of kids. Madam stayed in bed a whole fortnight. A fortnight! My mother used to stay in six days and Gladys said her mother used only to stay three days. Who was going to look after the other mob? Her mum used to come down and start scrubbing and it never did her any harm. And then she fed the babies as well as doing all this work in the house.

They say once you start work you can't feed the babies, but it's all my eye and Betty Martin. Of course you can – especially if you drink a lot of beer like Gladys's mum did.

And I don't blame her for drinking it either. If I was living in Stepney and had had swarms of kids I would be drinking beer all the time too.

Having a working-class baby was a very casual thing. You never made many preparations beforehand. Naturally you got a few clothes in for it and the midwife would call some time near the date. Nowadays too you get all this talk about new psychological methods and a husband being in the room at the time of birth because it's good for him – it gives him a kind of feeling of oneness with the mother and baby. They talk this high-faluting rubbish as though it was a new thing. In working-class households the husband always was there. My dad was – there was only him and the midwife. And he was kept running in and out with kettles of hot water because we didn't have any hot water laid on. We only had an old sink and an outside lavatory. So Dad was in the room nearly the whole time. And so were other working-class husbands.

The way they talk now as though that's why all babies are wonderful and that's why there's such a feeling of affinity between parents because the father was in the room when the baby was born – it's all rubbish. There was no psychology as far as Dad was concerned – it was sheer necessity – lack of money. And as soon as the baby was delivered Dad did everything, the washing – and there's a whole lot of washing after you've had a baby – and clearing up. He took over and the next day Mother would do as much as she could from the bed. Like preparing the vegetables. Anything she could do with her hands.

So when Gladys and I saw all this paraphernalia of having a baby as though it was something out of the ordinary, we wanted to spit. People had kids like a bet on the Derby – once a year. Well, why not if you can? And why was there all this fuss? It's not as if having children was going to alter their lives. Where I was in service the mothers upstairs had nothing to do with their children. They saw them once a day. They never had the pleasure of them.

Surely to have the pleasure of children is to be with them when they're young and to give them the love and security that they can only get by knowing that their parents care about them. It's only then that you get something in return. It's nothing to do with money. I don't think these children were lucky – only in as much as they had all the food, the clothes and the toys that they wanted. But they weren't lucky in having the kind of things that we had in our home without money.

I often think, looking back, and because of the letters I've had since I wrote *Below Stairs*, that we were the fortunate ones. I've had letters from people who were children in these opulent homes. They say, 'We never had such a good time. You think because you were down there slaving away that you were the only ones that suffered, but you weren't.' One person wrote and said that she only saw her parents once a day when she went in the drawing-room at five o'clock after tea and that she had a cruel nurse, but felt so divorced from her parents that she was frightened to tell them how unkind she was, because she was sure that her parents wouldn't have done anything about it except to tell the nurse what she'd said, and that she would be even more ill-treated. So you see, she wasn't any better off than children in an orphanage who are given every material comfort but haven't got some one person who really cares about them.

But the nurse where I was working – in spite of the fact that we didn't like her – wasn't like that. The children thought the world of her – so she must have been kind to them and given them love. I could tell by the way they used to run after her and climb over her. So although to us she seemed stand-offish and snooty she couldn't have been so bad.

But what sort of life did she have to look forward to? They just lived for a time on borrowed affection. Then the children they had taken care of went away to boarding schools and they'd have to take another job and start all over again. What sort of existence was that? Although life below stairs was rough and ready, at least it was life. The rigid social divisions in any of the houses I worked in were generally carefully defined. You knew your place and you kept in it. You worked and played within certain limits and under certain terms and rules and it was seldom that these were ever broken.

I only remember one place where this happened. The goings-on there would have interested even Mr Sigmund Freud.

11

IT WAS AFTER I'd been in service in London for some years, I thought I'd like to be a bit nearer home for a change, so I came back to Hove and I worked for a Mr and Mrs Bishop.

It was a very peculiar kind of house in many ways. No one could say that they belonged to the gentry.

Mrs Bishop was a woman of about sixty who made herself up to look about thirty-five to forty and she did it extremely well. She led her own life – at the weekends at any rate, which was the only time they were in Hove. The house was filled with young men – young in comparison to her that is – and it was a very lively forty-eight hours indeed, though for most of the time Mr Bishop wandered around looking like a lost soul. But then he had his own little bit of fun during the week.

He would come down on his own to satisfy his particular aberration. And that was to inveigle one of the maids into his bedroom late at night when they were wearing their hair curlers. Then she'd sit on his bed while he fingered her curlers. That's how he got his pleasure. He was what I believe they nowadays call kinky.

Another expression you hear today is 'permissive society' as though it's something new. But the only difference from when I was young is that now this permissiveness applies to everybody – not just the rich. There's always been a permissive society for the well-to-do because if you'd got rank or wealth it excused a multitude of evils. Also rank and wealth gave you the opportunities and the facilities to be permissive.

Take the kinky Mr Bishop. If he hadn't had a house of his own and servants and hadn't been able to come down and live alone with us in the week, he wouldn't have been able to indulge in his peculiar habit of wanting to feel the servants' hair curlers.

The working classes couldn't have done it. Well we didn't have that peculiar taste. I suppose some of us had peculiar tastes but how, when, or where they could be satisfied is beyond me.

And although the maids used to profit by this peculiarity of Mr Bishop's by gifts of chocolates, stockings, and theatre tickets, we were contemptuous of him. We thought that somebody with his money and education shouldn't indulge in these footling pursuits. That they should be above such things. We weren't to know, as people do now, that this kind of obsession couldn't be helped.

Among ourselves we used to make fun of him and, when Mrs Bishop wasn't around, wouldn't give him the respect that we would a normal employer. We never used to call him Sir and we would grin like hyenas when we met him.

Well, what more could he expect? But we liked him because he was pleasant, gentle, and kind.

Yet after I'd been there about six months something happened that made me change my opinion of him completely. And it will show you how much I respected him when I tell you I never said a word of what I found out to another soul. And this at a time when precious little of interest or excitement came into our lives, so that we had to embroider the more mundane things to make them dramatic.

It happened one night when I was coming home from a dance. I'd been with a boyfriend who didn't bother to escort me home when he found that there wasn't going to be anything on the end of it. After an evening out I always believed in making the position clear. You might just as well be friends when all's said and done because some of them used to get very annoyed when they had taken me home and all they got for it was a goodnight kiss. I learnt this early on when one night I was being escorted back from another dance by a fellow. I didn't take him right to the door – fortunately. We stood in a turning parallel to it and he began to get extremely frisky. He was about twice my size too. Well, I got very nervous – matters were getting out of hand – so I said to him I needed to go to the loo. So he said, 'Where?'

'I live the next turning to this. I won't be long.'

He said, 'You won't come back.'

'Won't come back?' I echoed, making as though I was simply dying to come back. 'Of course I'll come back.' I said, 'You'll wait here for me, won't you?'

So I dashed to the house, bolted the door and got out of that awkward situation. The excuse of going to the loo has been very useful to me on occasions. Perhaps that's why they called it a convenience. That's a bit of a deviation from my story but it accounts for me coming home from the dance alone.

As I was saying, I was walking by the Hotel Metropole on the seafront, when who should be coming out of the hotel but Mr Bishop and a woman. She looked about forty – nothing particular about her – quite plain – and plainly dressed, too. It was all very embarrassing because I didn't know what to do. I'd almost bumped into them. Mr Bishop said, 'Good evening,' and she looked a bit odd. I muttered something and that was that.

But the strange part was that in the normal way when I'd got in I would have come out with it about seeing Mr Bishop with another woman. But I didn't. I don't know what restrained me then because I was quite young and hadn't got much sympathy for anyone who deviated from the norm.

I'd almost forgotten the episode when two or three days later I received a letter from a stranger and on reading it, it transpired it was from this woman. She asked me if I would go and see her at her flat in Brighton. 'Well,' I thought, 'it can't do any harm to see her.' So I went on my day out.

The first thing she asked me was, 'Have you said anything about seeing me with Mr Bishop?'

I said, 'No, I haven't said a word. It's strange really because we do talk about him.'

So she begged me not to either to the other maids or

to Mrs Bishop. I told her of course that I wouldn't. She didn't have to implore me – I wasn't going to say anything anyway. Now of course I wouldn't. I didn't want to spoil things for other people. Then she went on to tell me a story that could have come straight out of a novelette.

Her name was Dora and she'd been a housemaid with Mr and Mrs Bishop many years ago. There was a son of the house who seduced her, got her into trouble and landed her with a baby. As soon as Mrs Bishop heard of it, although she knew it was her son who was responsible, she dismissed Dora without a reference. So as well as the stigma of an illegitimate child, she had no money and no chance to get another job. I asked her why she didn't sue the son.

She said, 'Well how could I? By the time I'd had the baby he'd been sent to Australia as a ticket of leave man for forging his father's cheques. In any case it would only have been my word against his and I wouldn't have stood a chance.'

It was always the same then. It was always the girl's fault if she got into trouble. Nobody ever blamed the man. It was considered natural for a man to pursue and to get everything he could and if he could find a girl that was muggins enough to give it him – well, she deserved what she got.

She went on, 'I knew he was a bit of a ne'er-do-well but he told me he was emigrating to Australia and that he'd take me with him. But it was the old story. He didn't care about me any more when I told him I was pregnant. And the next thing I knew was that he'd gone.'

So I said, 'What did you do then?'

She'd written to Mrs Bishop asking her to help out with money but she never got a reply. She'd managed to borrow a bit but when the baby, a boy, was two months old she was at her wits' end. There seemed to be no hope at all. And then out of the blue Mr Bishop wrote to her and suggested that they meet.

She said, 'He came to see me and was marvellous. He paid off my debts and set me up in this flat. And he's looked after us both and paid for the child's education. But the reason you saw us together is that now my son is married and I'm on my own Mr Bishop comes to see me once a week on a Wednesday night.'

Well I couldn't help grinning thinking about what might be happening.

So she laughed, too, this Dora, and she said, 'I know what you're laughing at.'

I said, 'Well, I wouldn't really have asked you outright – but it's the hair curlers.'

We both went off into fits of laughter about this.

Anyway it transpired that half of every Wednesday night was spent fixing and playing with hair curlers. They used them on each other – not only on their heads but in other places as well.

'Don't you get fed up with that sort of queerness?' I said. 'After all, it's hardly the kind of thing that you expect to find in normal society, is it?'

So she said, 'Well, if normal society means that when you take a wrong step people treat you like dirt as I was treated, give me abnormality every time. Apart from this oddness

Mr Bishop has always been kind and generous to me. He knows I've got another man friend and he doesn't mind in the least so long as he can come here Wednesday nights.

'For him,' she said, 'it's an oasis of quietness after the racketty life that his wife leads.'

I never saw her again after that, and although I never mentioned it to a soul I used to wake up at nights and roar with laughter thinking about an elderly man and a middle-aged woman experimenting half the night with hair curlers.

But it showed, didn't it, that it couldn't really pay you to step outside your own social circle. If you did it was a near-certainty that you would be the one to get hurt.

Mind you, even flirting with the trades people could have its dangers as I was to find out.

12

WHEN I WAS in domestic service we didn't have any super-markets but we certainly had super service and super food. No shopping had to be done by the cook. Occasionally if she went out in the afternoon she would look round the shops to see what new things were in. But she didn't have to. The tradesmen called every morning. By tradesmen I mean the owners or managers or their assistants. They would take the orders, talk about any special things they'd got in and then later the errand boys arrived and delivered. The cook would make them come right into the kitchen and she'd examine what they'd brought and if it wasn't right there would be no question of making do – she sent it back. For instance if you ordered a particular slice of rump steak or fillet steak or fillet veal and the cook thought that it wasn't up to standard, she wouldn't keep it; the errand boy would have to take it away and come back with something that she thought was.

Incidentally Albert my husband was a butcher boy at one

time; he said that often when they took something back all the butcher did was chop a lump off the end and return it again and it was always accepted.

When the tradesmen called all the under-servants, the under-housemaid, under-parlourmaid and me, we used to try to make ourselves look as nice as possible. I noticed that the under-housemaid and under-parlourmaid always seemed to be below stairs at these times. The under-parlourmaid had a legitimate excuse to be down because of the butler's pantry being there, but the under-housemaid's work was upstairs.

The under-parlourmaid used the butler's pantry for washing up all the silver – none of it was washed up in the scullery. The silver and the afternoon tea things were washed up in the pantry. Then there were cupboards to put silver away in and green baize covers to fit everything into. There were shammy leathers galore for polishing and special cloths and papier-mâché bowls so that the silver didn't get scratched. All very different from the stinking old sinks I had out in the kitchen.

But back to our hovering around the tradesmen. It was really an absolute waste of time because the ones who called for orders were either already married or, if not, were far too old, and the errand boys that came with the things were always much too young.

The butcher's boy at my first place in London was the only errand boy I really fancied but unfortunately it was all too obvious that he didn't fancy me. He was tall and hand-some like an Adonis and he had wavy hair. He was a real heart-throb. Agnes the under-parlourmaid used to vie with me for his favours. She was a sentimental girl and had a real crush on him, but like me she was wasting her time. All her sweet words and languishing looks were repeated ad infinitum by the servants wherever he went. He had marvellous opportunities so you can be sure that he shopped around for the best and the easiest. I adopted a sort of a hard-to-get attitude, completely ignoring this Adonis – I thought that this might intrigue him enough to make him become interested in me. But what a hope! I might have been empty air for all the notice he took of me. When I think about it now it's obvious that if you want to intrigue somebody you've got to look intriguing yourself and I certainly looked far from intriguing. Not many kitchenmaids could look intriguing, especially just after they've done the kitchen range.

When I later became a cook I acquired a position of authority over the tradesmen and at one time I did contemplate a life of bliss with a fishmonger. Well, not a life of bliss exactly but life with a fairly substantial income. I know that sounds a materialistic approach to matrimony, divorced from the sort of romantic ideals, but unless you're so violently in love that time and motion cease to exist, money does count. I mean, in exchange for a nice home, nice clothes, and good food you can look at any man through rose-coloured glasses. Well, I thought I could.

This fishmonger, Mr Hailsham, certainly needed looking at through rose-coloured glasses. He resembled nothing so much as one of the large cod fish that he used to bring – considered very suitable for servants' meals, being very nourishing, you know. His flesh was dead white and it was always cold, and he had tiny little expressionless eyes. But he had a very flourishing business. He used to supply far larger establishments than ours was and, according to Mr Hailsham, his father and his grandfather supplied the gentry and nobility. He showed me photos – so I suppose there must have been some truth in what he said.

The only time Mr Hailsham showed any sign of animation was when we were talking about fish. You might think it was difficult to wax poetical over a salmon or a turbot but Mr Hailsham could. He used to go to the market every morning and he'd start off on a great rigmarole about looking into their mouths, studying their scales and their tails – ecstatic he used to get. And that's why he got to look like his fish. You see, he lived, thought and breathed fish.

He was about twenty years older than me so not unnaturally I assumed that he was married. One really cold morning I invited him in for a cup of coffee – what with the fish being so cold and him looking so cold I took pity on him. And he got a bit forthcoming. I found he lived with a brother and a sister and none of them was married. I kept on with the recipe of a cup of coffee and after a few weeks he thawed out even more and became quite friendly towards me. Then I commented on the fact that all three of them were still single.

'Oh,' he said, 'my dear mother, God bless her, made us promise before she died to keep together and always help each other.'

'But surely,' I said, 'she didn't mean that you'd got to

look after each other to the extent that you couldn't ever get married? She couldn't have meant that. After all the name's going to die out if you don't get married and with your business so long established you don't want that to happen.'

So he said, 'Well, we've never had any inclination to get married up to now.' And he looked at me in a meaningful way.

At least I thought he looked at me in a meaningful way. I suppose it was a meaningful way – it was difficult to tell with his eyes. He certainly looked at me. So I continued to cultivate him, to sort of get closer to him, though the all-pervading odour of fish that hung around him was hardly an inducement for closer proximity.

Then the other servants said, 'You'll never get him, you know. He's been a bachelor far too long and his sister looks after them both too well.'

This was a bit of a challenge. It's amazing what a determined woman can do. I find even the most rigid and intractable of men lose their powers of resistance where a woman's concerned. You've only got to look at Adam and Eve, haven't you? – going back to Biblical days. Adam could have refused to bite the apple, couldn't he? The reason he didn't refuse it was because he knew that Eve had already had a large bite out of it and that she'd be banished from the Garden of Eden in any case and he didn't want to stop there without her, so he thought he might as well have a bite too and then they'd both have to go. That's the reason. Not because she really tempted him but because he thought what was the good of the Garden of Eden if he was living in it on his own?

Mind you, I had to put in an awful lot of spadework to bring this Mr Hailsham up to scratch. Cups of tea and home-made cakes, and listening to long dreary anecdotes about the fish business and Mr Hailsham's acumen and judgement and that he'd made it such a flourishing concern – not his brother. You see Mr Hailsham did the buying and the orders and the brother did the selling in the shop, and according to Mr Hailsham it was the buying that was the main thing because if you didn't buy well you wouldn't sell well. There was something in that, I think. Then when his sister was ill I made nourishing dishes for her – egg custards and things like that. It paid off eventually because there came the fateful morning when Mr Hailsham said to me, 'Don't call me Mr Hailsham, call me Cyril.' Cyril – I ask you – anyone less like a Cyril I've never met in my life. And this was the prelude to Cyril asking me to go out with him on my next evening off. I agreed, though with some trepidation. I wondered what he'd look like when he was dressed up. But never in my wildest imaginings did I visualize the figure that I saw waiting for me at the end of the street when I went out. Talk about Beau Brummell and Beau Nash rolled into one. He was wearing spats and he had a flyaway bow, yellow shammy-leather gloves and a silver-topped cane, and he was holding a bouquet of flowers. Well, I nearly died of mirth. Talk about seeing Mr Hailsham the fishmonger turned to Cyril the fop. And yet despite this he still had the odour of fish pervading him and it was hard to associate this sort of Beau Brummell with the fishy smell.

Anyway I went out with him on several occasions and

eventually it led to an invitation to tea with his brother and sister. His sister was something of an invalid – she enjoyed bad health. They lived over the fish shop – quite a lot of rooms they had because there were two floors, but they were the kind of rooms that gave me claustrophobia. They were so heavy, crowded, and ornate. They had flock wallpaper in a dark red colour and I felt as though the walls were pressing in on me all the time. And they were full of things that had belonged to 'dear Mother' and were kept for sentimental reasons. 'Dear Mother' had collected these little small pieces of china from wherever she went on holiday. There were things from Margate and Ramsgate and Broad-stairs, little bits of crest china, a whole cabinet full of them, with antimacassars on every chair and stuffed birds in cages. And wherever you sat the beady eyes of these things followed you.

I must say though that they were all very nice to me. I'd been a bit scared about meeting the sister. After all, every-one had said she wouldn't let any female get her claws into either of her brothers. She was charm itself. 'Miss Langley – or may I call you Margaret?' That sort of thing. And she showed me over the flat. No, I was welcomed with open arms. It wasn't until a bit later that I realized the full Machiavellian plot that was being hatched over me. It was only disclosed when Cyril and his brother had gone out to get a drink and to bring in a bottle of port for her and me. She was drinking it for medicinal purposes and I would be drinking it for never you mind what. They hadn't been gone five minutes before his sister came over and put her arms round me, and if there's anything I hate it's a woman mauling me around. I'm not that keen on some men mauling me around, but a woman – never.

Then she said, 'Oh, I'm so very glad that Cyril's found a friend like you. You know one that can cook well and look after a house. We need another pair of hands here – now that I'm an invalid. Cyril and Harry, they're so fond of their food and only the best is good enough for them. You being a cook will appreciate that.'

And she went on, 'I can't tell you how glad Harry and I are that Cyril's found you.'

I was absolutely dumbfounded. As far as I was concerned we were only in the very early stages.

So I said, 'Aren't you going ahead a bit? We don't know each other all that well yet.'

'Oh, but you will,' she said. 'I know Cyril's made up his mind. He talked to us about you and about how domesticated you are. We shall all live here so happily together.'

I nearly passed out. Here had I been thinking it was me that was doing the chasing and I'd swum straight into the fish-net. You can just imagine. I mean married to old cod's eyes Cyril. It mightn't be the realization of a maiden's dream. But taking on Cyril, his brother, his sister, and all the Victorian impedimenta as well – well it was a life sentence that I wasn't prepared to serve, I can assure you. Maybe a ready-made home and material comforts had to be paid for but not to that extent. Just a bloody unpaid housekeeper.

Then I visualized the night I first went to bed with Cyril. Those two would be holding their breaths and conjuring up the kind of orgy that they thought he and I would be conducting in our bedroom. And for all his lifeless exterior he might have been like that. These late starters often begin where others finish, on the assumption that now they've got the property they might as well make all possible use of it because they may not have what it takes that much longer to do it. So forewarned was forearmed. As soon as I possibly could with politeness, I dropped off inviting Cyril in for cups of coffee. And I certainly left off sending any delicacies round for his sister. And it was fortunate that at that time my mother became ill so that my evenings were spent going round and looking after her.

13

AFTER ALL MY efforts to get and keep a man I eventually found one right on my own doorstep. Somebody who'd been calling twice a day since I'd been cook in the house – the milkman. His name was Albert – Albert Powell.

I'd never thought of him as a possible husband because he was five years older than I was and I guessed he must be married. Most working-class men were married at his age, particularly with all the surplus girls there were about then – so I thought he'd already been snaffled.

I've written a lot about catching a young man and it may seem as though I never thought of anything else and that I was blatant in my efforts to get hold of one. But what you should realize is that everyone was the same then. The upper-class girls were just as keen to get married as we were. But they could do it in a more civilized manner. They had coming-out parties and went to theatres and deb parties and were introduced to men. The whole idea of being debs was that they should meet young men and get married.

Then of course more than now. In any class marriage was a career for a girl because on any level there weren't the jobs for women. But our efforts had to be blatant. The only way we could get young men was either to meet them at dances or pick them up in the cinema or in the parks. So although this method may seem vulgar it was the only way open to us. We would have liked to have been properly introduced to them but if we'd waited for that we would have waited for ever.

Another reason why I thought that Albert was married was that he always wore a ring on his wedding finger. Not many married men wore rings – never mind single ones. When I got married and I found that it wasn't compulsory for married men to wear wedding rings I promptly left mine off as well. This was one inequality between the sexes that I could do something about.

Ever since I'd been cook at that house I'd enjoyed seeing Albert the milkman, because he was always so lively and cheerful no matter what the weather was like. He'd always have a laugh and a joke – all tradesmen were like that. I used to see him regularly twice a day. But in all that time he never showed any kind of endearment. He never tried to get over-friendly with me or to kiss me, so I never really thought about him that way at all.

When I look back on it I often think that the reason that we got on so well, when we did start going out together, was because we'd seen so much of each other and knew each other so well that I didn't have to keep trying to impress him the way I'd done other men. And I don't have that horrible sick anxiety when I'd said goodnight and made a date to meet again as to whether he was going to turn up the next time. I knew I would see him the following morning.

Admittedly I didn't feel any transports of love but then I didn't want to feel them any more. You know, each time you met a boy you felt, 'This is the one I've been waiting all my life for,' and then you'd realize that if it was you'd have to wait alone because he certainly didn't feel that way about you. I was glad that was over. And we got on fine. He was kind and he was generous. Every time he met me he'd have a box of chocolates under his arm and it was the best seats in the cinema and sometimes even a taxi back home and flowers. He was a kind and generous man and I liked him very much. And he liked me.

We went out several months and eventually we decided that we liked each other enough to make a good basis to get married on. It might sound a bit cold-blooded now but I don't think it was. I mean we liked the same things. Perhaps there was not a lot of emotion – but I'd had emotion. This being up in the heavens one minute and down in the depths the next with a man is no basis for marriage. Because while you'll put up with it before marriage, you don't afterwards and that's the way the rows start. Then again he liked drinking and so did I. So we agreed that we'd get married.

As we'd got very little money between us we decided on a registry office because it was that or a white wedding with all the trimmings – and it doesn't matter who you invite, you never please everybody. You spend a fortune on guests and they go back and compare it unfavourably to other weddings they've been to. I know because I've done the same thing myself. Again, if we'd have had that sort of wedding we'd have had to buy our furniture on the never-never. So we decided on a registry office and furnishing our home for cash. The only thing we did get on hire purchase was the piano. And we had to have one because in those days no working-class home was complete without a piano. Neither of us could play it. I used to bang things out with one finger, same as I do with typing.

It was just as well that we had nothing else on the never-never because we hadn't been married six months when Albert lost his job. There was a dole by then but it wasn't very much money and he was out for a long time. He was just about to go on public assistance which meant having that horrible means test. It was a very lean time for us and the piano had to go back because we couldn't keep the payments up. This was terrible, you see, when they came to take it away. It had to go out the same way as it had come in – through our basement-flat window. It took so long to get that piano out that quite a crowd collected to watch and I felt so mortified. They must all have known that it was going back because we couldn't afford to pay for it. Albert said, 'Don't worry, maybe they'll think it's going to be tuned.' I didn't know whether to cry or laugh, so I said, 'Let's hope none of them heard that remark. It's bad enough them watching our piano going because we can't pay for it, without them knowing that I married a bloody ignoramus.' I didn't mean it of course.

When we got married we couldn't afford a honeymoon,

but Albert had a week off work and we went around looking at London. We used to enjoy going to the various markets. Like the Caledonian Market – it's gone now – where you could get practically anything. One of the stallholders there who spoke in a most cultured voice told us that after he'd put his stall up in the morning he'd wander round the others buying up stuff which he himself then sold. When you get that kind of thing happening there must have been bargains.

Another interesting one was Berwick Market. It was one of those where you could have your wallet stolen as you entered it and buy it back as you left the other end. I'd been there several times with Gladys. It was lovely. They had stalls all down the centre of the road with awnings on them, and the shops on either side had got their awnings out too – it was like a covered market. But it was no place to go alone – that is if you wanted to look at the shops. You had to go in pairs. Not because you might be assaulted physically but because of the strong, intense verbal barrage you were subjected to even if you stopped to look in the shop windows.

Every shop had a tout in the doorway – generally a man – and the moment you stopped and looked they started talking and gradually edging you inside. And once you were inside you were very lucky indeed if you got out without buying something – and generally something you didn't want. Part of their sales technique was to get you right to the end of the shop so that you couldn't slip out. Then it was talk, talk, talk.

I remember once being in one with Gladys. They were

selling her a coat. Normally I reckon I'm a person that can get a word in edgeways but I couldn't. Eventually I burst out, 'If you didn't keep up such a running commentary I might be able to tell my friend whether it suits her or not.' So the salesman whispered in my ear, 'You know, if the boss doesn't hear me talking all the time he thinks I'm not trying to make a sale.' It probably was like that too. If you showed any signs of leaving the shop without buying anything the entire family came in – the proprietor, his wife and any odd relations they'd got there. They would stand there and utter those obvious insincerities like, 'Oh, it's lovely, it makes you look years younger. It's just your colouring' – things like that – and you had to be more than strong-minded to resist their blandishments. We didn't. Gladys got a coat that she didn't want and hardly ever wore. But I hand it to those traders, although I got exasperated at their methods, they knew how to run a shop. After all, the idea of running a shop is to sell things – and they did. And although you vowed you'd never go back – you did.

Another market Albert and I went to was in Leather Lane. The day we went there there were two Indians selling mysterious ingredients from the East. One was an aphrodisiac to give you the sexual urge, well we'd only just got married so we hadn't found any dearth in that line, and the other was a powder – a panacea to cure all ills. They seemed to be doing more trade with the aphrodisiac than the panacea which must have proved something about us British.

Farther down the Lane there was a large crowd around two men. One of them was tying the other up in chains. He took his time but when he'd done it he asked any member of the audience to step up and try to extract him. A man stepped forward – part of the act I suppose – and he tried but couldn't do it. Then the chap who'd done the tying up said, 'Of his own volition and completely unaided he can get out of these chains in sixty seconds. But, before I start, I solicit your coppers.' And he went round with his cap. You should have seen the audience melt – and when the sixty seconds were up and he was out of his chains, there were only six people left and we were two of them. This again must have proved something.

Our two-roomed basement flat in Church Street, Chelsea, may have been a good address but it badly needed re-decorating and of course being newly married we were a bit houseproud, so Albert said he'd have a go at it. He'd never done anything like it before but I told him it was child's play because of my father and brother being in the game; the way they used to do it, it looked like child's play. Like all jobs which real experts do.

Albert decided that he'd paper the kitchen first. You never saw such a mess as we got into. None of the paper seemed to match up. We cut it wrong lengths and the pattern looked terrible. Then it tore because he put too much paste on it – and the last straw was when he stepped into a bowl of size and it shot all over the floor. Eventually it got done and we didn't think it looked too bad. We thought that the fact that the pattern didn't match didn't matter if you didn't examine it too closely. And when you're just married you only look at one thing closely.

Anyway I decided that it wanted a couple of pictures hanging on it – and I didn't want just reproductions that you can buy anywhere and that everybody has. I wanted something original. And I'd read in the paper that morning about an exhibition in one of those galleries in Bond Street. The pictures were by a new artist and the critic had said that the prices were within the reach of all. I imagined I'd get something for about a pound but when I got there, there was nothing under five pounds and the five-pound ones were only the size of a pocket handkerchief. I'd never seen such pictures, gloomy old things they were, dark and sombre scenes – all greys and browns. You felt as though you were in the depths of woe when you looked at them. I expect they were good but I thought they were miserable to look at.

I wandered around about three times. I wasn't going to buy anything. I decided that at first glance. But it looked a bit bad going in, giving it the once over and going out again and I wanted to look knowledgeable. Then one of those assistants came prancing up to me on the balls of his feet and said, 'Can I help you? Is there anything you fancy?' So I said, 'Well, no, they're all too expensive for me.' And I said, 'They're not very pretty, are they?' Well, by the look of horror that came over his face you'd have thought his trousers had just dropped down. 'Pretty,' he said. 'Pretty! Madam we sell paintings, not Christmas cards.' Well, I thought, that was a stupid way of talking. After all's said and done you want something that's going to liven you up, don't you? You don't want to look at the walls and think death's gradually coming ever nearer. We know it is, but we don't want to be reminded of it. Imagine getting up in the morning, going into the kitchen and looking at two of those things. It would drive you straight back to bed again. Anyway I felt very small, mortified, and ignorant at the whole thing – but you can't expect to know everything, can you?

Albert and I were very happy and comfortable in Church Street – though I did sometimes wonder after struggling all those years to get married what all the fuss was about. It didn't seem to me that it was anything to get over-excited about. Mind you, I wasn't any Lady Chatterley and Albert wasn't the gamekeeper. Somebody lent us a book very soon after we were married which I thought jazzed the thing up a bit. The *Kama Sutra*. I suppose you could call it Variations on a Theme. I put it on the bedside table – Albert's side – but as everything went on in the same old way I suppose it never got read.

I found that having a milkman for a husband was a far different proposition from having a milkman when you were in domestic service when you only saw him for a few minutes every day. There were quite a few disadvantages attached to being married to a milkman in as much as he did two rounds a day and for the first round he had to be up at half past four in the morning because he started at half past five. And then he'd come back at ten o'clock for his breakfast and then go off for the second round and back at three for his dinner. That's why of course we got used to such irregular meals and why we're so irregular now – in fact now we've got regular irregularity, if you know what I mean.

Being newly married I couldn't bear to think that he got up on his own at half past four so I got up too, made him a cup of tea and gave him a snack and a sandwich to eat on the round. But fortunately before my enthusiasm had waned he told me that he'd sooner do it on his own. What I think made him decide was that I'm one of those people who, the moment they get out of bed, start talking. I feel like that in the morning. I do more in the morning than in the evening. And I think Albert used to get fed up with my chit-chat. So when that stopped all I had to do was to get breakfast ready for him at ten o'clock. His wages were three pounds five and any commission he got for finding new customers, so we managed quite well. Our rent for the two rooms was fifteen shillings a week.

He went on his rounds by horse and cart. He had a very spirited animal with a disconcerting habit of rearing right up on its hind legs. Albert reckoned it had been a circus horse at one time. He really loved that animal. Agatha was her name but he called her Aggie. And he always used to be talking about Aggie. I got quite jealous. I felt at times he thought more of Aggie than me.

He had a terrible time one day in the winter when there was a thick fog. Aggie was so used to the rounds that while he called at one house she'd walk on to the next one. This particular day walking on in the fog she lost her way and Albert lost his horse and cart. He went wandering around asking people if they'd seen a milkcart anywhere. It took him over an hour to find them. But, jealousy apart, she was a lovely horse. When Albert used to stand on the footboard with the reins in his hand I used to think that he was Ben Hur driving his chariot. I used to feel really proud of him. Him and his Aggie.

His round took him to Maida Vale where some of the ladies of the night used to live. When he used to knock on the door once a week for the money they used to be in bed recovering from the rigours of the night before. Some of them used to offer to pay in kind, but of course as we'd only recently got married he insisted on the money. Other customers used to treat Albert as a bookmaker's runner as well as a milkman. He'd take the slips and the money and pass them over to a bookmaker he knew.

One disastrous day a woman gave him five bob to put on a rank outsider and when Albert came in he handed it to me. 'I'm not putting that money on,' he said, 'the horse won't win – it can't possibly.' Well, the damned thing came in and we had to find three pounds out of our own money to pay her. It was a financial crisis for us.

Many of the customers used to ask Albert to do odd jobs for them – shifting furniture, rolling carpets, even fitting tap washers. We used to get a lot of things that way. Many's the piece of furniture Albert's come home with on the cart and, later, toys for the children. People used to make a friend of the milkman then. They saw him every day and sometimes twice a day. It isn't like now where you give a regular order and he leaves it on your doorstep and if you want anything different you put a note in one of the empty bottles and you only see him when you pay him.

Also of course not many women went out to work – not

working-class women anyway. Most of them had big families and the women used to get lonely. They'd ask Albert in for cups of tea and talk to him as a friend. Many a woman would look at him with a worried face and say, 'Milkman, I've clicked again,' meaning they were pregnant. 'What am I going to do about it?'

Of course Albert didn't know. The only things he knew about was the same old things that everybody knew – hot baths, Beecham's pills, Penny Royal, or quinine – and none of these are any good. I know because I've taken them myself. I remember going to a doctor once to see if he would give me anything and he said the only thing he knew was, 'The hair of the dog that bit you. And,' he said, 'it costs you nothing and you enjoy it.'

That then was Albert's life as a milkman. It was a full life and he enjoyed his work. I think that's what's the matter today with men. Everything is a production-line job with nothing to relieve the mundane. It's no fun. So the only reason they work is for money and when the money isn't right they strike for more. But when you like what you do and take an interest and a pride in it money isn't so important – you're happy – so you're contented. Albert was contented and so was I. It was a very good start to our marriage.

14

OF ALL THE places that we lived in in London Chelsea was the best. Of course it was very different then to what it is now.

The King's Road was a busy one, but none of the people using it looked like they do now – there was none of this Carnaby Street atmosphere. Maybe by the standards of those days the people seemed eccentric – well, the artists did – but there was nothing like the queer collection of bits and pieces that you see strutting up and down encumbering the road.

Some of the artists were indistinguishable from anybody else. Some of them walked around in velvet jackets with flowing ties and beards and perhaps long hair, but at the same time most of them were serious artists. And you felt that their clothes were a necessary corollary to their way of earning a living. They didn't obtrude as though they were some sort of freak society as they seem to now. Most artists have been priced right out of Chelsea now that it has become a popular neighbourhood.

Of course even in those days you'd get the show-offs. Some of them came into our local pub – especially the less serious artists. They'd come in with their clothes and hands all painty and they'd lounge about at the bar talking about perspectives, high-faluting stuff like that. The Chelsea trippers as we used to call the people who came into Chelsea as voyeurs used to buy their drinks under the mistaken impression that they were hobnobbing with some future Turner or Landseer. We used to laugh to watch them being conned.

You could see them lapping it all up. I think they were titillated by the thought that they were mixing with the loose-livers. No doubt some of them were. There's been loose living from time immemorial, hasn't there? But people that are living loose don't go around shouting it from the house tops. It was a fallacy to think that those indulging had it written all over their faces. Many a person who looked the epitome of respectability might have been living the most lurid life.

The artists had their models and they used to come into the pub with them, but whether they were living in immorality you couldn't tell – and you couldn't ask them, could you?

The people there seemed to go with the surroundings. Of all the boroughs I've lived in, Chelsea was the only one that seemed to have a communal society. Everybody seemed to mix easily. The business people, the shopkeepers, the artists, and just ordinary working-class people like us – you didn't feel a class difference somehow. You were some sort of whole.

The nearest we got to any kind of intimacy with an artist was with our landlord and landlady who lived above us. But he wasn't a real artist, he was a sort of amateur dauber. He worked in an office all day and only painted in his leisure time.

Mr West was his name. He was a very short man, and like a lot of very short men he was pompous and wanted to throw his weight around. A lot of short men feel that you're going to overlook them or that you think they're not real men. For instance, he'd been married eight years and they'd only got one child although they really wanted more and Mr West used to consider that this was some kind of reflection on his virility. It wasn't true really because I've known quite a few extremely insignificant men with huge families. I think their wives sort of carry them forward, if you know what I mean.

Anyway this Mr West used to paint his wife in the nude. He painted her naked body and then he'd put different heads on it. He wanted me to sit for him in the nude, too. He promised he'd put a different head on me, too, so that nobody would actually know it was me. That's what he said – there may have been a more obvious reason of course. But Albert wouldn't let me. He wouldn't have minded me sitting for the head and putting it on some nude figure, but for me to be the nude figure, he just wouldn't stand for all that. I didn't really mind. I didn't particularly want to do it. Personally I think any female looks better with some clothes on. Mrs West certainly looked better with hers on. Very few females really look at their best without.

Today nobody takes any notice of nudity – not only in paintings but in real life. But even then to paint nudes was considered a very sort of way-out thing to do. No doubt that was the reason Mr West did it. He wanted to prove something. Real artists don't have to bother whether they look Bohemian or not but Mr West wanted to look like a Bohemian because he wasn't a real artist.

One of the next-door neighbours Albert and I had was a Russian, Boris Borovsky – I forget how it was spelt but that was his name. His wife was English – her name was Stella and a very nice person she was too.

Boris used to wear one of those Cossack hats all the time so that everyone could see he had affiliations with Russia and in the privacy of his own home he used to wear his shirt outside his trousers. He said all the Kulaks did that. I didn't even know what a Kulak was – and I don't now. He was always talking about what a wonderful place Russia was since the Revolution and I couldn't help wondering sometimes why, if it was that good, he didn't go back, but I reckon he knew where he was best off.

I don't know what sort of work he used to do – accounting I think it was. It was something whereby he had to work a lot on his own, so when he came home he was very glad of an audience. He'd talk about the heroism of the Russian workers. He was a great one for the Russian workers. Then he'd say, 'Look at the sailors on the *Potemkin*.' I'd never heard of the *Potemkin* – I didn't even know what it was. It was a long time before I realized it was a battleship. Apparently they had a mutiny on board.

He used to compare the sailors on the *Potemkin* with our sailors that mutinied under Captain Bligh. He said that there was all the difference in the world because the sailors that mutinied on the *Bounty* only mutinied to better themselves, whereas the sailors that mutinied on the *Potemkin* mutinied to better the lot of the workers in all Russia. I hadn't got the courage to tell him that I didn't know anything about the country, that my knowledge of Russia could have been written on the back of a halfpenny stamp. I knew they'd had a Revolution and that they weren't much good in the First World War, that they'd departed from the battlefield with great speed, and that was about all. But when he used to talk like this he used to talk to *me* personally. I thought it was wonderful that someone should talk to me like this and tell me these things. I thought that I was really seeing life on a grand scale.

When I was in domestic service all the maids were interested in was the bits of scandal from upstairs. They didn't come down and talk about culture. Nobody cared about culture then. Mind you, while I listened I used to think that his wife must have got bored with that kind of conversation. I suppose with me you couldn't call them conversations. I mean, they were more monologues in as much as all my part was, 'Oh, really! Well, fancy that! You don't say!' and other equally inane remarks.

Boris had also got very strong views about the place of women in the home. He thought that women's only place was the home and that their whole purpose in life was to look after their husbands and children. They'd got five. In fact he reckoned that half the trouble in Russia was because of the Czarina. That if the old Czar had knocked her about a bit, instead of letting her have her own way in everything, there'd never have been all this trouble with the old mad monk Rasputin.

He said, 'Don't you agree?'

And I said, 'Yes, you're right.'

I'd never even heard of Rasputin. If he'd asked me I'd have said he was some West Indian chap. But I didn't ask questions – just agreed. Because that way I got more conversations. Sometimes he used to act the big man with me. 'I'm master in my house,' he'd say. 'What I say goes. Stella's mind is as my own.' Good solid masculine horseshit.

Little did he know that Stella had a secret life that was nothing to do with him at all.

This Stella was a good milliner and she used to make hats for quite a few of the neighbours. She could have earned very good money in a shop, but he wouldn't let her because he didn't want her to be financially independent. But while he was at work she used to make hats in secret and there used to be a man call regularly. She said he came to buy the hats. Maybe he did but he stayed a very long time doing it, and I wouldn't have thought you had to draw the bedroom curtains to look at hats. No. It's my opinion Stella had an interesting side to her life if Boris had but found out. It's just as well he didn't know as much as he thought he did.

When I got to know her better, we were talking one day and I mentioned Russia.

She said, 'For God's sake don't you start on about that bloody place.' Then she poured out her feelings of boredom and frustration to me.

She said, 'If you'd known Boris as long as I have you wouldn't sit there listening open-mouthed and looking at him as though he was the Great Panjandrum himself like you do. I've heard it all so many times I feel as though I'm going stark raving mad. Why doesn't the stupid bombastic nitwit go back to the Russia he's always talking about, where the workers are so free and where he says they can divorce their wives so easily and where there's free love?

'Love,' she said. 'He doesn't know what the word means. He thinks it's that five-minute exercise I have to suffer with him once a week.

'And the bloody farce is,' she said, 'he doesn't know a thing about Russia – only what he's read. He left there when he was three years old and yet he talks as though he was responsible for the Revolution. I'm sick and tired of it.'

After this outburst I explained to Stella about my lust for knowledge and culture, and how although I was enjoying marriage I got a bit bored. So we thought it would be a good idea if we could collect a few young mothers and have a kind of a club and meet once a week.

We got together about six or eight mothers and we arranged to meet in each other's houses in turns. The idea was that whoever's turn it was should study some political, social, or cultural event and speak about it and then we would have a debate. In that way we thought we'd be able to give our brains a sort of turning over. We thought that we might create some kind of miniature Fabian Society, but instead of promoting socialism alone we were going to promote culture as well. For a while everything went well and then one day someone hadn't had the time to prepare anything, so we hadn't got a subject to discuss and before long this was happening with increasing regularity and the whole thing degenerated into the usual stupid women's chit-chat about what little Mary said, what little Johnnie did, what they'd told the teacher or what new thing they'd bought for their home. And there was nothing we could do about it.

Looking back on it I suppose it was rubbing shoulders in the pubs with the artists and thinkers that made me feel I could change the set ways of women's lives. I couldn't. But eventually I did change my own and I think it was living in Chelsea that opened my eyes to my own educational deficiencies. I wouldn't have missed it for the world.

15

ALBERT GOT CALLED up for the Forces in 1941 – they were having anybody then, as he said.

I'll never forget the day he went because his sister and I saw him off. She was weeping buckets of tears but I wasn't weeping at all. Not because I wasn't sorry to see him go – of course I was – but one gets philosophical about these kind of things. It wasn't as if he was going into the front line. He went into the RAF and not on flying duties – posted to Yorkshire. I was left in London in the front line with three children.

We were living in Lewisham at the time and we had one of those shelters in the garden – Anderson shelters – corrugated-iron things. You dug them down in the garden. And we'd had raids night after night without a break. So he was lucky – he was leaving that. Mind you, Albert never used to turn a hair. He used to sit in the shelter totting up his day's work. He was a marvellous person to have during a raid because he literally didn't feel anything. It wasn't that he was consciously being brave and heroic. It just didn't worry him. He thought that the probability that a bomb would fall on our particular little shelter was mathematically impossible. But I used to dread it because the railway used to run at the back of our garden and the sparks from the trains used to shoot up in the air. Why we troubled about blackout I don't know.

We had no end of incendiary bombs. We were supposed to rush out and throw earth all over them. But Albert would never come out because he hated talking to the neighbours. We spent hours and hours in that shelter in the garden. I used to be afraid; I'm not going to pretend I wasn't. I was deathly afraid, night after night, but I had the children to think about and if you don't show fear the children are not afraid either. So I couldn't show fear for their sake. If it had been just me and Albert I'd probably have been a quivering wreck.

But when they called him up I didn't really see the sense in staying in London with three young children on my own. My parents were still living in Hove and they told me they could get me a house down there to rent since a lot of people were leaving because of what they called the hit and run raids. They weren't really that. I mean there was nothing to hit in Hove, but the German planes unloaded their bombs there because then they had more chance of getting back. As a matter of fact it was funny that the house we eventually lived in there got more damage than our place in London.

But of course I'd lived in Hove as a girl – and in a way

it was like going back home for me. We also used to take our annual holiday there but we had to give that up – not because we couldn't afford it; after all we could stay with Mum. We couldn't afford the consequences. You see we'd taken our holidays in June, July, and August for three years running and our three children were born in March, April, and May. Well, if we'd kept on going down Lord knows how many children we would have had.

We couldn't really afford three children anyway. We should have stayed at two but as the first two were boys I was dying to get a girl and the doctor said to me when I told him this, 'Feed your husband up on pickles, spices, and onions and then you'll probably get one.' So I did that. I rather like spicy foods anyway. Albert didn't know what I was doing. But it was all rubbish because I still got a boy, and yet everyone had told me it was going to be a girl. All those wise women said, 'Oh, you're carrying it different this time – it's all round instead of being stuck out in the front.' People tell you this nonsense when you're carrying a baby, and they are mainly spinsters who do so. It's a funny thing to me that people who have never had any babies always seem to know more about it than those that have. To my mind that doctor should have been struck off for giving me that load of cobblers, or I should have had my head examined. I don't know which.

Anyway it was a boy, born on a Sunday. All my children were born on Sundays. I don't know whether that means anything – all were boys and all weighed eight and a half pounds. You couldn't have anything more monotonous than that, could you?

With the last one, when Albert went down to get the mid-wife in the morning she said, 'Oh, I'm just going off to church.' Very annoyed she was that I was having it then. What did she expect me to do – wait until after the service? It's true, I did – until after the evening service, much to her annoyance.

It took ages. It always did take me ages to have children. Some people can drop them like a hot cake. I do think they're lucky. The first of my babies took nearly three days to arrive. When they do it's never worth it. I mean, when you see them, little miserable-looking red objects they are, bawling away and all the relatives come and say; 'Oh, isn't it lovely!' and even a mother's eye can see it isn't lovely at all. I like them eventually but I've never been blind to the fact that they don't look anything at all to start with. But your relatives tell you it's marvellous. Then they say it looks like Albert or it looks like you and you don't want it to look like either of you because you know perfectly well it won't get on in the world if it does.

At any rate when this one was finally born it was about seven o'clock in the evening. I suppose the midwife did think it was a long time in coming but she didn't think it was as long a time as I did. When it arrived she said, 'It's an-other boy, Mother.' And I said, 'I don't care if it's a monkey so long as it's got here at last.' She was really taken aback. I could sense that and she said, 'I look upon every child I deliver as sent down from heaven, planted in earth's soil to grow up as a flower.' But she was a spinster and had never planted anything in the ground, otherwise she wouldn't have talked like that.

It's all daft, isn't it? This rubbish you read in romantic magazines – Charles Garvice and Ethel M. Dell – as if it was something mysterious and beautiful. It's a revolting business. People walk in and out the room when you're in the most peculiar position, you're looking your worst and you're suffering the tortures of the damned. It isn't a bit like what you read in books. Not for the mother. It's all right for the father – he just sits around.

The reason I had three children was because birth control at prices the working class could afford was only just beginning to come in. The well-to-do have always been able to have birth control either by doctors providing them with things, or with cosy abortions if they didn't work. But all we did was try to be careful. Nobody told me about the 'safe' period. We didn't chat about those sort of things then.

Mind you, I don't think there is any safe period. The Catholics call it Roman Roulette down our way. I'm not one but when you look at some of the huge families that Roman Catholics have, either they wanted a huge family or they kept slipping up badly. It depends a lot on the sort of husband you've got, doesn't it? I mean if a husband can regulate his desires to the safe period it may be all right. But what I know about men, they never regulate themselves. It just depends on how they feel. If they've had a damned good day at work they feel like a kind of a whoopee at night and they don't bother to inquire. Or if you tell them it's not all right they say, 'Oh well, let's take a chance.' They don't have to have them, you see. Makes all the difference in the world.

After I'd had two children I heard about a birth-control place in Ladbroke Grove for working-class women. It was in a very poor neighbourhood next door to the employment exchange; at that time there was a lot of unemployment around and the men used to hang about outside. The premises were a converted shop, and though it wasn't labelled birth-control clinic all the men knew what it was; the women who went there used to feel so conspicuous, we used to slink up to and into the place as though we were doing something really depraved. The men used to grin as you went in – but it was worse when you came out. 'All ready for it now, darling,' they'd say – or words to that effect.

The methods they had then weren't nearly as convenient as they are now. They were somewhat irksome to say the least and you had to keep coming back to be refitted. The thing was unattractive to look at and uncomfortable to wear. And you had to wear it most of the time. I mean you couldn't ask your husband after you'd given him his supper whether he would be liable to require the contraption tonight – it's not a sort of fireside conversation, is it? Anyway people like us didn't discuss things like that – not working-class families. The whole thing was shrouded in gloom and mystery. You went to bed and you drew the blinds and you put the lights out and everything went on in the dark. It was all bound up with the way English people felt then about sex. Even amongst married people it was sort of faintly illegal. I suppose we consider that anything that's nice and that we get for nothing must be illegal. As far as that contraption was concerned, if you went to bed without it and then discovered that it was required, it was either too late or it was the death knell of that spontaneous combustion that the love act ought to be. I mean, you just imagine when you're sort of full of love and somebody nudges you and says, 'Have you or haven't you?' If you haven't, you've got to get out of bed and do all the preliminaries, so by the time you get in again all the emotions you had have evaporated in the cold night air. So that's why we had three.

After Albert joined up I moved down to Hove. My mother got me a six-roomed house for a pound a week. It was cheap even then. Of course we'd not had a house in London and we'd only got enough furniture for three rooms so I put a bit in every room. At least everybody had a bedroom to themselves. The boys thought it was marvellous all having a room each instead of all being in one as they were before.

In spite of the fact that people were leaving the town there still seemed to be plenty about and a fair amount of life considering that it was wartime. And there were the troops, Canadian troops, not American. It was really too marvellous for words after living in London, where the ratio of women to men was about five women to one, to have all these spare men knocking around. And they'd come up and talk to you. They used to spin you the tallest yarns how they'd got ranches out in Calgary and Alberta and places like that and hunting lodges in the mountains. I didn't believe them, of course, though I pretended to. What did it matter – they looked so marvellous in their uniforms?

Our local pub used to be full of them and six formed

themselves into a singing group and they'd entertain us. They're very sort of forthcoming, Canadians; they don't suffer with inhibitions like the English. And they used to start singing and the whole pub would join in. Even Albert when he was on leave liked it and he's not very gregarious. We used to have marvellous times at the local. Mind you, anywhere looks better to a female if there's a lot of men about even although you're not having anything to do with them – just the fact that they're there and they're surplus.

In a way I felt sorry for the British soldiers because these Canadians took the girls away from them. If you went into a pub with one of ours, he'd buy you one half-pint and you'd have to sit and sip it the entire evening. Whereas of course the Canadians could afford to buy whiskies and gin. Can you wonder that all the girls went stark raving mad for them? This business of everybody being so virtuous and all walking on the straight and narrow path – it's only because the opportunity is lacking.

At that time I was doing daily work, charring. With the boys to keep, Albert's money as a corporal wasn't enough so I had to go out. The lady at one of the places I worked kept open house for the Canadians: officers of course not troops: and from time to time these officers would start chatting me up. They loved Brighton. When they had left Canada they thought they were in for a grim time but as they said, it was not only a home from home but it was far more. I remember Madam colouring up a bit when one of them said this, perhaps she thought I didn't know what was going on. Then they'd say how hospitable people were over here and I'd say, 'Yes, but you wouldn't find them like this in the normal way, it's just that the war brings out the best in people as well as the worst.' That was a sort of innuendo.

Well, month after month went by and then one morning I woke up and somehow I could sense a difference in the town, a kind of quietness. I couldn't think what it was. Something seemed to be missing. Anyway I went to work and the lady said, 'They've gone.' 'Who's gone?' I said. 'All the Canadians have gone.' 'They couldn't have,' I said, 'they were here yesterday.' 'But didn't you hear, all through the night those lorries? They've all gone. I shall be absolutely lost having nothing to do for them,' she said. I wasn't quite sure what she meant by that.

I've often wondered though what became of them all. I've never met any who came back. Some girls I knew got married to them and left to join them after the war, and of course there was the quota of unmarried mothers. But Brighton was like a gold-rush town around that time – like Canada had been with the Klondike – one moment it was filled with riotous assembly, with laughter and noise and then it was as if the mines were depleted. Suddenly the men were gone. Mind you, I think the publicans thought the gold had gone too; their trade fell right off.

Then gradually the town got back to normal as the local men came out of the Forces, but before that happened it seemed to me like a ghost town and my idea of a ghost town is a town full of females.

When Albert was demobbed in 1945 we were faced with a problem. He could have had his old job back but that meant moving to London and we couldn't get anywhere to live there. Also the boys were doing well at school. So we decided to stay where we were. Albert tried to get a job as a milkman but at that time there weren't any going.

When he went to the labour exchange there was the choice of two places. One was with the gas company as a kind of stoker and the other one was a furniture remover. So he went to the furniture removers and they offered him the job. The wages were very low, only five pounds a week which even in 1945 wasn't much. But even at that it was better than it had been. In the old days it was like being a docker. You went into the warehouse and if there was no work you got sent home again without pay. But although the wages were low the work was interesting which I think is important. I mean it's far more important to have low wages and do a job that you really like doing than to have high wages and grind away week after week at something that bores you to tears.

It wasn't static, not sitting on your backside in an office from nine to six. It wasn't even like a milk round where you're going around the same old customers for seven days a week twice a day. You're going everywhere or anywhere. Albert went up to Scotland, into Wales, right down into Cornwall and he was meeting different people all the time. And he learnt about furniture and antiques of all kinds.

Eventually he became a packer because he was such a careful workman and he used to see to the most expensive china – like those Dresden figures that were in all nooks and crannies and worth thousands of pounds. He still got the same money but he looked on it as a sort of promotion. The hours were irregular – when you're moving someone's furniture you can't say, 'I'm knocking off now,' when it comes to five or six o'clock. It can't be left in the street, can it? But we didn't mind irregular hours because we'd been used to them when he was a milkman.

At first I got very worried when he was late coming back at nights. I used to think of all the terrible road accidents that there were and wonder if something of the sort had happened to him. But, as he said, if anything did hit their pantechnicon they wouldn't have suffered I remember one very foggy night, it was ten o'clock and they should have been back at five. I was that worried I rang up the manager of the firm to see if he'd had any news of them.

He said, 'Mrs Powell, I'm worried too. They've got ten thousand pounds' worth of antique furniture on board.'

There's words of comfort for you!

I said, 'To hell with your antiques, I'm thinking about Albert.'

That riled him. 'Well,' he said, 'what do you think I can do? Take a lantern out to look for him? If so, you've got another bloody think coming.'

And he slammed the receiver down. Talk about old-world courtesy.

Albert's had some strange jobs. One place they went to was an old lady's house where she kept twenty-four cats. The council had put a compulsory moving order on her. It was too terrible for words. The place smelt like a sewer. And this old dear was in tears because these cats had got to

369

go to a cats' home. She knew them all individually – she'd lived with them for years. They'd each got their own basket with their name on. Albert and the others hated doing it but if it hadn't been them it would have been someone else.

At another place they were getting a piano up the stairs and halfway it stuck and they couldn't move it up or down. Well the old dear whose piano it was came down with plates of Hovis bread and butter. She said, 'Hovis gives you strength.' Well, I don't know whether it did or not, but when they'd eaten it they gave a mighty heave gouging a great lump out of the wall and the piano went up. The company had an extremely irate letter from the landlord afterwards and they had to repair the damage. But as I said they ought to have passed the letter on to the baker, it was his fault.

Then there was a couple of young men that lived together – they had to move six times. Very charming young men so Albert said, but probably they got so charming around the place that they had to move on. Anyway every single thing in the house was marked with their initials. Except the pots under the bed – they were marked HIS and HERS.

16

THE THREE MONTHS that I spent in hospital – I had two periods of six weeks each – were very different indeed.

I first went because I had a gastric ulcer. It was in 1944 and there was no National Health Service then. I was suffering from indigestion according to my doctor.

I said to him, 'I can't understand why I can't breathe properly.'

But he said it was indigestion and indigestion it had to be till I had a haemorrhage and was rushed into hospital to have a blood transfusion.

I often think that these people who talk about blood and breeding and who have to have blood transfusions don't know what poor old plebeian stuff they've got knocking around in them. I remember when they were giving it to me I said, 'I hope you're giving me blue blood, I'm only used to the best.'

The nursing was splendid but the food and amenities for the patients in the public wards were deplorable. And the lack of privacy most distressing, especially for older people and particularly for those who had gone into hospital for the very first time.

None of the beds had curtains and only in the direst circumstances did they put screens around them. Some of the old people used to complain bitterly about this but it never did them any good because the more they complained the less consideration they got.

I always found during my stay in hospitals, and that includes before and after the National Health Service, that it's best to accept everything that happens to you with the spirit of Job because that's the only way you can really enjoy it. That way you get a reputation for being long suffering and uncomplaining and you're held up to the other patients as a shining light.

The nurses say, 'Look at Mrs Powell, she doesn't ring her bell all day long and she doesn't ask us to keep doing this, that and the other for her.'

The fact that all the other patients get to detest you doesn't matter because they're not looking after you. It's the nurses you've got to rely on for your comfort. So I never complained about anything. I just let it all happen to me.

Once I had recovered sufficiently to be able to walk around the other patients soon forgot their animosity because I did little jobs for them – like getting a jug of water or something out of their locker or bringing them their tea. And then patients are always dying to talk to someone about their home, their husbands and their children. Curiously enough I never found many patients wanted to talk about their operations or what they were in there for. Not then.

When they get home they do, but I think it's too near to them in hospital. They try to pretend almost that it doesn't exist. It's rather like a conversation I once overheard between two women.

One was saying to the other, 'Oh, I've got such pains in my stomach and I have to keep on taking these Rennies to relieve it.'

So the other said, 'Haven't you been to the doctor, then?'

She said, 'No. I'm scared to go to the doctor because he might send me to the hospital and they might say it's cancer.'

Well, the pain wouldn't go away would it? But she thought that if she didn't give it a name, it wasn't there. And that's how I found they were in hospital.

Although as I've said I kept quiet, before the National Health Act there was plenty to complain about in the public wards.

The meals were the worst thing. They used to be served on battered old tin trays with no cloth on of course, and as I was in there with ulcers it was mainly cod that tasted and felt like cottonwool. And the mashed potatoes had hard concrete lumps in them and were nearly always stone cold. You really had to be hungry to eat it. Mostly the sweet was a milk pudding and it was either so stiff you could have bounced it on the floor, or it was hard grains floating around in milk.

And when it was time for the bedpans the nurses used to

deal them out on beds as you would a pack of cards. And there we used to sit parked on them, in full view of each other, and there was one toilet roll between four. And we'd throw it from bed to bed and sometimes we'd miss and it would roll down the ward like a large streamer. And we'd go into hysterics of mirth. It was the only way to accept the humiliation of it all.

That was my first stay in hospital and I hoped it would be my last.

But some years after, by this time there was the National Health Service, I discovered that I had a lump about the size of a small marble underneath my breast. I went straight to the doctor and he sent me to the hospital for an examination.

And what a change I found. You were treated as though you mattered. Even the waiting-room was different. No dark green paint, whitewash, and wooden benches. There were separate chairs with modern magazines – not the kind that Noah had around in the Ark.

They told me that I should have to have a minor operation for the cyst to be removed, but that I would only be in there about a week.

And again what a difference I saw. The beds for instance. The bed that I'd had before was like lying on the pebbles on Brighton beach. I got to know every lump in it and used to arrange myself around them. But now I had a rubber mattress. I felt as though I could have lain there for ever.

And the food was beautiful. All served on brightly coloured trays with the right cutlery. I remember one day I was waiting for my lunch when the matron came round; she saw my tray and said to the nurse, 'Isn't this patient having fish for her lunch today?'

And the nurse said, 'Yes, Matron, she is.'

'Well why hasn't she got a fish knife and fork then? Change it instantly.'

I was amazed. I couldn't have cared less because we hadn't got any fish knives and forks at home. But that just shows you, doesn't it?

And there was variety. I don't think we ever saw the same meal twice in one week and that needs some doing. It just showed what kind of kitchen staff they'd got. Presumably under the National Health Act they could afford to pay them more wages than before. When I was in service you were considered the lowest of the low if you worked in hospital kitchens.

And every bed had got curtains and they were drawn not only at bedpan time but at any time you were attended to.

There was only one thing that was exactly the same and I suppose always will be and that is that neither nurses, house surgeons nor the visiting specialists would ever answer any questions about your condition. In fact they never stayed long enough by your bed for you to get the question out.

I think that a generation that's brought up on *Emergency Ward 10* and *Dr Kildare* must suffer great disillusionment when they go into hospital. In all the time I've spent there no doctor or house surgeon has ever sat on my bed talking to me about my complaint.

As for the specialists they don't even look at you. They seem to stare right over your head. They frighten you to death. They stand there looking so stern you feel you've got every ailment under the sun and you're not likely to last much longer and they're weighing up who's coming into your bed when you've gone.

And the nurses seem to think that along with physical deterioration goes mental deterioration. You get these young nurses saying, 'Come along, Mother, be a good girl. Put your nightie on and pop into bed.' As though you were suffering from senile decay and didn't understand plain English. It riled me the way they did that. I hate being jollied along at any time, let alone when in hospital.

As I said, I went into this hospital to have this cyst removed from my breast and the night before the operation the Sister stuck a form under my nose for me to sign. I hate forms at the best of times and when I'd recovered from the shock I read it and discovered that I'd got to agree that in the event of them discovering that I needed major surgery I was prepared to have it done. At once I knew that they were going to slash my breast off otherwise why go into all this palaver if it was just a cyst.

So I signed – and I knew what it meant.

I wasn't shocked when I came to after the operation and found I was bandaged up in miles of bandages. I knew it hadn't been just a cyst.

I asked the nurse of course but she just said, 'Go to sleep, Mother.'

But Mother knew. The nurse wouldn't tell me because she felt I was going to suffer from the shock. But I'd suffered from the shock the night before when I read that form.

About a couple of days after the operation the house surgeon told me that they had found a tumour there and had to
remove the breast, but that it was a non-malignant one and
I would be going home shortly. It didn't take me long to get
over the operation and I was soon able to get up and help a
bit.

We had some lively people in that ward. There was an
unfortunate woman there who used to suffer with the most
rude noises. She couldn't help it. But when she let one go
the patients would call out, 'There's a bomb just gone off,
Nurse,' and then a little later, 'It's all right, the all clear's
gone now.'

There was another woman. She was only in there to have
her bunions done. She was a card if ever there was one.

She said to me, 'This is the first time I've had a bed to
myself for forty years.'

So I said, 'Is it? It must be awful being separated after all
those years.'

'It isn't,' she said. 'It's bloody marvellous. Sharing a bed
with my old man is nothing but sweat and swill.'

She said she wasn't going back to sharing a bed, which
shows that hospital life has a lot to answer for.

Some of the patients looked at me a bit queerly. They told
me later that they thought I'd have delayed reaction emotion about losing my breast. But strangely enough I wasn't
ever really upset.

My mother was more. She kept weeping like mad by my
bedside. But if you're a young girl and you're hoping to get
married it's a far more serious thing, isn't it? You'd have to

tell your young man and explaining it away would be a bit embarrassing. But I'd got a husband who I knew wouldn't think any the worse of me because of it. And when they told me it was non-malignant I was quite happy about it. Naturally I would have preferred to have kept it. It wasn't the kind of thing that I could chuck off and not know I hadn't got. It's not the kind of an appendage that doesn't matter whether you have it or not. It's not like your appendix. But no, I wasn't too upset about it.

Then three days before I was to go home they came up to me again, put the curtains round the bed and I prepared myself for another shock.

In came the Sister this time. I'd always thought of her as a bit of a martinet. Mind you, you need a Sister that's a martinet because the other hospital I was in the Sister was very strict indeed and I used to feel sorry for the nurses, but we realized when she went on holiday what a difference a strict Sister made to our lives because once she was out of the way the nurses didn't care a bit. They used to laugh and joke and make the most terrible row and we never got half the attention that we had when she was there. But this one I'd thought was a hard woman – unfeeling – but what a change. She was kindness itself to me. She sat there by my bed for half an hour. She told me that they'd got a report back from the Marie Curie hospital in Hampstead that my growth was malignant and that I'd got to go there and have radium treatment.

It was only then that I really thought about cancer. As soon as she mentioned the Marie Curie I knew what the hospital was for so I knew I'd got cancer and I was very upset then for the rest of that day. I know I wept a few times to myself and that. The thing I asked Sister to do for me was to catch my mother before she came in to visit me and tell her because I didn't feel as though I could. I knew she'd be terribly upset about it, which she was.

But strangely enough by next morning I'd recovered. I thought – oh, well, here goes. Lots of people go to the Marie Curie and they don't all die. I mean if you've got to have cancer you couldn't have it in a better place than in the breast because once you've had it removed most of it's gone.

So by the next day I'd got over it and as I wasn't due to go for a week I asked if I could go home. 'No,' came the answer. They wouldn't let me go because they were frightened I wouldn't come back. But after a day or two I got lively and me and this woman with bunions kicked up such a shindy larking around that Sister said, 'All right, you've won, you can go home for the weekend but don't forget to come back.' Of course, I would come back in any case.

When I got to this Marie Curie hospital in Hampstead I found there were many far worse than me because they'd let it go such a long time before they'd been to a doctor, and it had spread and gone into an arm as well. So really and truly it really does pay to see a doctor in the very early stages because it never affected me in that way.

I used to go every day for radium treatment – just five minutes a day. It was in a little room that there was this sort of Heath Robinson contraption that hovers over you. You have to lie down and there's a door about a foot thick, which is closed on you and of course I suffer appallingly from claustrophobia. I didn't mind the radium treatment but the thought of being shut in that room was almost too much for me. But the nurses were very good. There was a little glass window and they'd look at me. But although it was only five minutes it seemed like half an hour and I'd imagine they'd forgotten the time.

Anyway I had six weeks of that treatment and then I went home. I had to go back once a month for the first three months and then once every three months and then once a year. I still do now although it was over ten years ago and I've never had a recurrence.

When I got back came the problem of a bra. The old bras I'd got were no good at all. The Marie Curie had given me the address of where to go for one on the National Health Service. Maybe now it's a better model but at that time, believe me, it was pure stodge. An appalling pink-coloured thing, a cross between a liberty bodice and a strait jacket. I've never seen anything like it in my life. I thought they would have tried to do something better than that. I mean just at a time when you feel mutilated and even though you try to laugh about it, you do feel mutilated, you'd have thought they'd have produced something artistic.

Well I accepted it because it was on the National Health but I didn't wear it. I bought myself a pair of falsies and a bra to go with them. I only needed one falsie, but they wouldn't sell them singly. There's a waste of money. It was the cult of the huge bra à la Jane Russell and breasts was all coming in then and everybody was endeavouring to look twice the size they really were. So perhaps it was as well I didn't get them singly otherwise I'd have looked unbalanced.

Of course wearing a falsie can be a very tricky thing. The first time I put a bathing costume on and went swimming I was very disconcerted to see it bobbing merrily around on top of the waves. I hastily stuffed it back but I felt awful. I don't know whether anyone noticed or not but it was a pale pink colour and it looked most peculiar. Anyway after that I used cottonwool. I thought of buying one of those bras that you blow up and you're provided with a little pump. I would only have blown up one side but then I thought it would be a bit awkward if I had a puncture. I couldn't really carry a repair outfit around with me, could I? So I gave up that idea.

But though I joked about it then and joke about it now, losing a breast does something to you in a sort of psychological way. You never feel the same person again. Not to yourself. Maybe you seem the same to other people. In the beginning you feel degraded and then you don't feel a complete woman any more. All right there's things on the market to make you look the same externally but there's nothing on the market that makes you feel the same internally.

But don't let me make a big thing out of this psychological feeling. What I would say to anyone would be if they suspect anything like that is to go straight away to a doctor. Mine was only a breast operation – one amongst many, but I made a friend at the Marie Curie who was there for an internal cancer operation – and a very big operation indeed. She was in hospital for months, but now she's out, she's doing a full-time job in domestic service and she still only has to go in once a year like me. She caught it in what were the early stages and although the operation was a big one because it was internal it hasn't spread all over her body. But I had a sister-in-law who suffered the pains and wouldn't go in and when she had to it was far too late. If it's caught early mostly it can be cured and even if you have to have the operation I had you can still live a very happy life.

17

SOME PEOPLE JOIN evening classes because they're bored and want company. I didn't. I just wanted to be able to converse with my sons. I found that I wasn't able to do this because they'd all won scholarships and gone to the grammar school. There they were, eleven and thirteen and fifteen, sitting at the table talking among themselves and Albert and I were completely left out. It didn't worry Albert – he didn't care whether he conversed or not. He likes to be quiet but I enjoy making conversation and I hated being excluded from it.

You hear children say that they've got nothing in common with their parents and the psychiatrists tell you that parents mustn't become divorced from their children, that they must make efforts to understand them. They say you don't understand them because if you never talk to them you can't understand them. As well as cooking, washing and doing the cleaning for them you've got to be able to talk to them otherwise they consider you less than the dust. They won't realize that you've worked so darned hard looking after them that you're tired. Oh no, if you're not bothering to keep your old brains exercised then there's something wrong with you. There's nothing wrong with them if they don't understand these things.

Anyway I found that conversation was reduced to the weather and the headlines in the newspapers and after you'd said that there was nothing else to say. Then I read an article that said that the more one soaks up knowledge the more the brain expands to absorb it. Something like Parkinson's Law where the work expands so as to fill the time available for its completion, which is the truest law I've ever known. You've only got to look at our town council's employees. They demonstrate Parkinson's Law to a tee. So I decided that although I'd never believed in keeping up with the Joneses, I'd try and keep up with the boys – and that to do this I'd got to start educating myself by going to evening classes. I thought, well, I'll try this theory out.

It didn't work with me this Parkinson's Law – maybe because I started too late. I thought, oh, well, the more you take on the more your brain expands – and I took on three things straight away – French, social science, and something called metaphysical philosophy. This last one I took as a sort of status symbol. The very name of it! I imagined myself surprising all my sons with some gem of intellectual conversation that I'd got through this metaphysical philosophy. A sort of female Oscar Wilde I visualized myself as, with repartee and wit flashing round the table. But after six weeks of classes I hadn't understood a word of metaphysical philosophy. The dictionary defined it as abstruse and abstract and, believe me, the dictionary definition was correct. Certainly it was abstruse.

We had to do homework on it and we were picked at random to get up in class and explain in layman's terms what we'd written. Well, I copied mine clear out of the book. I hadn't any idea what it meant. I was just hoping that I'd get away with it. Unfortunately I was picked one night to get up and I couldn't say that I'd copied it out of the book. It would have been too terrible for words, especially when you want to be a big noise and I always liked to be the big noise. So I stumbled through it somehow or other and the teacher said, 'I don't really think you've grasped what it means yet.' I thought – no, you and me both because even if you've grasped what it means you can't explain it in lay terms. So after six weeks I gave it up. I didn't bother about metaphysical philosophy any more. But I did keep on with the French and social science.

Social science I thought would have some bearing on life; the social approach, not history with dates and figures or what's been. I thought it would enable me to co-relate the sort of life I was leading to the world around and would give me an idea of what made people tick – that kind of thing. It didn't, but that's what I thought it would do.

I suppose I started where most people were leaving off. There must have been a lot that I should have studied before I even took on social science but I didn't know. People used to say, why didn't I take up a craft, but I didn't want to do things with my hands – tatting, lampshade-making, glove-making and things like that. I'd quite enough to do with my hands running a home and I didn't want to start threading beads or petit point or making pictures out of bits of felt. That sort of thing's all very well if you've got an artistic sense, but I haven't. I'm devoid of it. No – I wanted to use my brains; I wanted to be able to talk to my boys. I wanted to be able to baffle them with social science, then we could sit at the table and have unintelligible conversations, all of us, because as soon as there was a gap in what they said I could rush in with mine, and they wouldn't be able to understand me any more than I could understand them.

The French course was ludicrous. In my imagination I thought that as they were learning French they would help me. I didn't realize that the rot had set in with regards to children and their parents. My generation had revered their parents; whatever their parents said was law and gospel and you believed what they said and you gave them respect as well as love. But by the time I became a parent children no longer thought that what their parents said was true or gave them any respect at all. When I used to come out with my little *bons mots* in French they hooted with laughter at my pronunciation. I pronounced the words as they looked. I got old Hugo's French dictionary out at the table and I'd say, '*Voulez vous passer le sel s'il vous plaît*,' saying it like you see it in print.

And they'd say, 'Mum wants the vinegar? Pepper, Mum? Pass Mum the mustard, Dad.'

The little blighters knew I meant pass the salt but they purposely misunderstood.

When I said, '*Chacun à son goût*,' they'd say, 'Get up, Dad, you're sitting in something. You've got your arse in the goo.' They just made fun of me all the time. But I plodded on. Once I start anything I do it till the bitter end, except for metaphysical philosophy.

The teachers, too, vary in their approach. I've had ever so many kinds of teachers. Some of them have the idea of ramming a lot of facts and figures down you – perhaps it's because they were taught that way themselves and they haven't been able to get out of it, but students who go voluntarily want the lessons made interesting. They naturally find facts and figures unpalatable and that's why I think attendances fall off. Some teachers don't make allowance for the fact that all we go there for is leisure-time activities, that we haven't had much schooling and that we require time to assimilate knowledge. They get impatient. And you have only got to make people who are a bit insecure about their early education feel that they don't know enough for them not to come any more. They're very vulnerable. You're vulnerable with your children but at least you can laugh it off. It may hurt you – it got beneath my skin even in my own home. But in classes if you have a teacher who makes you feel that you're ignorant, you think well what the bloody hell am I doing here? You haven't gone there to be humiliated so you stay away. Not all teachers are like that. Some are very good indeed. But still you can sense that some are thinking to themselves, she couldn't understand this when she was young so what hopes has she of understanding it now?

We students know that teachers are often tired. That they've been teaching all day and that this is only an extra to them because they want to earn a bit more money. The advantage is that with us at any rate at the beginning everybody is very enthusiastic. They want to learn. And yet again it's funny because in any class where you have to use your brain attendances keep dropping. You may start with about thirty and you're lucky to have got ten by the time the course is over.

1 don't know about the handicraft courses. I only attended one. It was flower-arranging and that was a lark if ever there was one; it was an absolute riot. The teacher must have had a marvellously aesthetic eye because she could make the most wonderful arrangements out of next to nothing, from the most unlikely materials.

She set us a task one week. She gave each of us a list of things that we had to make an arrangement with; my list said two or three smooth round pebbles, a piece of driftwood, a cabbage leaf and a stick of celery. I thought to myself: this is me, it's right up my street. I got the stones and the driftwood down on the beach and it didn't take me long to get a couple of sticks of celery and a cabbage leaf. First I tried arranging it on a flat dish among some wire mesh in a sort of – well it was a kind of . . . I thought it was a . . . but it wasn't, so I took it all out and I got a lump of plasticine and started again. I stuck the stones round it and the cabbage leaf (wilting) and the two sticks of celery (brown at the ends). You ought to have seen the result. I carted it up there just for a laugh. Everybody had got their arrangements, some had very fine muslin cloth draped over them, some in cardboard boxes and all were very lovely – even I could see that. And I came up with mine in an old brown carrier bag.

So they said to me, 'Where's your arrangement?'

I said, 'In this bag.'

'In a bag,' they said. 'Well, what is it?'

'Well,' I said, 'it's a cabbage leaf and two sticks of celery and pebbles.'

When I got it out everybody nearly died of laughter. They made ever such rude remarks. So they lost one pupil at handicrafts.

It was when I was fifty-seven that I decided that I would study in real earnest, not just as a leisure-time activity but where I really sat for something. Mind you, I'd been in earnest about the other things. I'd enjoyed them, had a lot of fun, made a lot of friends, and acquired a lot of knowledge. But I thought I'd like to do something in competition with the younger ones. So I went to the technical college.

I found joining the class there a far different proposition from joining the leisure-time activities. In the leisure-time activities most of the people were about my age because we were doing things because we'd retired or because our families had grown up. But studying for 'O' level were young people who for some reason or other had failed when they were fifteen and were trying again. So when I tried to sign on I thought I might be rejected on account of my age.

I waited for hours in the queue; on the signing-on days there are queues everywhere. You'd think that half the town was dying to go to learn. So I waited in the queue and when I finally reached the young man who was behind the desk he looked at me in amazement.

He said, 'What are you doing here, this isn't a leisure-time activity, you know? This is studying leading to an examination.'

'I know that,' I said.

So he said, 'Well, you obviously don't want to do that. You're in the wrong place.'

I said, 'I know what I'm doing. Is there any reason why I can't take "O" level English literature?'

That and the way I said it put him back on his heels. 'So he said, 'Well, no, I suppose there isn't really.'

Anyway I finally convinced him I was serious. But he wouldn't sign me on.

He said, 'I think you'd better go and see the principal.'

I don't know why. So I had to join another queue. Anyway when I finally got to the principal he also looked astonished.

He said, 'You know this is a two-year course at least. It could be three if you don't pass it in two years. Are you prepared to do all that? It's not much good starting and then leaving because you might be taking somebody else's place.'

That was all a load of my eye and Betty Martin, believe me. By the time the first year ended there was room for another half as many again. I made what I thought were keen noises.

'Oh, well,' he said, 'I suppose it's all right,' in a very half-hearted manner.

He thought it was a waste of his time and my time.

Mind you, he was quite right. He's not there for benevolent reasons. He's there to see that young people who
haven't got an education get one. And I didn't blame him
in the least. Why should he bother about the older people?
It was up to the older people to be very self-assertive for
themselves and I certainly was.

Anyway I joined the original queue again. I was in
queues about two hours that night. Finally I got up to the
young man again.

'Oh, it's you is it,' he said.

So I said, 'He says it's all right.'

'Oh, well,' he said, 'then it must be. Anyway you'll be
glad to know there's another old lady in the class apart
from you.'

When I got to the class I found the other old lady was
around forty so it was really very flattering. I thought
that either she was a lot older than she said or I was a lot
younger-looking. Still, contrary to all scepticism, I was in.

The class started off about thirty strong. Some took their
exam in a year because they'd only just failed before they left
school and all they needed was a bit of brushing up. I think
it's stupid that when you've failed an examination they don't
tell you what particular thing you failed in – whether it was
grammar, the essay, the dictation, the spelling, or what. It's
left to you to realize for yourself. So you don't know what
you should be swotting. I felt sorry for the youngsters, they
were so confused. But some of the class took the exam after
a year and as they never came back I assumed that they had
passed. My guess had been quite right: the class started off

with thirty but it had dropped right down to fourteen and by the end of the second year there were only ten of us left to take the exam. I suppose it got boring for some of the young ones. There was so much else in life, so much else they could be doing. And it's not just the evenings that are taken up. You've got to study at home. As well as the homework that you're set, you're expected to read books. So inevitably people did drop out. It wasn't the quality of the teacher – we had a fine teacher. And as I hoped I would, I enjoyed being with and working with young people. They were great fun.

I felt embarrassed at first – especially the first night. I got there about a quarter of an hour before the class started, thinking I might be able to walk into a more or less empty room and that the others would come in gradually and I wouldn't have to meet them all *en masse* so to speak. But when I got there the class was nearly full up and what made it doubly embarrassing was that they thought I was the teacher. It was terrible. They jumped up when I went in and came forward, said who they were and asked me what my name was. Then I realized what they thought.

I said, 'I'm not the teacher.'

'Not the teacher,' they said. 'Well, then you're in the wrong class.'

'No, I'm not,' I said. 'This is English "O" level, isn't it? The first year of English "O" level?'

They said, 'Yes.'

'Well, I'm one of the students.'

And they all laughed, though I must admit in a very nice way.

There were more girls than boys in the class, but apart from this woman of forty I could have been grandmother to any of them. It wasn't long before I was left in splendid isolation because the forty-year-old soon dropped out. Apparently she'd gone into it because although she was married, her children were off her hands and she'd taken up working in an office again. This entailed a lot of letter writing and she wanted to get her grammar right, but she reckoned this course didn't really do anything for her. I think it would have if she'd stayed.

But the young ones were fun and I never once had any embarrassment. The fact was that they were there because they were keen on being educated and getting on. They weren't a lot of hooligans or layabouts.

Two years later when I went to take the exam I got a terrible shock. It was held in a church hall and I thought there'd just be me and the nine youngsters who were left in the class. When I got there, there were about ninety-nine youngsters from other places – and me looking like Mrs Methuselah. I managed to find my own nine that I'd gone through with and I stuck to them like a leech. I didn't want to feel out of it. We stood around with everybody saying that they knew they were going to fail. You have to say that before because it sort of lets you down lightly if you do fail.

Eventually we filed into the hall. It was all very austere and frightening. Every desk at a certain distance from the next, and you're not allowed to touch anything till you're given the word to go. Then they come round with the list of questions and when you look at it you nearly die. Your mind is a complete blank and you're sure that you're never going to be able to answer any of them. Then you sort of pull yourself together and things become a bit clearer and you think well I've got three hours. Three hours seems a long time at first but the trouble is to keep writing. Your hand aches; during the last hour my hand ached so much I thought I'd never be able to keep going. Then I glanced around at this sea of earnest young faces and I couldn't help wondering what all these young people were going to do if they passed. How intent they seemed on striving to go one better. And I thought of what my life might have been like if I'd been able to take up the scholarship that I'd won when I was thirteen. And then I thought, well maybe it would have been like the verger in that Somerset Maugham short story.

He'd been a verger for years and he couldn't read or write and it hadn't mattered. But a new vicar took over and found that he was illiterate. So he was sacked. He was wandering around disconsolate and he saw a tobacconist shop for sale. He bought it and he did so well that he ended up with a chain of shops. One day he went to the bank and the manager said, 'Why don't you invest your money?' And handed him a prospectus.

So he said, 'It's no good showing me this, I can't read.'

The manager said, 'Can't read and you've done so well? Imagine where you would have got if you could have read.'

And the man said, 'Well, if I could have read I would still have been a verger.'

So I often think if I could have taken up the scholarship

and become a teacher, as was my ambition, life might not have been nearly so interesting as it has been.

Anyway even though I allowed my thoughts to wander I managed to get through the paper. I couldn't answer all the questions, simply because the time limit beat me. I suppose when you're younger your mind is more agile and certainly your hands are.

When we came out we all got together and had a celebration, coffee and cream cakes, the school tuckshop sort of thing. Then we all said how badly we'd done, once again preparing the way in case we'd failed. We all said we knew we hadn't passed and yet we were very cheerful about it. But when we got the results we had all passed.

This success spurred me on. I thought: well I've got 'O' level so why not have a go at 'A' level. Mind you the 'A' level was a very different proposition from 'O' level. There was Shakespeare, Tennyson, and Huxley and books like that to be read and *I, Claudius* by Robert Graves. I thought I'd never get through it, what with everybody getting murdered and what not all the way through the book. Then just after we had started we were told that we'd have to complete the course in a year instead of two years. This was because the numbers were so low that if we didn't the class would have to close. This I felt was asking a lot – and it might be expensive because the examination fees were quite high.

But I'm glad I took the chance. We had a marvellous teacher, I've got to hand it to him. Anyone who couldn't assimilate the knowledge that he dished out and couldn't understand the books when he explained them should have stayed at home and done fretwork or tatting. He was wonderful, but all too fast the examination day came round. It was the church hall again. This time when I got there, there was a bottle of smelling salts and a bottle of eau-de-Cologne on my desk with a card saying 'Good luck, Gran' – was my face red? I asked the others afterwards who put them there but none of them would admit to it. They were another grand set of youngsters.

Well, as you must have gathered, I passed. Once again success went to my head. So now I'm studying for my 'A' level in history. I've done one year and have got one more year to do and I hope to pass that as well. After that who knows? Has anyone ever got a university scholarship at the age of sixty-five?

People ask me what value has it been to you? What have you got out of it? This kind of remark sends me screaming up the wall. It's as though you're expected to show them money – or some object that you've been able to buy because you've acquired some knowledge. I suppose it's the sort of bloody ignorance you've got to expect in a materialistic world.

I'll tell you what I've got out of it. I've increased my fluency of self-expression both in the spoken and written word. I've got a new confidence. I've found beauty that I didn't know existed in the English language – and you tell me where you can buy beauty.

Studying for the 'A' levels has given me an insight into books that I hadn't got before. I never did read rubbish but when you come to books by people like Shakespeare and Tennyson and the teacher opens your eyes for you, it's like Ali Baba and the treasure cave. I'd never liked poetry because I hadn't been able to make head or tail of what the poet was getting at. But when you have a teacher whose whole being radiates as he talks about it, who so obviously loves it, who wants you to love it too and who takes the trouble to explain it to you, a new life opens for you. So even if you only get more pleasure out of reading it's worthwhile.

Who wants money when you've got public libraries? Your life can be very rich when you have these so rich in knowledge and beauty. And this is what that teacher gave me: not just knowledge but the desire for and the direction to go to acquire more. And any man who can do that for people has reached the peak of human achievement. Well, that's what I think anyway.

18

BEFORE I STARTED studying history for my 'A' level at the ripe age of sixty-one you could have written all that I knew about history on a single page. And that all boils down to the way I was taught at my elementary school. We weren't taught that history was a record of the living past but that it was a record of a dead one. Nothing was presented as the vivid pageant of the times or the fascinating study of the people who'd lived in those times. It was nothing but a collection of facts, figures, and dates.

When I left school all I really knew of history was that King Alfred burned the cakes, King Harold got shot in the eye, and King Richard had a humpback. What a heritage to leave school with. Another bad thing about school in those days was that you never left with a desire to learn more, which surely is the whole reason for education – that you leave with a desire to learn more and that you know how and where to find knowledge. Mind you, you left school knowing the three Rs which is more than many do today.

But looking back I can't really blame the teachers because the same teacher had to teach every subject; not like now when you have specialist teachers for each subject.

Since I've been studying history I've listened far more attentively to my mother's tales about Victorian life – she was born in 1880. Before I never used to take much notice of her. I used to let her drone on.

She says – and it's true – that people think that life for the poor is as hard now as it was many years ago. I must confess I used to think the same. She tells me about her grandparents. Both of them had to go to the workhouse when they were old because the Government gave no money, they only provided workhouses. And none of their children could afford to keep them so they just had to go there.

My mother's grandmother died in one and because of one. She was over sixty and you might say she died of old age, but the conditions there accelerated it. My mother's grandfather lived on, though he couldn't walk, and when his sons used to go and see him he'd cry and say to them, 'Oh, get a cart, get a wheelbarrow, get anything – only get me out of this terrible place.'

Eventually my mother's father did get him out and took him home. And the old man used to tell my mother the most harrowing tales. What an appalling place it was.

It was a workhouse and an asylum all in one. The laundry used to be done down in the cellars and the reek of that yellow soap and decaying bodies was always with them. The sick and the infirm just lay in the wards with no one to look after them – only the other inmates, if they felt like it.

When it got dark there was just one oil lamp for everyone and they had nothing to do but just sit and gaze at each other. Most of them were illiterate so they couldn't help themselves.

Things like this don't happen now. It's history. But it's history within living memory and it's history which accounts for the way some people think and behave today.

When my mother was a girl, the workhouse was at the end of their garden and the children from there used to go to the same school. They used to be known as the workhouse brats, with their grey woollen dresses in the winter and grey cotton dresses in the summer. In the area where Mum lived whole families used to go into the workhouse in the winter and in the summer when there was more work about they'd come out again. But while they were in they would be separated, the women from the husbands and the children from both. The shadow of the workhouse hung over every working-class family.

My mother went into domestic service in 1895. The people she worked for had acquired their wealth in trade as so many middle-class people had at that time. They had sold their town house and bought a big one in the country, filling it with the latest in Victoriana.

She got ten pounds a year there, paid quarterly as it was too small an amount to be paid oftener. Out of this she had to buy herself one new dress a year. She wore the same dresses summer and winter. But then of course you couldn't buy anything ready-made. She's told me it took seven yards of serge material and seven yards of lining and of course not only did she have to buy the material, she had to pay to have it made as well. So she had very little money left out of her ten pounds.

In this particular job, the under-servants were expected when they went out to wear a black bonnet provided by the employers. Mother simply hated wearing this bonnet. She was always a bit on the militant side. To her that bonnet was a sign of servitude and she thought it should be resisted. So one day she went out in her own hat and she was seen from the drawing-room. When she came in she was called for and she got a severe telling off. She didn't dare do it again but she looked for and got another job.

At the next place she got twelve pounds a year, paid monthly, with a Lord Jisson, VC. He lived outside Chichester at a place called Bosham. It was a much larger grander place, and he kept a pack of hounds. But it was run on military lines and everybody's task was allotted to them. There was a housekeeper there who kept tabs on the women and a butler who kept tabs on the menservants, and for everyone a list of duties was laid down. Whereas in the other places she was at the beck and call of all and sundry, here she had to stick rigorously to the duties. And the housekeeper saw to the standing orders.

All the servants had beer supplied twice a day, even the under-servants. Mother didn't drink hers, she used to save it for the organ-grinder. Apparently an organ-grinder used to come twice a week with his monkey and this monkey had developed a taste for beer. So the organ-grinder used to drink what he could and give the rest to the monkey.

After which, Mother said, that monkey used to cut the most unusual capers and this would be a talking point and an enjoyment for the servants for days.

Of course today it sounds trite and shows a lack of education. But those were the kind of events that you had to look forward to. Some form of variety to relieve from the humdrum. You had no education and little hope of advancement in position or in money, and no security at all of course.

As for the advanced education, that was still a pipedream. And it wasn't until the poor did get an advanced education that they were able to speak up for themselves, that they became, as you might say, powerful advocates for their own class. Left to the upper class nothing was going to be done. Why should they kill the goose that laid their golden eggs.

But things were improving even then, compared to my grandmother's days, because when my grandmother was in service there was a sort of feudal system.

She worked in a large manor house and the man who owned it owned the entire village; all the land for miles around and every cottage were owned by him too and he was very particular indeed about how they were kept. Nobody from outside could come and live in his village. He made sure that nothing and nobody changed. As Grandmother said, this system had its advantages because when the villagers were ill, medicines and food were sent down from the big house. But, she said, even so the villagers weren't grateful. They used to detest having to doff their caps to the squire who they felt was rude and arrogant to them. Still Grandmother reckoned that the villagers then had a better life than when things became freer for the working class. Because then nobody really cared at all.

This was always a point of disagreement between my mother and grandmother. Mother was a stickler for her rights, not women's rights but her rights, and as far as she could she fought for them. Of course she couldn't break the system, but occasionally she bent it.

One thing she couldn't bend however was the business of waking up in the morning. It always had been a servant's nightmare. At one place, though, she came to a good arrangement with one of the gardeners. Every night she would tie a piece of string to her big toe and throw the string out of the window. When the gardener used to come round at five o'clock in the morning he'd give it a mighty yank and so wake Mother up. Apparently she was never late, though on more than one occasion she hobbled round her work for the rest of the day.

The saying 'early to bed and early to rise makes a man healthy, wealthy, and wise' I've always thought a stupid one. Yet there must be something in it since at any rate for much of our lives my mother, Albert and I have had to get up very early. It hasn't made us wealthy or necessarily wise but we've certainly been healthy. Albert and I are both now drawing the old-age pension. So I suppose that proves something.

19

WHEN I SEE the words Retirement and Old Age I ask myself why are the two coupled together? Why does retirement suddenly and automatically mean old age? Retirement shouldn't make a radical change in life. But it does, especially for men. When they retire their life changes completely but a woman's doesn't because she still goes on doing more or less the same things, particularly if she's a woman who hasn't gone out to work. She still does the housework, the shopping, the cooking, and the laundry.

Before a man retires he should start thinking what it's going to mean. But he doesn't so when the time comes the conditions take him unawares and he's not able to adapt himself to them. What he often mistakenly thinks is that when he retires it's going to be a marvellous existence. All the things he's not had time to do when he was working he's going to be able to do then. Perhaps he's got a hobby. Perhaps he likes to make things at home or collect things or look after the garden. But what he doesn't realize is that these things that fitted in nicely in his spare time are nothing like sufficient as full-time occupations.

I think men become so apathetic and that's why life seems to hold so much less happiness for them in retirement than it does for a woman. I'm going by the old people where I live and where my mother lives. I do quite a bit for them and there's hardly any men left there now. Amongst all the families, in about forty houses, there can't be more than six men. And it's not because the women were so much younger than the men, it's just that the men didn't adapt themselves to a life of leisure, didn't know what to do with themselves and so like the old soldiers in the song they just faded away. Men are not as resourceful as women, nor do they adapt to new circumstances.

A man leaves school, he gets his job and he plods along till he's sixty, sixty-five, or seventy and when work ends he doesn't know what to do with himself. He feels he's got no place; he's in limbo. The wife doesn't want him at home. She loves her husband, of course she does, but she loves him to go off to work at eight or nine in the morning and come home at five or six at night. She doesn't want him under her feet all day long. She likes her life, a life whereby he's not in the home all day and she can go out and visit her cronies and do her shopping. All of a sudden he wants to join in with these things, he wants to go shopping with her; he wants to know where she's been and what she's been talking about, and very soon acrimonious discussions start between people who have lived as Darby and Joan all their lives. It's only because the man doesn't think and doesn't try to make a place for himself in the world of retirement. Mind you, the wife can help. Together they can plan his life – make some sort of timetable. They don't have to stick to it religiously but it will give them something to go by until the man has worked out a definite way of life for himself.

I often think it's a great pity that a man can't retire gradually, doing half a day for a time while he sorts himself out. The trouble is he believes that all the week life will be just like it was at weekends. And while he's enjoyed his weekends when he was working all the week, he hasn't realized that it's because he's working that he enjoyed them. He doesn't understand that it was the change he enjoyed and that there's no longer going to be any change.

Another thing, most councils like ours run courses on retirement but they don't get the people they should. They don't get the working-class person, the man who has done a physical job and is going to find it harder to use time than a person whose work has employed his brain. A man who does a hard physical job all week doesn't come home at night and pick up a book and read, he probably just turns the telly on. He doesn't think about using his brains. He probably thinks he hasn't got any. I've heard many old men say, 'Oh no, I've never done anything like that and I'm too old to start now.' But they're not too old. It's the middle class who go to these courses but the others need them even more. And the things that you can learn to do now! Every occupation, every hobby is covered so you don't have to be intellectual if you don't want to. This is something to think about and to do that will make for a happy life in retirement.

But no, these men don't. Then I hear them say they've got time to go and visit their children, and see more of them. They don't realize that their children have got a life of their own by now, a life in which their parents have not played a part before; and you can't expect them and their families automatically to alter their way of life because you have leisure time on your hands. Married children have got their own work and their own friends and they haven't much place for you in their life and there's no reason why they should have, because if they're relying on the companion-ship of their aged parents, their own lives must be very barren, indeed. But the parents won't realize this. They get disgruntled and say, 'Ah, there you are. You get old and even your own children don't want you. You might as well be on the scrap heap.'

I don't see why you should expect your children to devote their lives to you. When your family get married you've given them up. You've done your duty in life. You've brought them into the world, you've fed them, clothed them and educated them to the best of your ability. Let them lead their own lives, I say. Don't make them feel that their mother and father are sitting stewing over in their minds about what they do or don't do for them. Everybody should be complete in themselves and you shouldn't have to rely on other people to provide a purpose or to make you feel that you're important in life.

I think nowadays that old people are lucky. There's never been so much done and thought about for them as there is today, but they must help as well.

Those I feel really sorry for are the ones who live on their own and who have no one to visit them or care for them. Perhaps they've driven people away by their cantankerousness but to be old, poor, and cantankerous is the last word in a lonely existence.

Another sad thing to see is those people who've lived in council houses and who have to move to a small flat. You can't blame the council because they've got a long waiting list of young people with families who need houses. Obviously it's only right that one or perhaps two people living in a three-bedroomed house should move out but they're taken away from everyone that they know. Some of the council flats for old people in Brighton for instance are sited in a road where they are isolated. No one goes up that road unless they live there or unless they have to deliver there. So sometimes from morning to night the old people, particularly those who can't get out, never see anything of life at all. It's a terrible existence for them, a kind of apartheid. Then they start to realize that they're in a kind of a special category. They're a race apart. They're no longer Mr and Mrs Smith, a couple with a grown-up family, but two people who've joined the ranks of the drop-outs, the problem people, the 'senior citizens' as they choose to call them. But the old people don't call themselves the senior citizens – they call themselves the second-class citizens.

How can they be other than second-class citizens surrounded as they are by people all like themselves, all old, all living in the same road or block and all with the same problems and the same incomes? How much better it would be if the old were mixed up with the young. Most neighbours feel kindly towards elderly people, especially elderly people who are not capable of getting out themselves. They'd help in so many small ways. Carry coal, do a bit of shopping and explain the forms that they get sent and that simply plague them.

Another thing that neighbours could do is to persuade some of those who are living on a pittance to accept social security. It's amazing the number of old people that won't take social security. They look on it as their parents looked on the old parish relief. My mother remembers it well – when the authority used to come round, open all your cupboards to see how much food you had and tell you what they thought you could do without. Then any furniture that they didn't consider you needed they told you to sell it before you asked for money. It isn't anything like that now. They help old people as unobtrusively as they can. They make you feel that it's not a charity but a right.

Another type of old person I feel particularly sorry for is what I think they call 'distressed gentlefolk'. Mind you, I suffered at the hands of gentlefolk when I was in service, but that's forgotten now. One of these ladies said to me, 'It's the cold winters I worry about – you see I can't afford much coal and it makes all the difference to being up and around or staying in bed all the time.' When I asked her what she missed most from the comfortable life that she used to have she said, 'Most of all I miss not being able to afford a private doctor.' And I felt a fellow feeling with her because that is one of the things I would like. She said, 'I never go to the doctor now unless I've really got to. There's four doctors in a group practice where I am registered and I hardly ever get the same one twice so I've got to explain my symptoms each time I go. While I'm doing this he's writing on a pad and when I've finished he just hands me a prescription without a word and out I go. I'm sure all the doctors in that group favour contraceptives for the unmarried, abortions for the married and euthanasia for the unwanted like me.'

She herself believed in euthanasia.

She said, 'I consider that when we become a misery to ourselves and our relations we should have the privilege of removing ourselves from life if we want to.'

I think I agree with her. Old age can be, and should be, a time of gracious living and companionship. But it can also be a time of loneliness and wretchedness. There's precious little dignity about coming into the world so let us at least leave it in the best possible way that we can.

20

DIGNITY WAS SOMETHING that in my early life the working classes were not supposed to be able to afford.

As a kitchenmaid I was at everyone's beck and call and the kind of work I was doing meant that I always looked scruffy. So I felt what I was called, a skivvy, and feeling like this gave me an inferiority complex, or what we call today a chip on my shoulder.

When I was going out I would make what I thought was the best of myself but that was only my opinion at the time, and looking back on it my opinion must often have been wrong. Of privacy we had none. Working and sharing a bedroom as I did meant I was never alone; my life was what you would call an open book. I don't think I resented this at the time – open book it might have been but it wasn't a very interesting one.

But dignity and privacy are two things that I have since thought go side by side. So when I saw how more and more country houses were being opened to the general public I

411

wondered how their owners felt about this invasion into their lives.

I knew of course that their education had prepared them to meet any situation but I wondered – if they showed any emotion – whether their feelings were the same as mine.

It was with a very strange sensation and a not altogether agreeable one that I went to Woburn Abbey to interview the Duke of Bedford for the BBC. Although during my years in domestic service I'd never worked in such a grand establishment, nevertheless for me to go in at the front door instead of the basement and talk to the owner – well, it was something I never thought would happen, not in my wildest dreams. In domestic service the only time you ever went in by the front door was when you went after the job, never for the rest of your time there did you ever sully it except by cleaning it.

I had read about the Duke, how he was sociable and happy-go-lucky, but that didn't mean a thing to me because people that are sociable and happy-go-lucky were, in my experience, only sociable and happy-go-lucky to people of their own class. The sociability and affability got shed like a snake skin when they were dealing with what they designated the lower classes. So I thought, maybe he is all they crack him up to be but if he knows what I was originally he won't be the same to me. So I felt a bit nervous at the thought of the coming interview.

But I must say His Grace surprised me. He was not a bit like I expected. On the contrary he made me feel as though I was really welcome. He chatted me up over a glass of sherry. And his comments on his ancestors were witty and often far from flattering. I mean describing some he said 'the only sensible thing they'd ever done was to marry money'. And then he went on to describe the things that some of the others had done which were unprintable. So I felt at my ease from the start instead of feeling that I'd got to be on the defensive all the time. By defensive I mean I went there all tensed up, ready to be aggressive if I felt that he was going to talk down at me. I thought: 'Never mind, just because I've been in domestic service, I'm not working for him so I haven't got to be feeling as though he's "Sir" to me. Naturally I'll give him his title. But he needn't think that I'm going to be subservient. Jack's as good as his master.' I know he isn't really but then I always sort of build myself up with the fact that he is, you see.

But he took the wind right out of my sails and so did his house – it was absolutely wonderful. I still think about it now, that marvellous place. It was full of the most beautiful things, and as he took me around I realized the deep feelings the Duke had in owning them. I've never felt any desire to own things, even valuable things, but I sensed that he looked at them as something in trust from his family. He hadn't actually bought them for himself and he was honouring that trust by his determination to keep them.

I began to realize more how one does feel towards really beautiful though inanimate things. We've got nothing in our house that the dustman would give us twopence for – it's all utility stuff, stuff you can't really feel a pride in, and the house is just a place where we live and that's all you

413

can say about it. But that house was where other people had lived and the things in it were things they'd used and loved and it needed very little imagination to visualize what it must have been like when they were used to the full, when it wasn't just a place where a small part was used by the family and the rest had to be thrown open for every Tom, Dick, and Harry who cared to fork out half a crown to come round and stare at. I could visualize, having been in domestic service, the large parties and balls that were given there and the rank and nobility that attended them.

All right, they'd never done a stroke of work in their lives but I could forgive them that. I could see them under the chandeliers and walking down the staircases. And now these things were just there for people to stare at. But it was good to feel they were all in use at one time, that they had to be kept clean by servants, that they weren't always show pieces.

I thought what a retinue of servants they must have had below stairs to wait hand and foot on those people above. And I was glad that there were lovely houses like that even though I didn't admire them when I was working. I'm glad too that they are open to the public to see. It's not the same thing reading about them as being able to visit them.

Nevertheless, I felt a kind of discomfort going round Woburn Abbey. It seemed an invasion of people's privacy, that my strange eyes should peer at things that the Duke's grandmothers and great-grandmothers and great-great-grandmothers had loved, used, and handled. I was violating these things with my eyes. Maybe the Duke doesn't feel like that but I did. That I really shouldn't be there – peering into private places because through force of circumstances or economic or political pressure they're no longer able to be kept in peace. When I look at lovely things, see them in a home and part of a home, they take on a far more personal and appealing appearance than they do in a museum. Museums are soulless places.

And then there's the Duke of Bedford not only enjoying taking me round but talking about other visitors that he liked sharing his possessions with. He didn't feel that fate had dealt him a harsh blow in any way. He really seemed to enjoy the fact that he could share them and that it was by people's half-crowns that he was able to keep the whole thing going. He thought, it's just one of those things and that all the stately-home owners were in the same boat and that it was far better than having to give them up altogether.

Although he spoke in a flippant way, too, about his ancestors, I don't really think he felt flippant. Perhaps to people whom he must realize have got no ancestors they want to acknowledge it's just as well to be flippant, particularly about those you've got hanging on your walls, unless you want to hear some peculiar remarks. None of my ancestors would I ever want hanging on walls, I can assure you. But then I don't come from the line of stately homes.

Anyway during this personally conducted tour His Grace certainly was lighthearted. He wasn't in any way condescending. Of course I was interested in the mechanics of throwing a stately home open to the public – how it was kept clean? What kind of floor covering they had? And he described the kind of material which was the most hard wearing. Then he told me he had a dozen or more people coming in from the village every day to dust – thank heaven I wasn't one of them! I'd have been frightened to pick up anything, let alone put a duster around it.

And it isn't only the house. The Duke of Bedford's got a lot of outside attractions as well. You might say he's an impresario; he believes in giving value for money. Some owners consider they're doing a great service by allowing the public to see how the wealthy live. For half a crown you see them in the lap of luxury then you can go back home and have a big moan about bloated aristocrats. You've got ammunition for your gun, haven't you?

At some of these stately homes you get a sort of potted history lesson while they take you round. I was glad the Duke didn't because history as presented by people whose ancestors have lived it on the upper level is not the same as the history you read. Give me the Industrial Revolution and the poor old down-trodden working class of the Victorian days, that's the kind of thing I like, not how well the wealthy lived.

Then you get other stately-home owners who light-heartedly say there's nothing to being a lord. In fact if you read some of the remarks of the aristocracy you would think that they feel that there's a sort of special privilege in being a non-privileged person. It's a kind of inverted snobbery. But the great British public love them, otherwise they'd get rid of the House of Lords.

I think it's an anomaly. One peer even had the nerve to

say that the House of Lords was the last bulwark against democracy. What he meant by that I don't know, but it sounds pretty inflammatory. I reckon it's the working class that need the aristocracy; we have got something to fight against. So keep them there and keep up the struggle. We must continue to fight for the fact all men are equal regardless that some of course will always be more equal than others.

All the time I was going round Woburn Abbey these thoughts were going through my head. The interview went well, largely because His Grace made it all so easy. We talked in his private sitting-room. Afterwards I happened to notice one of the oil paintings on the wall, a Rembrandt it was, the companion picture to one that had recently been auctioned and sold for three-quarters of a million pounds.

When the Duke told me this I said, 'And is that one worth that much?'

'Yes,' he said, 'I should think so – possibly a little more.'

So I said, 'Well, why don't you sell it?'

'Oh, I don't know,' he said, 'it looks rather cosy up there don't you think?'

Cosy! I ask you. But after that remark I thought perhaps we'd better keep the House of Lords after all.

Then he delivered his *coup de grâce* which showed me that I'm the same sort of snob as all of them. As we got up to leave, to my amazement he said, 'But surely you're staying for lunch?' And to my absolute astonishment and fury the producer said, 'I'm very sorry, we really haven't time. We've got to get this tape to the BBC. It goes out this evening.'

I nearly died with mortification when I heard him say this because to have been able to have gone back to my home and said to my neighbours in the course of conversation, 'When I had lunch with the Duke of Bedford,' you can imagine what that would have done for me. It was no good saying, 'The day the Duke of Bedford asked me to lunch.' I mean, the idea that I'd refuse! As we drove back home in silence, because I wasn't speaking to the producer by then, I thought of the number of things that would have reminded me of the day I had lunch with the Duke of Bedford. Then it struck me what the Duke had done for me. He showed me that in spite of all my talk about 'them up there and us below stairs,' if one can possibly associate with them, one does so – which makes us all really snobs at heart, or perhaps just ordinary mortals.